DICKENS AND THE RISE OF DIVORCE

For my parents, Lewis Hager and Faye Paxson Hager

Dickens and the Rise of Divorce

The Failed-Marriage Plot and the Novel Tradition

KELLY HAGER
Simmons College, USA

ASHGATE

Published by
Ashgate Publishing Limited
Wey Court East
Union Road
Farnham
Surrey, GU9 7PT
England

Ashgate Publishing Company
Suite 420
101 Cherry Street
Burlington
VT 05401–4405
USA

www.ashgate.com

British Library Cataloguing in Publication Data
Hager, Kelly.
   Dickens and the rise of divorce : the failed-marriage plot and the novel tradition.
   1. Dickens, Charles, 1812–1870 – Stories, plots, etc. 2. Divorce in literature. 3. English fiction – 18th century – History and criticism. 4. English fiction – 19th century – History and criticism. 5. Feminism and literature – Great Britain – History – 19th century.
   I. Title
   823.8'093543–dc22

Library of Congress Cataloging-in-Publication Data
Hager, Kelly.
   Dickens and the rise of divorce : the failed-marriage plot and the novel tradition / Kelly Hager.
         p. cm.
   Includes bibliographical references and index.
   ISBN 978-0-7546-6947-0 (hardback : alk. paper)—ISBN 978-0-7546-9711-4 (ebook)
   1. Dickens, Charles, 1812–1870—Criticism and interpretation. 2. Domestic fiction, English—History and criticism. 3. Divorce in literature. 4. Marriage in literature. 5. Divorce—Great Britain—History—19th century. 6. Marriage—Great Britain—History—19th century. I. Title.

PR4592.D57H34 2010
823'.8—dc22
                                                                                    2009026053

ISBN 9780754669470 (hbk)
ISBN 9780754697114 (ebk)

Mixed Sources
Product group from well-managed forests and other controlled sources
www.fsc.org Cert no. SA-COC-1565
© 1996 Forest Stewardship Council
FSC

Printed and bound in Great Britain by
MPG Books Group, UK

Contents

Acknowledgments

It is a pleasure and a privilege to acknowledge all the friends and readers this project has had over the years. My teachers at the University of California, Irvine—Robert Newsom, the late Homer Obed Brown, and John Carlos Rowe— and at the University of California Dickens Project—Murray Baumgarten, Edwin Eigner, John O. Jordan, and especially Hilary Schor—deserve my first thanks. My colleagues in the Expository Writing Program at Harvard, the English Department at Yale University, and the Departments of English and Women's & Gender Studies and the Center for the Study of Children's Literature at Simmons College have been unfailingly enthusiastic in their support for this project; I thank the late Richard Marius, Nancy Sommers, Anne Fernald, Kelly Mays, and Rhonda Rockwell; Sarah Bilston, Laura Green, Vera Kutzinski, Linda Peterson, Michael Trask, Ruth Bernard Yeazell, Alexander Welsh, and Katharine Weber; Pamela Bromberg, Suzanne Leonard, Lowry Pei, Jill Taylor, Mary Jane Treacy, Susan Bloom, and Cathryn Mercier. I am also grateful to James Eli Adams, Beverly Lyon Clark, Linda Peterson, and Garrett Stewart for enormously helpful readings of the almost-final manuscript, and to the reader for Ashgate, Deborah Denenholz Morse, who not only responded to the project with an enthusiasm beyond my wildest dreams, but whose suggestions also made the book's introduction more focused and its Podsnappery more precise. My undergraduate teachers at Rice University, especially Walter Isle and Susan Wood, merit special gratitude for their inspiring teaching.

James Buzard, John Picker, and Leah Price, chairs of the Victorian Literature and Culture Seminar at the Harvard Humanities Center, invited me to present a portion of this project to the seminar; William Cohen and Mary Ann O'Farrell, chairs of the Prose Fiction division of the MLA, invited me to present at the convention in 2005. I am grateful for those invitations and for the opportunity to present my work in such wonderful forums. An early version of Chapter 3 appeared in *ELH* as "Estranging *David Copperfield*" (1996); an excerpt from Chapter 2 appeared in *Victorian Literature and Culture* as "Jasper Packlemerton, Victorian Freak" (2006). I thank the editors and referees of these journals for their generous responses to my work. I am indebted to my editor at Ashgate, Ann Donahue, who is as patient as she is perceptive. I would also like to thank Terri-Leigh Hinkle at Beatley Library, Simmons College, and the extraordinarily efficient Interlibrary Loan department at Beatley, as well as Mary Haegert and Heather Cole at the Houghton Library of Harvard University. I thank the Houghton Library for permission to publish Phiz's illustration, "Mr. Carker in his hour of triumph," from the 1848 edition of *Dombey and Son*.

To Mary Jean Corbett, who never tired of reading multiple manifestations, and Deidre Lynch, who has been a friend, a teacher, a reader, and an example beyond compare, I want to express my deepest gratitude and my sense of how very fortunate I am to have friends and colleagues of such rare quality.

I dedicate this book to my parents, Lewis and Faye Hager, and I thank them, as well as my sister, Jennifer Hager, and her husband, Julian Bray, for their love, their encouragement, and their unfeigned interest in divorce Victorian-style. I am also more grateful than I can say to Jewel Otten, Julia, Brian, and Isabel Knier, and Jim and Mona Otten for their enthusiasm for this project, even though it meant that many visits were long postponed and too many phone calls were unreturned.

It's hard to know how to thank Tom Otten; all the things I want to say are Walworth sentiments, and I know that he, like Wemmick, firmly believes they belong there, not on this page.

I never congratulate any girl on marrying; I think they ought to make it somehow not quite so awful a steel trap.

The Countess Gemini in Henry James's *The Portrait of a Lady* (1881)

Wedlock is a padlock,
When you're married to a no-good man.

Laura Lee, "Wedlock is a Padlock" (1971)

Introduction

In May of 1858, in a letter to her daughter Vicky, Queen Victoria wrote, "I think people really marry far too much; it is such a lottery after all, and for a poor woman a very doubtful happiness." Seven months later, in another letter to Vicky, she wrote, "I think unmarried people are very often very happy—certainly more so than married people who don't live happily together of which there are so many instances." And two years later, in May of 1860, she wrote to Vicky again about the shortcomings of connubial bliss: "the poor woman is bodily and morally the husband's slave. That always sticks in my throat. When I think of a merry, happy, free young girl—and look at the ailing, aching state a young wife is generally doomed to—which you can't deny is the penalty of marriage" (Hibbert, *Queen Victoria in Her Letters and Journals* 104, 105). These excerpts from her letters to her (newly-wed) daughter reveal that the Queen, symbolic center of the culture and one of the most public advocates of the domestic sphere and its delights, regards marriage with deep skepticism. Despite her very public advertisement of her own marriage (and her prolonged and extreme mourning of her husband), she calls matrimony a lottery and likens it to a physical illness.

The Queen was not, of course, alone in her distrust of, and discomfort with, marriage. In *The Subjection of Women* (an essay Mary Lyndon Shanley calls "one of the most devastating critiques of male domination in marriage in the history of Western philosophy"), John Stuart Mill also compares marriage to slavery and argues that women are forced to submit to the tyranny of matrimony because society only gives them a "Hobson's choice" ("that or none") when it comes to determining their future (Shanley, "Marital Slavery" 230, Mill 156). Indeed, Mill's celebrated essay focuses almost exclusively on women's subjection as it relates to marriage and might more accurately be titled *The Subjection of Wives*. Mill's emphasis on the conjugal in theory and in practice is clear from the first paragraph, where he announces his conviction that "the principle which regulates the existing social relations between the two sexes—the legal subordination of one sex to the other—is wrong in itself," to the slippage in his language throughout from men and women to husbands and wives, a slippage which reveals that when he says men he really means husbands, and when he speaks of women, he is quite specifically referring to those who are married (125). That is, even when Mill refers to men and women and so posits the individual *as* an individual, he is actually assuming that these men and women are husbands and wives. For instance, Mill's assertion that the present system of subordination has lasted so long because it is "not confined to a limited class, but common to the whole male sex" gives way, in the next sentence, to his admission that this power is especially seductive because it is not power in the abstract but, rather, power that "comes home to the person and hearth of every male head of a family" (136). Whereas Mill's use of the word "women" might signal that attention will be paid to governesses and other unmarried female domestics or to the economic exploitation of women who work in factories, the essay maintains an almost obsessive interest in the plight of wives, women who

> live under the very eye, and almost, it may be said, in the hands, of one of the masters—in closer intimacy with him than with any of her fellow-subjects; with no means of combining against him, no power of even locally overmastering him, and, on the other hand, with the strongest motives for seeking his favour and avoiding to give him offense. (136)

Further, Mill's detailed explanation of the benefits to "mankind" that would result "if women were free" quickly boils down to an explanation of how his proposals will improve "the condition of women in marriage," thereby "laying the foundation of domestic existence" and thus guaranteeing the basic principles of "social justice" (216, 220). As Victor Luftig points out, "though the problem continually acknowledged in the *Subjection* is the absence of opportunities for women beyond marriage, Mill's images of improved circumstances continually return to the married couple in the individual home" (36). Perhaps it is that unshakable belief in the heterosexual couple that explains Mill's otherwise curious reluctance in *The Subjection* to endorse divorce. On the one hand, Mill seems squarely in favor of remarriage, reasoning that

> if a woman is denied any lot in life but that of being the personal body-servant of a despot, and is dependent for everything upon the chance of finding one who may be disposed to make a favourite of her instead of merely a drudge, it is a very cruel aggravation of her fate that that she should be allowed to try this chance only once. The natural sequel and corollary from this state of things would be, that since her all in life depends upon obtaining a good master, she should be allowed to change again and again until she finds one. (161)

But Mill hastens to add that he is "not saying that she ought to be allowed this privilege." "That," he maintains, "is a totally different consideration. The question of divorce, in the sense involving liberty of remarriage, is one into which it is foreign to my purpose to enter" (161). When he mentions divorce again a few pages later, he suggests it as a remedy only for those yoked to the truly unreasonable:

> there are, no doubt, women, as there are men, whom equality of consideration will not satisfy; with whom there is no peace while any will or wish is regarded but their own. Such persons are a proper subject for the law of divorce. They are only fit to live alone, and no human beings ought to be compelled to associate their lives with them. (172)[1]

Finally, in his last mention of divorce, at the end of the same chapter, he makes it clear that he is talking only about a "separation on just terms." "I do not now speak of a divorce," he insists (179).

Mill's reluctance to address the question of divorce seems strange, not only because divorce seems to have everything to do with his concerns in *The Subjection*, but also because divorce was now possible, having been made legal (although not affordable, and not equally available to men and women) in England 12 years before the publication of *The Subjection*, in 1857. In a letter to John Nichol after the publication of *The Subjection*, he explained that he steered away from the question of divorce in the essay not only for political reasons ("from the obvious inexpediency of establishing a connection in people's minds between the equality and any particular opinions on the divorce question"), but also because "I do not think that the conditions of the dissolubility of marriage can be properly determined until women have an equal voice in determining them, nor until there has been experience of the marriage relation as it would exist between equals" (qtd in Rossi 60). Mill's reluctance to take up the issue until marriage has been reformed indicates his basic belief in the institution and his hope that once the conditions between men and women are made more equitable, marriage will improve to such a degree that divorce will not be necessary. And indeed, for all of its strenuous critique of marriage as it was actually practiced by the Victorians, *The Subjection* envisions a future in which the union involves no "obligation of obedience" and is "no longer enforced to the oppression of those to whom it is purely a mischief" (Rossi 179). As Sue Lonoff reminds us, Mill concludes *The Subjection* "with a forecast of the happiness to be gained by both sexes when women become men's equals," when what Susan Hardy Aiken calls the "paradisial state" of "this new form of relationship" has been realized (Lonoff 81, Aiken 365). Perhaps we are to assume that no one would want to leave such a paradise, and so the question of divorce would then be moot. "Like the sacred marriage at the climax of Revelation," Aiken argues, "the marriage Mill envisions is the goal of historical evolution, the sign of a transformed civilization" (366). And to take up, even to entertain, the idea of breaking the contract that signals such an advanced state of society would be to blight the vision at the heart of Mill's essay.

What are we to make of the fact that one of the most powerful and celebrated documents in the crusade for women's rights has as its ultimate goal the improvement of the institution of marriage, even the establishment of a domestic paradise? Why did Mill, the liberal thinker *par excellence*, the theorist who, in *On Liberty*, derided those social strictures that limit the variety of experiences open to persons, maintain such a deeply normative vision? Conversely, what does it mean that Queen Victoria, the monarch Margaret Homans and Adrienne Munich describe as "so matrimonially devoted, so excessively maternal (nine children), and then so emphatically widowed," wrote to her newly-married daughter on more than one occasion about marriage's discontents (2)?

One thing these curiously contradictory cultural facts suggest is that marriage is a vexing institution, one that keeps the politics of mid-Victorians confused, constantly under revision, and divided in their aims. While Mill explicitly and powerfully uncovered the monstrosity of the institution in terms of both its legal implications and the actual horrors to which the doctrine of coverture and the patriarchal nature of nineteenth-century culture gave rise, he dedicated his protofeminist essay to proposing ways in which the institution could be improved. Similarly, while the Queen was clearly aware of the evils the relationship entailed for women, she publicly celebrated her own marriage, extolling "the mutual love and perfect confidence which bound the Queen and Prince to each other" (qtd in Houston 174). Further, she valorized her status as wife over her status as queen in a very public manifestation of the doctrine of separate spheres, endorsing the ideal of the Angel in the House and of woman's limited and private domestic role. And finally, in her pronounced mourning for Albert, she enacted the myth of the modest heroine, who only loves once and loves forever—a strange pose for the woman who professed to "hate marriages" (Hibbert, *Queen Victoria in Her Letters and Journals* 287).

Perhaps it goes without saying that marriage is a vexed and vexing institution. At this particular moment in twenty-first-century culture, when it is a truism that the divorce rate is 50 percent but reality television celebrates the courtship plot in its innumerable versions of *The Bachelor*, perhaps we should not be surprised to notice the paradoxical nature of the Victorians' attitude to matrimony.[2] Indeed, this was an age that saw the rise of a powerful women's movement, the passage of numerous laws respecting the rights of women (from the first Custody of Infants Act in 1839 to the first law protecting women against matrimonial cruelty in 1878), and the phenomenon of the New Woman, but also a century that gave us Coventry Patmore and his domestic angel, Ruskin and his queen confined to her domestic garden, and Sarah Stickney Ellis's conservative prescriptions for the women of England.

Accept, even assume, that the rhetoric surrounding marriage will be confused and confusing, then. Accept that such rhetoric will be full of self-censure, contradictory in its aims, constituted by tensions between public image and private admissions, and of norms that remain the norm even as they are hard to swallow. But why, then, given that such confusions, hesitations, and contradictions characterize marriage in the Victorian period, has the courtship plot remained the defining model for studies of the novel? Why does our most basic understanding of the plot of the domestic novel suggest that we have overlooked the crisis of marriage the Queen's letters, Mill's essay, and the furor over the Woman Question so clearly point to?[3] We need to appraise the relation between marital discontents and the courtship plot, and in this era of interdisciplinary studies, critical legal studies, and new historicism, we have many models for such a study. Indeed, twentieth- and twenty-first-century critics of Victorian literature and culture have focused on married women's property, on prostitution, on the New Woman, and on the questions of women and work and women and education and their relationship to the Victorian novel, although in so doing they tend to subscribe to the basic tenet of Ian Watt's *The Rise of the Novel* that "the great majority of novels written since *Pamela* have continued its basic pattern, and concentrated their main interest upon a courtship leading to marriage" (148–9). Such allegiance to the courtship plot suggests that even in uncovering a more historically specific and skeptical understanding of gender and culture in the nineteenth century, we still accept the notion that marriage provides closure for the domestic novel.[4] Our commitment to the courtship plot also leads us to overlook important parallels such as the fact that divorce was legalized in the same year that *Little Dorrit* (a novel that includes a breach of promise suit, an extralegal separation, and a marriage described as a "jolt through a Slough of Despond, and through a long, long avenue of wrack and ruin) concluded (in 1857) or that the divorce bill was debated in parliament as Thackeray was writing *The Newcomes* (a novel that stingingly critiques arranged marriages, includes a spectacular divorce case, and leaves the reader to imagine, if she can, that its hero and heroine eventually unite in "Fable-land") from 1853 through 1855 (*Little Dorrit* 668, *The Newcomes* 818).

Important work has been done on the mutual relationship between the Woman Question and the Victorian novel and on the mutual relationship between the Woman Question and the development of laws protecting wives, their property, and their children; I want now to apply that work to our basic understanding of the nineteenth-century novel and its prevalent plots, an application that seems especially important given that the novel anticipated much of the legislation that gave women rights to their children, their property, and their bodies, and given that the novel, in portraying the dissolution of marriage before it was, strictly speaking, legal, provided the law with plots by which it might sever the matrimonial bond. While critics do acknowledge that novels treat marital failure (essays on Trollope's *He Knew He Was Right* [1869] or Anne Brontë's *The Tenant of Wildfell Hall* [1848], to name two of the most popular examples), the multitude of novels that plot the failure of marriage—before and after divorce was legalized, long before the advent of the sensation novel or the daring plots of Thomas Hardy and George Meredith—suggest that the novel is just as often (often at the same time as it plots a courtship and ends with a wedding) dedicated to showing how a marriage unravels, to uncovering the myth of matrimonial bliss, to revealing how many husbands and wives were trying to escape or miserably enduring the wedlock they had so eagerly sought, as it is to plotting courtship. Or to put it another way, we recognize that novels plot marital failure, but we have yet to revise our understanding of the genre with those plots in mind. One way to think about both the prevalence of this plot and the fact that it has not been accounted for in our theories of the novel might be to posit that the novel's predilection for the failed-marriage plot is "a corollary of the importance of marriage to the novel form" and that it in fact "reinforces the romance plot."[5]

Indeed, it sometimes seems as if marriage is everywhere written against, even as it is everywhere desired or assumed. Thus one reason we do not see the nineteenth-century debates over marriage reflected in later criticism of the Victorian novel is that even those Victorians who exposed the problems of the institution believed in it in a very fundamental way and insisted that it was crucial, for individuals and for society. While Mill admitted that it was "next to an impossibility to form a really well-assorted union" and suggested that marriage makes men monsters, he did not want to consider divorce in his proposals for the reform of marriage, and he believed women wanted to remain in the home, in the domestic sphere—that they wanted, in other words, to remain wives (233). By the same token, even though the Queen believed marriage to be "sad and painful," when she herself was released from the "ailing, aching state" of marriage, she engaged in a bout of spectacular and spectacularly long mourning and dedicated herself to memorializing her husband ((Hibbert, *Queen Victoria in Her Letters and Journals* 233, 105).

In a somewhat similar fashion, the work by historians on marital failure in the Victorian period has helped us understand how and why the failure of marriage became a public, juridical matter in the nineteenth century, while literary critics have made important connections between the legalization of divorce and its dissemination in the public press and the enormous popularity of the sensation novel, with its reliance on bigamy and adultery as pivots of the plot. But there exists a marked reluctance to consider the ramifications of the public failure of marriage on our understanding of the courtship plot (and especially on our understanding of the novels written before, say, the 1860s), just as, I think, we are reluctant to entertain the notion that the examples of failed marriage we do admit are so numerous as to suggest they are representative, rather than remarkable. For instance, one of the most astute critics of Victorian gender politics, Mary Lyndon Shanley, argues that "Mill's depiction of marriage departed radically from the majority of Victorian portrayals of home and hearth," citing Ruskin's "Of Queens' Gardens," Coventry Patmore's *The Angel in the House*, and James Fitzjames Stephen's vehement assertion that he disagreed with *The Subjection* "from the first sentence to the last" ("Marital Slavery" 233). But, in fact, Mill's argument dovetails quite closely, as we have seen, with Queen Victoria's private assessment of the institution, and it also resonates with the portraits of unhappy marriages that frequently shape Browning's poems ("My Last Duchess," "Andrea del Sarto"), with George Meredith's sonnet sequence devoted to the failure of marriage, *Modern Love*, and with Frances Power Cobbe's diatribes against matrimonial cruelty and the doctrine of coverture more generally in her essays "Celibacy v. Marriage," "Criminals, Idiots, Women, and Minors," and "Wife-Torture in England," not to mention the sensation novel's fascination with bigamy and adultery.

This book, then, reads the Victorian novel with the vexed nature of marriage firmly in mind. It seeks to build on recent feminist and New Historicist criticism of the domestic novel by inserting the marriage debate into novel theory. Specifically, *Dickens and the Rise of Divorce* argues that marital failure appears so often in the novel that it constitutes a plot in and of itself. The failed-marriage plot—the story of a marriage that disintegrates into mutual alienation or dissolves in separation or divorce—complements and competes with the courtship plot and enables the novelist to write beyond the third volume, as Thackeray puts it in *The Newcomes*.[6]

The history of the English novel is incomplete without the failed-marriage plot, for this narrative is the necessary, if often ignored, second half of the story of courtship the domestic novel is so eager to tell. In Chapter 1, I contextualize this plot by interrogating those theories of the novel that leave little room for the discontents of marriage, by revisiting a series of novels of the eighteenth and nineteenth century in order to uncover those failed-marriage plots we have been trained to overlook, and by tracing the legal history of marriage and divorce that makes available alternatives to the courtship plot.

As the title of this book suggests in its echo of Watt, one of my main purposes in *Dickens and the Rise of Divorce* is to analyze—and break—the lock Watt's thesis has had on our understanding of the novel for over 50 years. As the title also suggests, I do so in large part by concentrating on the novels of Charles Dickens. The novels of Dickens are, perhaps unexpectedly, fertile ground for a case study of the failed-marriage plot: their conservative, domestic plots notwithstanding, in each and every one there exists at least one failed marriage and at least one plot which revolves around breaking wedlock. The disintegration of a marriage is, in fact, one of the things that Dickens makes fictions from, and he gives the failure of marriage a surprisingly high degree of visibility. All of Dickens's novels are concerned—in a multiplicity of ways, both large and small, and in a manner that is alternately comic, tragic, melodramatic, and ironic—with the phenomenon of failed marriage. As I discuss at length at the end of Chapter 1, Dickens cannot quit bringing up the matter of failed marriages. In Chapters 2–5, I examine some of those instances in which he presents the breaking of the matrimonial bond with extraordinary clarity, as well as those moments of marital dis-ease in his novels which we may have read over, ignored, or dismissed in our concentration on the courtship plot. Moving from an exploration of the way Dickens utilizes the failed-marriage plot in three early novels—*Oliver Twist* (1837–39), *Nicholas Nickleby* (1838–39), and *The Old Curiosity Shop* (1840–41)—to three novels written in the middle, and perhaps at the height, of Dickens's career—*Dombey and Son* (1846–48), *David Copperfield* (1849–50), and *Hard Times* (1854)—I read the novels of Dickens in dialogue with parliamentary debates and the articles they appeared alongside in *Household Words*; I analyze his fictions in the context of popular entertainment like Punch and Judy shows and Madame Tussaud's waxworks exhibitions; and I set his fictions alongside the conduct books of Sarah Stickney Ellis, the novels and essays of Caroline Norton, and the journalism of Eliza Lynn Linton. In my chapters on Dickens at mid-career I am especially interested in Victorian protofeminists like Norton and Linton, whose work in reforming the laws of child custody, divorce, and married women's property stands in a curious and contradictory relation to the apparently conservative plots and politics of their own novels and essays—plots and politics which seem to have much in common with those we find in Dickens. This apparent inconsistency suggests not only the need for a more nuanced account of the Woman Question, but also a reassessment of Dickens's own gender politics.

I concentrate on the novels of Dickens, then, as a case study of the failed-marriage plot, a means of uncovering a very different Dickens than we have previously admitted, and an attempt to develop a more accurate picture of what we think of, anachronistically, as Victorian feminism. In the failed-marriage plot, we see Dickens's relation to the Woman Question—its defining issues, its leading intellectuals, its strategies of persuasion, its narrative techniques—come to the fore. Encompassing the issues of child custody, property rights, matrimonial cruelty, and the law of separation and divorce, the Woman Question is important to consider in the context of this study for two reasons. First, the failed-marriage plot is a woman's plot—a plot that concerns itself primarily with the matter of female agency: it tends to revolve around a wife leaving her husband, an act that was both illegal and unacceptable. Furthermore, the ambiguity with which the Victorian monarchy and the legislature dealt with matters of sexual politics, the contending images of the domestic, and the contradictory policies concerning the family which were at work during the nineteenth century make this a period of particular richness for my project. Further, while I find the failed-marriage plot a suggestive and productive one whenever it appears—whether in *Mansfield Park* (1814) or *Wuthering Heights* (1847) or *Jude the Obscure* (1895)—the plot is of special significance when it appears at the same time as the first stirrings of an active woman's movement. In other words, the cultural context of the Victorian novel enables us to see quite clearly the kinds of social and legal forces to which the failed-marriage plot was responding, as well as the kinds of institutional changes that followed in its wake.

The failed-marriage plot works against the energies of the traditional courtship plot and points to the nature of the problems that bring about the failure of marriage, both in individual instances and as a social institution. Both plots are necessary, and both plots read each other (often within the same novel) and contribute to our notions of marriage, as well as to our sense of the patriarchy. Yet the failed-marriage plot allows us to see that there is a possibility for change, that there is a weakness in the hegemonic force, that there is a way in which a wife can break free from what *Dombey and Son*'s Captain Cuttle calls "the house of bondage" (794). Although the women who manage to escape their failed marriages tend to wind up in other patriarchal institutions—Edith Dombey with her doddering Cousin Feenix in Italy, Louisa Bounderby back home with her father—it is still important to note that they have done much more than simply trade one form of imprisonment for another. The fact that their return to a father-figure is of their own choosing is crucial, and it points to both the victory and the limitations of these narratives of disrupted matrimony. The failed-marriage plot, then, simultaneously points to the power of a society to dictate behavior and to the ever-present possibility of flying in the face of those dictates. Raymond Williams reminds us that the hegemonic force "does not just passively exist as a form of dominance. It has continually to be renewed, recreated, defended, and modified. It is also continually resisted, limited, altered, challenged by pressures not at all its own" (*Marxism and Literature* 112).

In showing us the possibility of such resistance, the novel of failed marriage suggests the possibility of alteration and modification.

D.A. Miller suggests that "perhaps no openly fictional form has ever sought to 'make a difference' in the world more than the Victorian novel, whose cultural hegemony and diffusion well qualified it to become the primary spiritual exercise of an entire age" (*The Novel and the Police* x). The Victorian novel is, then, a felicitous point at which to study the failed-marriage plot since in it we can see the paradox of what has been called Victorian hypocrisy. Just as strenuously as marriage was presented as the goal of every British girl and the cornerstone of British society, the social and individual conflicts that were supposed to be set to rest by marriage are often, in the Victorian novel, highlighted by the failed marriages they chronicle. As Judith Walkowitz points out, "marriage no longer resolved the female dilemma; it compounded it" (13). If we would take seriously those stories of marriage the novel so often tells, if we would direct our attention away from the courtship plot, we would see that this is so; we would begin to notice all the husbands and wives clamoring for our attention, all their stories of marriage and its discontents, all the warnings their plots give, and the ramifications of their plots for the genre. In other words, if we concentrate on the stories of marriage as much as we have attended to the stories of courtship, we would begin to put together a rather different history of the novel, a more nuanced sense of the genre, and a more precise understanding of the culture that produced that object, that told such distressing stories and so often sounded the alarm over the institution. It was the Victorians who brought us both the popularization of the novel form and the legalization of divorce; the chapters that follow suggest that coincidence is no accident.

Notes

1   It must be admitted, however, that those "with whom there is no peace while any will or wish is regarded but their own" is a pretty capacious category. Certainly there are more people who fit that description than there are women who have committed adultery or men who have committed adultery aggravated by incest, bigamy, rape, sodomy, bestiality, cruelty, or desertion, to compare Mill's grounds for divorce with the legal standard in 1869.

2   In the *New York Times* on April 19, 2005, Dan Hurley debunked the myth that "one in two American marriages end in divorce." Hurley found that "the rate has never exceeded about 41 percent" and that rates vary so much by age, gender, and level of education, that it is difficult to calculate an overall rate. He also found some sociologists skeptical about this apparently lower rate of divorce. "About half is still a very sensible statement," according to Dr Larry Bumpass, Professor Emeritus of Sociology at the University of Wisconsin's Center for Demography and Ecology. Bumpass's insistence on the 50 percent rate bears out my larger point: that we believe in marriage and seek it like the grail, even as we assume that it will fail at least half of the time.

3   I am not suggesting that Victorianists have overlooked the crisis of marriage, but rather that we have not considered the ramifications of that crisis for the novel as a genre. While work on coverture, divorce law, matrimonial cruelty, and married women's property law (the work of Mary Poovey, Lee Holcombe, and Mary Lyndon Shanley deserves special mention in this context) has caused us to reexamine our notions about Victorian gender politics, they have yet to influence our understanding of the novel. By the same token, historians have long been concerned with the intersection between marriage law and the Woman Question, and studies by James Hammerton, Maeve Doggett, John Gillis, Roderick Phillips, and Allen Horstman are not only careful and perceptive analyses of the way in which the institution of marriage became increasingly codified and policed, moving from a private sacrament to a civil matter made very public, but they are also highly suggestive for any student of the novel. In other words, these studies have considered the history of divorce and its cultural and ideological consequences, but literary critics have yet to examine the significance of marital failure in terms of the novel's emphasis and dependence on the courtship plot.

4   Recent studies of matrimonial cruelty by Marlene Tromp, Lisa Surridge, and Kate Lawson and Lynn Shakinovsky draw much-needed attention to one specific kind of marital failure and what the representation of domestic violence in the novel reveals about marital cruelty in Victorian culture, just as work devoted to the sensation novel, with its reliance on plots of adultery and bigamy, often suggests the degree to which Victorians were chafing at their matrimonial bonds. While work like this, inaugurated by Elaine Showalter's analysis of the novels of Mary Elizabeth Braddon and Ellen Wood in the 1970s, poses the important question as to whether the wedding that shores up the social system inevitably leads to a happy union, that questioning has led to a more informed understanding of Victorian marriage itself rather than a reconsideration of the genre that so often devotes itself to a sustained portrait of domestic life.Similarly, Andrew Dowling's seminal essay, "'The Other Side of Silence': Matrimonial Conflict and the Divorce Court in George Eliot's Fiction," explores what the new divorce law reveals about Victorian assumptions about privacy, marital felicity, and the more nuanced meaning of cruelty operative in the cultural and juridical ideology of the second half of the century. But while he argues that the divorce court's proceedings "fueled an interest and created an audience for tales of matrimonial breakdown," his cause-and-effect logic precludes any exploration of the ramifications of this popular plot for our allegiance to the courtship plot (328).

5   I am indebted to James Eli Adams for this insight.

6   As Mrs Mackenzie tells the narrator of *The Newcomes*, "You gentlemen who write books, Mr Pendennis, and stop at the third volume, know very well that the real story often begins afterwards. My third volume ended when I was sixteen, and was married to my poor husband. Do you think all our adventures ended then, and that we lived happy ever after?" (230).

Chapter 1

Contextualizing the Failed-Marriage Plot: Ian Watt, the Domestic Novel, and the Law of Marriage

In *Aurora Floyd* (1863), Mary Elizabeth Braddon sets the agenda for the present study as she asks her readers,

> Yet, after all, does the business of the real life-drama always end upon the altar-steps? Must the play needs be over when the hero and heroine have signed their names in the register? Does man cease to be, to do, and to suffer when he gets married? And is it necessary that the novelist, after devoting three volumes to the description of a courtship of six weeks' duration, should reserve for himself only half a page in which to tell us the events of two-thirds of a life-time? Aurora is married, and settled, and happy; sheltered, as one would imagine, from all dangers, safe under the wing of her stalwart adorer; but it does not therefore follow that the story of her life is done. She has escaped shipwreck for a while, and has safely landed on a pleasant shore; but the storm cloud may still lower darkly upon the horizon, while the hoarse thunder grumbles threateningly in the distance. (163)

Dickens and the Rise of Divorce focuses on the "storm cloud" and the "hoarse thunder" as it seeks to contest the privilege students of fiction have accorded the courtship plot since Ian Watt's *The Rise of the Novel* (1957). It questions the critical commonplace that marriage establishes closure and demonstrates instead that marriage is just as frequently the impetus for further, often highly-elaborated, narrative development. More specifically, *Dickens and the Rise of Divorce* uncovers and argues for the existence of the failed-marriage plot: the plot Braddon has in mind when she suggests that "half a page" is not enough "in which to tell us the events of two-thirds of a life-time," the plot that considers at length and in detail the failure of the wedded relationship. The goal of this chapter is to understand why the history of the English novel has ignored or overlooked the failed-marriage plot, a project I begin by exploring theories of the novel that fail to take into account the unhappy marriages that litter the pages of the domestic novel and by trying to figure out why marital misery has received so little critical attention in narrative theory. I then canvas eighteenth- and nineteenth-century novels for examples of marital dis-ease and the strategies novelists have employed to construct narratives from what happens after the vows have been exchanged and the courtship plot successfully resolved. I conclude by looking at the legislation enacted from 1753, when clandestine marriages were forbidden and marriage more stringently codified, to 1857, when divorce was legalized. Looking at the legal versions of the courtship plot, the failed-marriage plot, and the divorce plot helps us see, in another register, just how pervasive and perplexing the interrogation of marriage was in eighteenth- and nineteenth-century Britain. The matrimonial legislation enacted in that period suggests yet another reason to insist on a more balanced and complete view of the institution of marriage as it was reflected through the medium of literature. As Niklas Luhmann reminds us, the codification of relations between men and women "not only regulated behaviour, but also documented its own recurrence in the very area of behavior it regulated" (32). Specifically, "codification becomes reflected" in the novel, and "already by the seventeenth century it was common knowledge that the lady had read novels and therefore knew the code" (31). Luhmann draws attention to the way in which cultural systems (which include literature and the law, not to mention the economy, politics, and science) both influence and depend upon each other for their successful reception.

The Courtship Plot and the Novel Tradition

Ruth Yeazell points out in her study of the modest heroine that the period of courtship is traditionally viewed as "the special province of the English novel" (*Fictions of Modesty* 50). As Yeazell's phrase implies, it is a controlling assumption of the history of the novel that Continental novelists of the eighteenth and nineteenth centuries wrote novels of adultery, concentrating on extramarital liaisons which occur after the marriage ceremony, while their English counterparts produced novels of courtship, relying on a narrative culminating in the exchange of wedding vows to provide closure. But this assumption deflects attention from the fact that many English novels pay attention to the wedded relationship itself, that many novels of courtship also examine the events that take place after the courtship plot has been resolved. In other words, the strong critical emphasis on the courtship plot has led many critics to ignore another, equally important, generic impulse. All English novels of the eighteenth and nineteenth centuries do not, in fact, end with the marriage of hero and heroine, and the domestic novel does not always establish closure and ask its readers to believe that society has thus been stabilized. Indeed, the novel of courtship's plot-motivating tension between hero and heroine that must be resolved in order for them to marry is often mirrored in the tension between husband and wife. Privileging the courtship plot effectively preempts a theory of the novel that takes into account the prevalence of postmarital plotting and that recognizes the failure of marriage as the subject of this plot. That is, while the courtship plot certainly emerges in the eighteenth century with novels like Samuel Richardson's *Pamela* (1740), formalist critics like Dorothy Van Ghent and J. Hillis Miller—and even a Marxian historicist like Mary Poovey—have established this plot as a critical paradigm, a formalization critics abstract from the messy and uncontainable history of the novel and thus one continually questioned in the novels themselves. While no one would argue that there are no unhappy marriages in English novels, critics of the British novel tend to abstract as a norm a version of union that the texts themselves everywhere put in jeopardy. Hence critics as various as E.M. Forster, Leslie Fiedler, and Nancy Armstrong (all of whom at times write skeptically about heterosexual union, whatever their other differences) have viewed marriage as the goal of the domestic novel and have written histories of the novel that take for granted that the marriages depicted in the English novel are successful.

I want first, then, to think about how and why students of the novel subscribe so faithfully to Watt's theory of the novel, how even the most subversive of critics base their understanding of the domestic novel on a theory that has shaped our understanding of the genre for over 50 years. I want to examine why Mary Poovey, a critic who is otherwise impatient with received wisdom and critical truisms, accepts that a "generically new novel" that "would take as its subject marital unhappiness as well as bliss … of course, would not begin to appear in Britain until the very end of the century, when Thomas Hardy finally broke the stranglehold of the marriage plot with a mode of realism that denied readers the gratification of romantic wishes fulfilled" ("Recovering Ellen Pickering" 448). The strength of Watt's hold on novel criticism reveals itself in Poovey's "of course," and in what follows I want to articulate some of the reasons for that powerful grip, to provide an explanation for the overwhelming and long-lived success of his conservative thesis, and to suggest an alternative account of the domestic novel.

Poovey's assertions are symptomatic; her work has voluminously undermined any totalizing claim about the Victorians and their affective life, yet we see the persistence of the Victorian symbolic of contented marriages in her otherwise revisionary oeuvre. Poovey is also a good place to begin tracing the attractive power of Watt's thesis, for she, like so many other students of the novel, assumes that the end of the Victorian period (not accidentally) coincides with the end of the courtship plot, or, at the very least, the beginning of a move away from it. In *The City of Dickens* (1971), Alexander Welsh nominates E.M. Forster's insistence that "if it was not for death and marriage, I do not know how the average novelist would conclude" as "a fair description of the English novel before Forster's time" (220). Similarly, in *Tradition Counter Tradition* (1987) Joseph Boone argues that the "tragic wedlock plot" does not emerge until the end of the nineteenth century (10).[1] More subtly, Jonathan Loesberg, in his essay "Deconstruction, Historicism, and Overdetermination: Dislocations of the Marriage Plots in *Robert Elsmere* and *Dombey and Son*" (1990), invokes the passage in *Aurora Floyd* which is my point of departure in this chapter and argues that "when with casual humor and merely for heightening suspense, a suspense writer calls attention to the breaking of a novelistic convention, we can safely guess that the convention being broken is no longer an all-powerful one" (460). Loesberg's point here is especially significant, for while he points to the fact that the convention of ending a novel in marriage is "no longer an all-powerful one," he also implies that it was at one point a convention, and an "all-powerful" one at that. Indeed, he assumes this convention to be one that held before 1863. While his dating of the breaking of that convention predates Poovey's (Hardy) and Welsh's and Boone's (the end/turn of the century), his argument reveals that he, too, equates the domestic novel with the courtship plot. Whether critics point to Hardy or Forster or Braddon as the instigator of the move away from a conventional marriage plot, all of these moves are variations on Watt's theme that there is in fact a convention to be broken, whereas I would argue that the failed-marriage plot was a competing and complementary plot from the beginning of the novel's emergence in the eighteenth century.

Closely linked to Watt's thesis that the English novel most often finds its plot in courtship is the corollary thesis that there is no way to plot a marriage, that novels end in marriage not only because that institution marks the successful end of a courtship, but also because it puts an end to all narrative possibilities. This view is not unlike Forster's sense that death and marriage are the only ways to end a novel, and it is an important consequence of Watt's argument to consider in the context of my argument about the failed-marriage plot, for marriage does not always put an end to novelistic plotting (unlike death, marriage does not mean the end of a character's story), and marriage does not always establish closure—for the novel or for the characters the institution unites. Indeed, the preponderance of second-chance plots and remarriages in the English novel indicates that the form neither requires nor insists that its plots always end in marriage or that marriage is always a static state of affairs. Yet adopting too easily the courtship model leaves us without a theory of the novel that takes into account the prevalence of postmarital plotting. The implications of the many novels that take a more sustained view of the institution of marriage itself—that find their plots in the lives of husbands and wives—have yet to be taken up by novel theory.[2] Critical emphasis on the courtship plot has had the strange effect of occluding the plot that concerns the future of that desired end.

The kind of post-courtship plotting that forms the focus of my study is the failed-marriage plot, precisely because it is this plot that most explicitly contradicts the accepted notion that marriage establishes closure. But there are also, of course, novels devoted to the marriage plot in the most literal sense, novels of remarriage, as I suggest above, and novels in which a man and woman who have married for reasons other than affection—-the attraction may be one-sided, or they may have been forced to marry for economic or familial reasons or to escape some other fate—come to love each other. In novels like these, the courtship plot is almost exactly reproduced within the wedded relationship. Yet for critics as various as D.A. Miller, Mary Poovey, and Carolyn Heilbrun, marriage is "nonnarratable" (the term is Miller's); it has no capacity "to generate a story" (Miller, *Narrative and Its Discontents* 5).[3] Poovey assumes that marriage in general "brings the plot to closure and thus ends the writer's work" ("Recovering Ellen Pickering" 452, n. 5), while Miller finds that happy marriages, like those that mark the end of Austen novels, "inhibit narrative productivity"—that they have "no narrative future." "The 'perfect union' of Emma and Mr. Knightley virtually *must* end the novel," he argues, "otherwise, it would not be a 'perfect' union" (Miller, *Narrative and Its Discontents* 5). Carolyn Heilbrun shares Miller's view that marriages are not the stuff of fiction and that Austen's marriages are especially devoid of plot. In "Marriage Perceived: English Literature 1873–1941" (1977), she argues that until the beginnings of the modern novel (a line of demarcation fast becoming familiar), "marriage was not allowed to enter into literature, except as a condition universally acknowledged, but either unobserved, or glimpsed so occasionally that little was discovered beyond casual misery or boredom or both." She accounts for this omission on the grounds that marriage is "quotidian" and that happy marriages are "not news" (163).[4]

Three strands linking these various accounts are worthy of remark: the frequency with which Hardy or the modern novel is linked to the beginnings of the novel's exploration of marriage and its failures; the similarity between Carolyn Heilbrun's insistence in 1977 that marriage is "not news" and D.A. Miller's description of it in 1981 as "nonnarratable"; and, more generally, the surprising consonance between E.M. Forster and Jonathan Loesberg, Carolyn Heilbrun and D.A. Miller, Alexander Welsh and Mary Poovey, between pioneers of novel criticism and latter-day, more self-consciously historicist and more skeptical critics. I will return to these three correspondences in formulating an explanation of the longevity of Watt's thesis, but I want first to turn to some more scattered evidence of Watt's reach, to bits and pieces from recent studies of the domestic novel that suggest how widely scholars subscribe to the basic thesis of *The Rise of the Novel*. Consider, for instance, Ann duCille's *The Coupling Convention: Sex, Text, and Tradition in Black Women's Fiction* (1993), which begins thus:

> "It is a truth universally acknowledged that a single man in possession of a great fortune must be in want of a wife." This oft-quoted opening line from Jane Austen's *Pride and Prejudice* suggests both the degree to which the marriage plot is indigenous to the genre of the novel and the extent to which the middle and upper classes have historically been preoccupied with matrimony and affairs of the heart and pocketbook. It is a truth not so widely acknowledged, however, that the single everyman in Jane Austen's universal is not only wealthy but white. This study is concerned with what happens when the players change, when the fictive figures "in love and in trouble," to use Alice Walker's metaphor, cease to be white men and women of means and property and become black men and women, poor as well as propertied. What happens to the marriage tradition—to Leslie Fiedler's notion of love as "the subject par excellence of the novel," for example—when it is considered in the context of a literature by and about American men and women who for generations were denied the hegemonic "universal truth" of legal marriage? (3)

In her groundbreaking study of the courtship plot in African-American fiction, duCille applies Watt's thesis to novels by William Wells Brown, Frances Harper, Pauline Hopkins, and Zora Neale Hurston, but in so doing she accepts what she calls that "hegemonic 'universal truth.'" She extends the reach of the courtship plot when she argues that, "making unconventional use of conventional literary forms, early black writers appropriated for their own emancipatory purposes both the genre of the novel and the structure of the marriage plot" (3).

duCille's acceptance of *The Rise of the Novel*'s privileging of the courtship plot is similar to Mary Poovey's articulation, in *Uneven Developments* (1988), of the way in which a novel like *David Copperfield* both describes and reproduces "a specific model of desire" that "ideally" is "stabilized and its transgressive potential neutralized in the safe harbor of marriage" (90). duCille's approach also resembles Nancy Armstrong's groundbreaking (yet fundamentally Wattian) assertion in *Desire and Domestic Fiction* (1987) that

> when Austen and the Brontës sat down to write novels, they apparently knew they were writing novels, and they knew what a novel was. ... For by then it had been established that novels were supposed to rewrite political history as personal histories that elaborated on the courtship procedures ensuring a happy domestic life. (38)

Armstrong further reveals that her revision is one that works within the domain of a discipline-defining hypothesis when she argues that

> around the time Austen wrote, the novel was being defined by Scott, Barbauld, and others in a way that gave meaning to such narratives whose resolution depended on marriage. The novel was identified with fiction that authorized a particular form of domestic relations. But if Austen could not vary the form and still write a respectable novel, she could modify the content and thus the nature of the social conflict that marriage appeared to resolve. (50)

Her awareness of the ways in which Austen modifies the content of the domestic novel highlights our assumption that the form itself is inviolable and that we respect the boundaries established by Watt and the truths his thesis appoints as "universally acknowledged." Further, in the epilogue to *Desire and Domestic Fiction*, Armstrong demonstrates that the English novel presents us with the kind of heterosexual, normative, conservative plot that Watt has trained us to read for, and she suggests that this plot is one that she, and most readers of English fiction, have internalized. In the following passage she not only spells out what is at stake in her account of the domestic novel, but she also reveals the debt her revisionary thesis owes to Watt. I thus quote from her epilogue at length:

> I am convinced that the household Richardson envisioned for Pamela has grown more powerful during the time that has passed between his day and ours. This is true not only because the self-enclosed family often conceals a host of abuses, but also because, with the emergence of the professional couple as an economic reality, gender roles have changed in significant ways. The ideal of domesticity has grown only more powerful as it has become less a matter of fact and more a

matter of fiction, for the fiction of domesticity exists as a fact in its own right. It begins to exert power over our lives the moment we begin to learn what normal behavior is supposed to be. ... I feel this power keenly—the power of all the domestic clichés we have grown half ashamed to live by. And I have tried to demonstrate how this power was given to women and exercised through them. To that end, I have used certain novels to explain how a notion of the household as a specifically feminine space established the preconditions for a modern institutional culture. I have argued that, in the hands of an intellectual such as Richardson, the female was used to contest the dominant notion of kinship relations. The novel, together with all manner of printed material, helped to redefine what men were supposed to desire in women and what women, in turn, were supposed to desire to be. (251)

I want to expand on Armstrong's precise and probing reading of the English novel and take into account the fact that "the ideal of domesticity" is portrayed as imperiled as often as it is valorized. I want to complicate her assurance that "the fiction of domesticity exists as a fact in its own right" by considering those plots that undermine and parody and show us the discontented side of the myth of Victorian marriage. The fact that Armstrong accords the "ideal of domesticity" an increasing power suggests that Watt's thesis has become a cliché—something we may unconsciously assume and thus base our readings upon—which is all the more reason for us to shift our perspective on the novel's history.

The other thing that strikes me in this respect is that even when critics do notice the conservative basis of our theory of the novel, they attribute the conservatism to the novels they are reading rather than to our theoretical conclusions about them.[5] For example, Jeff Nunokawa, in *The Afterlife of Property: Domestic Security and the Victorian Novel* (1994), cites approvingly those "feminist assessments of Victorian domestic ideology in and beyond the novel [that] have exposed the cult of separate spheres as a means of strengthening and stabilizing the market economy by providing intermittent relief from their conflicts and contradictions":

The home whose ideological dimensions Mary Poovey and Nancy Armstrong survey is ... a place where the war of all against all, or the one between the classes, or the split of self within the self, brought on by this economy is suspended or cured. According to their various accounts, the domestic sphere, whose essence is the love of a good woman, offers a vacation from the pressures of the market economy, or translates the terms of its divisions and divisiveness from the marketplace where they are invented and exacerbated into a sphere of romance where they are resolved. Under the sharp lens of their scrutiny, a simple image of home as a haven in a heartless world gives way to the more complex vision of a site for the imaginary resolution of antagonisms that the market economy starts and cannot solve. The domestic devotions they examine assist the operations of the market economy exactly as Victorians themselves thought a wife should: by furnishing the place where the perturbations of the marketplace are put to rest. (12)

In this subscription to happy endings, Nunokawa (one of the most skeptical of novel readers) demonstrates that the model—a conservative view of Victorian marriage—exists in the midst of its own change.[6] The home he describes here as a "more complex vision" sounds as if it were presided over by a Ruskinian queen, while the idea that the domestic sphere "offers a vacation from ... the market" brings to mind Patmore's domestic angel. But the critique of the doctrine of coverture (the ethos responsible, according to John Stuart Mill, for all the woes of Victorian marriage) that we find in so many Victorian novels underscores just how very much "the perturbations of the marketplace" figure into and come home to disturb the domestic sphere, rather than to be put to rest.

Similarly, in "The Transport of the Novel," the introduction to their collection *Cultural Institutions of the Novel* (1996), Deidre Lynch and William Warner explain that many of the contributors to their volume understand the novel

> as a social machinery that helps produce individuals as subjects of sexuality and aligns their desires with the norms of family and/or the demands of consumer capitalism. For many contributors to this section, attending in this manner to what novels do in culture involves engaging the romance, construed either as the novel's figure for its own origins or as the generic location in which the narrative eludes the reality principle and responds to desire. (8)

In other words, they read the novel as a conservative agent (it "aligns" our "desires with the norms of the family") and as a kind of fairy-tale ("the narrative eludes the reality principle and responds to desire"). The novel, then, is a domestic genre and one that concerns itself with the desires—and even the creation—of an individual. This definition of the novel bears the imprint of Watt, not only in its all-encompassing identification of the novel with the domestic but also, and perhaps even more importantly, in its equation of a novel's plot with a story of an individual's desire, of her personal and private life. Indeed, individualism is the cornerstone of Watt's argument, and in nominating the story of courtship as the novel's most typical plot, Watt spotlights the emotional desires of an individual, training novel readers to look for them in determining the main action of a novel and to read a stabilized sexuality as the signal that the novel's story is over. Moving as it does from *Robinson Crusoe* (1719) to *Pamela*, *The Rise of the Novel* itself traces the perfect intermeshing of the sexual and the economic into the establishment of domestic stability with which Watt ends his account.

Watt's focus on individualism begins even before he advances his theory of the novel of courtship. His chapter on *Robinson Crusoe* is subtitled "Individualism and the Novel," and in it he argues that it was Defoe's emphasis on the individual and his distrust of marriage in *Crusoe* that brought the novel into being as a genre devoted to the courtship plot ending in marriage. Watt sets up his argument by suggesting that

> the novel's serious concern with the daily lives of ordinary people seems to depend upon two important general conditions: the society must value every individual highly enough to consider him the proper subject of its serious literature; and there must be enough variety of belief and action among ordinary people for a detailed account of them to be of interest to other ordinary people, the readers of novels. It is probable that neither of these conditions for the existence of the novel obtained very widely until fairly recently, because they both depend on the rise of a society characterised by that vast complex of interdependent factors denoted by the term "individualism." (60)

Reading backwards, we can see how Watt's specification of "daily lives" and "detailed accounts" paves the way for his assertion that Richardson's success with the novel form had much to do with the fact that "he avoided an episodic plot by basing his novels on a single action, a courtship" (135). That is, once we accept the notion that "the daily lives of ordinary people" are of interest, and once we begin to understand the appeal of "a detailed account" of those lives, then it is not too difficult to see the plot possibilities provided by focusing on the relationship between two people as they move toward marriage. I belabor this point not only because it is the foundation of Watt's argument, but also because it is the aspect of his thesis that crops up most often and in the most surprising places. Specifically, it is the importance of individualism to his theory of the novel that marks the parallels between Dorothy Van Ghent and J. Hillis Miller.[7]

In the introduction to *The English Novel: Form and Function* (1953), Dorothy Van Ghent generalizes that "the subject matter of novels is human relationships" and that "the procedure of the novel is to individualize" (3, 4).[8] Similarly, J. Hillis Miller finds that "Victorian fiction, like fiction in general, has a single pervasive theme: interpersonal relations" (*The Form of Victorian Fiction* 94). Both Van Ghent's and Miller's theories of the novel are not only consonant with Watt's way of thinking about the novel, but Van Ghent also anticipates his diction. Compare her "the subject matter of the novel is human relationships" to Watt's "Defoe's story is perhaps not a novel in the usual sense since it deals so little with personal relations" (92). Or lay her assertion that a novel proceeds by individualizing alongside Watt's insistence that the novel depends on a state of affairs wherein "the society ... value[s] every individual highly enough to consider him the proper subject of its serious literature" (60).

This echo becomes particularly clear when Watt defines for us precisely what he means by the term "individualism":

> the concept of individualism ... posits a whole society mainly governed by the idea of every individual's intrinsic independence both from other individuals and from that multifarious allegiance to past modes of thought and action denoted by

the word 'tradition'—a force that is always social, not individual. The existence of such a society, in turn, obviously depends on a special type of economic and political organisation and on an appropriate ideology; more specifically, on an economic and political organisation which allows its members a very wide range of choices in their actions, and on an ideology primarily based, not on the tradition of the past, but on the autonomy of the individual, irrespective of his particular social status or personal capacity. (60)

In Watt's scheme of things, the community (what he calls the "society") is organized in such a way that it permits the individual to concentrate on his or her own interest. By the same token, Hillis Miller argues that the characters in Victorian novels

who hold the center of attention have not yet fulfilled themselves by way of their relations to others. They exist as potentiality, not as actuality, as a hollow or perturbation in the midst of the surrounding community. This situation of unsatisfied desire makes them relatively introspective. The narrator concentrates on their sense of themselves as incomplete and follows their attempts to bring themselves to completion. (*The Form of Victorian Fiction* 93–4)

This part of Watt's argument makes it clear that the quotidian doings of ordinary people are of interest because these ordinary people are free agents: autonomous, independent, and possessed of unlimited possibilities and potential. Hillis Miller builds upon Watt's notion of autonomy in his emphasis on potentiality, on the possibility of fulfillment, and on the novel's dedication to chronicling these characters' "attempts to bring themselves to completion." Indeed, the importance of autonomy and possibility has much to do with the appeal of this argument. That is, one reason Watt's thesis is so attractive has to do with the fact that he works from the outset to define the plot of the novel as one we are invested in and one we are very reluctant to quarrel with. He turns the hero and heroine into fully realized characters (one almost wants to say "people") who have the right, the freedom, and the ability to search for fulfillment "irrespective of [their] particular social status." To suggest, as I am doing, that they would do so only to discover the failure of what they have so bravely and independently achieved seems churlish, to say the least. Indeed, once Watt turns to the matter of courtship, he invests it with such overwhelming significance that it is difficult to imagine that such an enterprise could fail. Because he connects the triumph of the courtship plot (i.e. marriage) with free choice, the rights of women, and with a Puritanism that imbued marriage with a "spiritual and social meaning," Watt ties up our subscription to his theory of the novel with our investment in the rights of the individual, a nascent feminism, and a view of marriage that rejects the conventions of courtly love for a more mutual and a more spiritual relation (167).

In what may be the most influential chapter of *The Rise of the Novel*, "Love and the Novel: 'Pamela,'" Watt begins by reminding us of Madame de Staël's theory that "the Ancients had no novels" because "the classical world attached relatively little importance to the emotional relationships between men and women" (135). And he reminds us that this devaluation of romantic love was, according to Staël, "largely" "a result of the inferior social position of women." Thus the chapter that pronounces that "the great majority of novels written since *Pamela* have continued its basic pattern, and concentrated their main interest upon a courtship leading to marriage"[9] begins by linking the rise of the novel to the advancement of women's social position. While the protofeminism of Watt's thesis has received very little attention, it surely has much to do with the fact that critics like Armstrong, Poovey, and Yeazell can so easily work from within the model Watt provides. Indeed, one of the reasons Watt's privileging of the courtship plot has had such an incredibly long half-life is that he identifies it as a woman's plot, that he makes it clear that by "individual" he means both man and woman, and that he argues, in 1957, that "the rise of the novel, then, would seem to be connected with the much greater freedom of women in modern society, a freedom which, especially as regards marriage, was achieved earlier and more completely in England than elsewhere" (138). This account of things not only helps us see how Tony Tanner's *Adultery in the Novel* (1979), on the one hand, and Ruth Yeazell's *Fictions of Modesty* (subtitled *Women and Courtship in the English Novel*), on the other, are, like most studies of the novel, direct descendants of *The Rise of the Novel*. It also helps explain the investment in Watt's equation of the novel with the courtship plot. Dickens's Podsnap would say that the failed-marriage plot is decidedly "not English!" just as quickly as he would banish an adultery novel lest it bring a blush to the cheek of the young person. Subscribing to Watt's thesis validates a world that allows for female choice, women's moral authority, women's new independence. Because these are all things we are deeply invested in, then, why suggest that this account is incomplete? Why bring up the failure of a relationship a woman chose to enter?

In the introduction to *Desire and Domestic Fiction* (aptly titled "The Politics of Domesticating Culture, Then and Now"), Nancy Armstrong suggests another reason we may be reluctant to look beyond the courtship plot: "as the heirs to a novelistic culture," she suggests, "we are not very likely to question the whole enterprise. We are more likely to feel that the success of repeated pressures to coax and nudge sexual desire into conformity with the norms of heterosexual monogamy affords a fine way of closing a novel and provides a satisfactory goal for a text to achieve" (6). While an important part of my project is devoted to uncovering the ways in which that "repeated pressure" comes from critics of the novel rather than from the novels themselves, it is true, as I will explore in more detail below, that the domestic novel does often encourage us to believe that marriage ensures a happily-ever-after, even as it portrays the failure of marriage in its subplots, for instance, or even as it suggests—while plotting a successful courtship—how naïve we are to succumb to such wish fulfillment. Joseph Litvak makes a related point. In laying out the goals for his study of theatricality and the nineteenth-century British novel, *Caught in the Act* (1992), he insists both that the nineteenth-century novel "marks the triumphant climax of the well-known rise of the novel" and that "it has been shown less to record than to help institutionalize what has been dubbed, almost as memorably, the fall of public man—a fall from the theatricality of eighteenth century culture into the world of domesticity, subjectivity, and psychology" (ix). While it is not clear if by "help institutionalize" Litvak is referring to the cultural work the novels themselves performed in the nineteenth century or to the work that we contemporary scholars do when we read into them, he does shed some light on novel theory's investment in believing that the novel represents and replicates an "intimate, personalized" world. Similarly, the Foucaldian conclusion of Litvak's sentence bears a marked resemblance to the way in which Poovey and Armstrong seek to expose the novel's powers of coercion:[10] "the world of domesticity, subjectivity, and psychology … far from providing refuge from surveillance, installs it, with remarkable hospitality, in an apparently infinite number of snug little homes, where it can go about its business under cover of an endlessly idealizing misrecognition" (ix–x). Litvak does, however, suggest most enticingly the appeal of these "snug little homes" and the lure of what we might call Watt's remarkably hospitable thesis.

It is important, too, to note that Litvak emphasizes the difference between eighteenth- and nineteenth-century culture. For one recurrent—and deeply implicit—assumption in the critical texts I have been examining is that, along with Jane Austen, the Victorian novel provides the most and the best examples of Watt's thesis. That is, I find a general willingness to admit the existence of the failed-marriage plot from Hardy on, and as Litvak's emphasis on the theatricality of the eighteenth century suggests (and as any student of Fanny Burney or Maria Edgeworth or Eliza Haywood well knows), marriage is not always represented as an institution of harmony or content in that period. But Victorianists seem more determined to uphold the conservative nature of the marriage plots we find in Dickens or Eliot or Gaskell.[11] This tendency is not unrelated to the fact that this period is called the Victorian period. The period immediately before it—Romanticism—is named for a way of feeling, for an emotion, or a style; the word "modern," as Carol Christ so perceptively notes, "means characteristic of the present as opposed to the past" (156). But the period in between is named after a queen, a nomination that is really a critical act (and one performed so routinely that it is rarely recognized as such). Indeed, Christ reminds us that "Paul de Man has argued that modernity is characterized by the desire to forget the past, to originate something wholly new"—a characterization which helps us understand the widespread sense that the novel only began to explore the stresses and strains of the wedded relationship in what we call the modern period (156). Christ goes on to argue that

> the way in which "modern" implies a present which displaces a past while "Victorian" describes a discarded past reveals much about the relationship of the two periods as constructions in literary history. Although they seem serial terms of historical description—after the Victorian period came the modern—

they are frequently oppositional—the modern defeats, displaces, overcomes the
Victorian. (157)

What it overcomes when it defeats the Victorian is, as I suggest above, an age
that is named after a figure of authority, an embodiment of tradition. The other
association we have with the term "Victorian" is a kind of fustiness, a general
conservatism, even a kind of prudery. To talk about the Victorian novel of failed
marriage, then, seems oxymoronic, counterintuitive, pointlessly radical even.

The survey of the English novel that follows will look at examples from the
eighteenth and nineteenth centuries that reveal the genre's interest in marriage,
as opposed to simply the courtship leading up to that relationship. But because,
as the preceding pages suggest, the Victorian novel seems to be the least likely
site for any kind of marriage plot (failed or otherwise), most of the examples
will come from the nineteenth century, and I will spend more time exploring the
occurrence of the failed-marriage plot in the Victorian novel than in eighteenth-
century fiction. The preponderance of Victorian novels of failed marriage leads me
to suspect that this era was perhaps even more interested in plotting the relationship
between husband and wife and in examining the failure of that relationship than
the period that preceded it. Similarly, in exploring the history of marriage law
from the beginning of the eighteenth century through the turn into the twentieth
century, it becomes clear that while sweeping changes were enacted to the law of
marriage throughout that 300-year period, it was in the nineteenth century, during
Victoria's reign, that legislation focused most exclusively on divorce: on codifying
and classifying the ways in which legal separations and divorces could be effected,
and then on the fates of the property, the children, and the divorced wives after
these marriages had been declared legally over. In fact, it is my sense of the
Victorian novel and the Victorian period as so very concerned with the institution
of divorce that leads me, finally, to my focus on Dickens. For if critics of the novel
have a blind spot when it comes to their classification of the Victorian novel and
its interest in courtship, then perhaps that blind spot also partially accounts for
their categorization of Dickens as the novelist of hearth and home, the inventor of
Christmas, genial paterfamilias.[12] Dickens is the Victorian novelist who perhaps
best embodies stereotypical notions of the age, and if we can find instances of the
failed-marriage plot in his fictions, then I think we have fairly conclusive evidence
that the failed-marriage plot is one of the Victorian novel's favorite stories. I thus
concentrate on the novels of Dickens in the subsequent chapters of this book, both
as a case study of the failed-marriage plot and in the interest of revealing a more
accurate and nuanced portrait of Dickens as novelist.

Plotting Marriage

I want to begin my survey of the English novel by going back to what I referred to
at the beginning of this chapter as the controlling assumption of the history of the

domestic novel: that there exists the Continental novel of adultery, on the one hand, and the English novel of courtship, on the other. Since English girls were thought to have greater freedom in choosing a husband than those French girls propelled straight from the convent into a *mariage de convenance*, there was a story to be told about an unmarried girl and her passage to matrimony, which would not exist for a girl raised in the Continental tradition. "It cannot be emphasized enough," Luhmann argues about the French novel, "that the freedom to choose someone to love applies to the *extra-marital* relationships of *married* persons" (50). Any kind of romantic tension, plotting, or complication could only come after the marriage ceremony for the *jeune fille*. Or as Luhmann puts it, "freedom thus began with marriage" (50). Thus, the novel of adultery is thought of as the other version of the novel of courtship. This version of the differences between the English novel and the Continental novel is, of course, a reductive one. But it is hard to quarrel with its general outlines, and it dovetails with what Luhmann identifies as "the differences between the *amour passion* complex of the French and the Puritans' notion of marriage based on 'companionship'" (10).[13] While I would not argue with this view of the novel of courtship, I would argue with the assumption implicit in this view that there is no post-wedding plot available for the British heroine. Perhaps, following this account, there is no such thing as a Continental novel of courtship, but it does not logically follow that there is no English novel of adultery[14] or that English novels typically do not explore marriages as well as courtships.

We quite often discover the same kind of post-wedding plot the Continental novel finds in adultery in the English domestic novel's treatment of the relationship between husband and wife, in its portrayal of marriage itself. The novel of courtship's plot-motivating tension between hero and heroine, which must be resolved in order for them to marry, is in many instances mirrored in the tension between husband and wife. In the "Finale" to *Middlemarch* (1872), we are explicitly told that such is often the case, that "marriage, which has been the bourne of so many narratives, is still a great beginning ... It is still the beginning of the home epic" (890).[15] It seems quite plausible then, that for every domestic novel ending in courtship, there is a domestic novel that paints the life of husband and wife.[16] Even those novels of courtship that do end in the marriage of hero and heroine often contain extended meditations on the married lives of minor characters, and these subplots both frame and serve as cautionary counterpoints to the more conventional stories of courtship they introduce and surround. In *Mansfield Park*, for instance, Fanny's and Edmund's courtship is played off against the unhappy marriage and eventual divorce of Maria and Mr Rushworth, just as the ill-assorted marriage of Mr and Mrs Bennett and the disastrous union of Lydia and Wickham in *Pride and Prejudice* (1813) provide a cautionary backdrop to the courtship of Elizabeth and Darcy.[17]

To assume—as we do when we accept that courtship is the British version of the marriage plot—that marriage provides no narrative motion is to subscribe to a belief in a partial generic history and to give many English novels only a partial reading. It is also to accept that marriages are static and cannot supply a novel's plot. We know almost instinctively that such is not the case, and the plots of *Daniel Deronda* (1876), *Vanity Fair* (1848), *Jude the Obscure*, and *Wuthering Heights* bear out our intuitions. That is, Gwendolen's marriage to Grandcourt is so miserable, so thoroughly failed, that the reader is strongly encouraged to believe her responsible for his death. Amelia's pathetic devotion to her husband, George Osborne, and Rawdon Crawley's naïve trust in his wife, the clever and ambitious Becky Sharp, lead to marriages that are shams of trust and devotion and that everyone, with the exception of the trusting spouses, Amelia and Rawdon, know to be models of infidelity. In *Jude*, the plotting of Sue Bridehead's marriage to Phillotson and Jude's to Arabella Donn suggests both that marriage is a trap and that people walk into it blithely and with their eyes wide open.[18] *Wuthering Heights* is just as cynical about the institution; full of characters who marry even though they should most certainly know better (Edgar Linton, Isabella, young Linton), it reveals a belief in the power of marriage to insure domestic comfort and social stability even as it demonstrates that matrimony is anything but comfortable or stable. Like our privileging of the courtship plot, characters' eagerness to marry suggests they want to believe in marital bliss despite all the evidence to the contrary; that eagerness provides Emily Brontë with three complicated plots to tangle and explore.[19]

It is not, then, that the English novel asks us to believe that stories always end in marriage or that marriage is always a static (or a happy) state of affairs. The examples I cite suggest just how much narrative energy the plotting of marriage can yield. It should, in fact, go without saying that the domestic novel is engaged in examining the institution of marriage and its relationship to society.[20] But the marriage plot has been overlooked as a plot of generic and cultural significance, perhaps because there has yet to be put forth an explanation of the way in which this dominant concern with marriage can exist in a form devoted to the process which only leads up to that state. Further, as my examples—which range from the highly canonical and widely taught to the lesser known—suggest, in order to uncover the prevalence of the failed-marriage plot, we need not only to give the canonical novel a more complete reading, but also to move beyond the limits of the canon in order to generate a more complex generic history. It only takes a slight shift in emphasis, in reading, to realize that the domestic novel, for all its allegiance to the courtship plot, also always reveals marriage under pressure. If marriage is the center of Victorian culture in some inescapable ways, then it is also inescapable that that center is dis-integrating, worried. As James Eli Adams has written, not of marriage but of masculinity, it "is exemplary of all gender norms in being always under pressure from the very social dynamics that authorize it, the changing consolidation of social authority through new varieties of suspicion, exclusion, and affirmation" (19).

The kind of "home epic" on which I focus in this study is the failed-marriage plot, because this plot most explicitly contradicts the accepted notion that marriage establishes closure and most tellingly reveals the "varieties of suspicion, exclusion, and affirmation" that simultaneously underwrite and threaten the matrimonial norm.[21] A taxonomy of the failed-marriage plot helps characterize the different

kinds of failed marriages that the English novel so frequently depicts. These
include the plot inherited from Restoration comedy (and rewritten so frequently by
Thomas Hardy) of the rake or dandy figure who destroys either his or his friend's
marriage; the Gothic bigamy plot, found most famously in *Jane Eyre* (1847) and
in the sensation novels of the 1860s; the plot that reveals the impoverished legal
status of wives (most notably in novels by crusaders like Mary Wollstonecraft
and Caroline Norton); the many stories of abusive marriages; and the plot that
unflinchingly—and sometimes even spectacularly—explores and dissects the
discontents of marriage.[22]

In the next few pages I will concentrate on two novels of failed marriage
which explore the discontents of marriage and reveal just how much plot the
story of a marriage can generate: Anne Brontë's *The Tenant of Wildfell Hall* and
Trollope's *He Knew He Was Right*. If, as Luhmann suggests, "thematic choices
and guiding principles ... of love are not arbitrary, but rather represent reactions
to the respective society and the trends for change within it" then these novels are
especially revealing in terms of the Victorians' vexed attitude toward marriage;
they highlight those curious contradictions I identified in Mill and in Queen
Victoria at the outset of this project and show them at work in the domestic novel,
determining some of its most powerful and pervasive plots (Luhmann 20). I also
want these close readings to serve as a point of entry for my discussion of the ways
in which marriage and divorce law developed in the eighteenth and nineteenth
centuries, and specifically, to suggest the role of the novel in bringing about
the legalization of divorce and the protection of wives' property, children, and
bodies.[23] Leo Bersani proposes that "both the reader and the society within the
novel stand in fascinated awe of those figures who embody that secret excess or
violence which perhaps prefigures a structural explosion but which also awakens
the self-preserving energies of a stable order" (70). In looking at the figures of
excess in these novels (and they are hero, villain, and institution, by turns), then, I
want to suggest how these plots anticipated the explosion of legal reform and also
the way in which they alerted more conservative readers of the impending threat
to the conventions and constructs of patriarchal marriage.

Brontë prefaces her novel by explaining her aim in writing it: "if I have ...
prevented one thoughtless girl from falling into the very natural error of my
heroine, the book has not been written in vain" (4). In other words, she frankly
admits that a failed marriage is a very real possibility. Indeed, *The Tenant of
Wildfell Hall* is a story of how to maneuver around a failed first marriage so
that a new, more perfect, union might be attained. But *Tenant* focuses on that
unwise first marriage, rather than on the more successful second one, as it records
Helen Huntingdon's trials as an abused wife and her various attempts to leave
her husband. *Tenant*'s heroine, unlike Rochester, Lady Audley, and Aurora Floyd,
who are similarly trapped, does not try to ignore the fact that she is married; nor
can the reader ignore the fact of her marriage. Thus in Anne Brontë's novel, even
more than in her sister's more famous work, we see the story of a failed marriage
deliberately and explicitly plotted. That is, while we hear little about the failed

marriage of Rochester and Bertha beyond the fact that Rochester was duped into it and that Bertha was both "intemperate and unchaste," and while the story of Lady Audley's marriage is almost as successfully buried as her first husband is when she throws him down the well, the failed marriage of Arthur and Helen Huntingdon is described at length, in detail, and over the course of 30 chapters (*Jane Eyre* 334). Garrett Stewart calls it "a brutal marriage plot," an apt description both because Arthur is so brutal to Helen and because Brontë gives us the story of their marriage in brutal detail ("Narrative Economies" 76). Further, Helen does not ignore her husband's existence or her legal status as his wife, as Aurora and Lady Audley almost succeed in doing.

Tenant is also more specifically a response to the state of the law with respect to matrimonial cruelty, for in 1848, when the novel was published, the punishment for husbands convicted of domestic abuse was remarkably light, while abused wives could claim virtually no protection.[24] This aspect of the law, coupled with the state of divorce law, meant that marriage was a highly claustrophobic institution (for wives, that is). Popular opinion also contributed to the cramped and confining nature of matrimony for an unhappy wife. The neighborhood vicar's response to the news that Helen has left her husband is typical: "nothing short of bodily ill-usage (and that of no trifling nature) could excuse such a step—nor even that, for in such a case she ought to appeal to the laws for protection" (442). His assumption that there are "laws" she can "appeal to ... for protection" reveals both a complacency and an absence of any real knowledge about the state of marriage law. It would not be until the Matrimonial Causes Act of 1878, which gave the courts power to grant judicial separations and maintenance to those women whose husbands had been convicted of aggravated assault, that Helen could hope for any legal protection from her husband.[25]

Similarly, *Tenant* responds to the current state of divorce law as it plots an extralegal divorce for its heroine, and it considers the ramifications of a divorce (the difficulty of earning her own living, the damage done to her reputation, the impossibility of maintaining custody of her child) as it chronicles the life of a separated wife, living under an assumed name. The novel narrates the failures of a marriage and the end of that union—and it also posits that a woman should be allowed to remarry, despite her mistakes and her previously wedded state. Helen's story revolves around what is unmistakably a second-chance plot, and, in writing this story, Anne Brontë wrestled with the status of marriage and the ways in which it might be brought to an end specifically so that a woman could remarry, just as Parliament would do a few years later in taking up the first of the Divorce Bills. In the portrait she gives us of the miserable marriage of Arthur and Helen Huntingdon, Anne Brontë insists that her readers recognize the existence of failed marriages and the shortcomings of the institution and the laws that define and govern it, just as surely as Parliament did in legalizing divorce nine years later. Or as Deborah Denenholz Morse so perceptively puts it, "the readership of the novel is asked to judge in lieu of a society that provides no forum for legal redress when women and children suffer the domestic abuses that are chronicled in the novel" (103).

Two other strands of the plot are even more directly related to the doings of Parliament. First, Helen tends to justify her decision to leave her husband in terms of her son, little Arthur. When her husband begins to teach her son to drink and to swear, she becomes convinced that she cannot let him stay in such an atmosphere, and that it would be "better far that he should live in poverty and obscurity with a fugitive mother, than in luxury and affluence with such a father." Here we see the first indication that she will use her son to justify her escape from her husband's abandoned ways: "I could endure it for myself, but for my son it must be borne no longer: the world's opinion and the feelings of my friends must be alike unheeded here, at least, alike unable to deter me from my duty" (336). While child abuse was not, of course, grounds for divorce or even for separation, neither in the 1820s, when Helen was married, nor in 1857, when divorce was made legal, a mother's right to custody of her children had been legally strengthened just a few years before the publication of *Tenant*. In 1839 the Custody of Infants Act was passed (largely due to the work of Caroline Norton, another abused wife who feared for her children at the hands of her husband). This Act allowed a separated wife to petition the court for custody of her children if they were under seven and she herself were of good character. Although this might seem like a very meager allowance, it did, for the first time, contradict the legal and societal assumption that a man's children were his inalienable possessions.

Tenant also responds to the issue of married women's property. While the first Married Women's Property Bill did not become law until 1870, the first of the many bills to be debated in the House of Commons and the House of Lords was introduced in 1856. Although Helen is initially uninterested in the issue of married women's property—when, in the context of discussing her engagement to Huntingdon, her uncle mentions the matter of settlements, she blithely assures him that "all I have will be his, and all he has will be mine"—she soon comes to understand the importance of being able to secure something for herself (168–9). In order to finance her escape, Helen plans to sell some of her jewelry and paintings, and also to continue to paint until she has enough money to leave her husband. But Helen confides all these plans to her journal, which her husband finds. After learning of Helen's plans, he seizes her keys: "Now then, we must have a confiscation of property," he tells her (350). This assertion is quite an accurate description of the right of a husband before the passage of the Married Women's Property Acts, and when we learn, just a page later, that he has ordered the destruction of her paintings and her painting materials, and that he has taken her money and her jewels in addition to "a few little trifles I thought it advisable to take into my own possession, lest your mercantile spirit should be tempted to turn them into gold," it is hard not to think about this aspect of the law which keeps Helen confined.

But what are we to make of the fact that that this novel, with its detailed consideration of a failed marriage, plots a second, happy, marriage for the heroine, that the story of Helen's first failed marriage is told within the context of a successful courtship plot? One conclusion that seems unavoidable is the generic one that the novel is, in fact, a novel of courtship, albeit the courtship of a married woman. Yet the embedding of a failed-marriage plot within this apparently conventional courtship plot suggests that traditional plot is being questioned from the inside out. The fact that the successful suitor tells us the story of his wife's first courtship,[26] the failure of her first marriage, and the two ways in which that marriage is brought to an end (when she leaves her husband and then again when he dies) should cause us to look more closely at both the story of her second courtship and marriage—which surrounds, and even protects and defends, the story of Helen's past, much as Gilbert defends Helen from the gossiping, suspicious villagers who surround her retreat at Wildfell Hall—and the more traditional frame narrative.[27] Anne Brontë interrogates the institution of marriage within the confines of the conventional "happily-ever-after" plot, it is true, but her interrogation is searching and explicit, and the fact that she spares no details in telling us of Helen's misery as Arthur's wife suggests that, like those subplots of failed marriage I allude to above, the interpolated story in *Tenant* is meant to be read alongside the courtship plot that frames it, as a cautionary tale that "reveal[s] the snares and pitfalls of life to the young" and that seeks to "prevent … thoughtless girl[s] from falling into the very natural error of my heroine" (4). Reading Brontë's preface after finishing the novel, we see that she does not mean the reader to privilege the ending, for to do so would be to participate in what she calls the "delicate concealment of facts." As D.A. Miller points out, novels "are never fully or finally governed by" closure (*Narrative and Its Discontents* xiv). Or as Janice Hubbard Harris argues, "there is a loss of insight … in focusing too intently on how a novel closes. Novels with ultimately conventional endings often leave a legacy in the mind that disturbs, teases, provokes" (186, n.13). And, indeed, Brontë makes it clear in her preface that she means her novel both to disturb and to provoke.

Similarly, Wilkie Collins's *The Woman in White* (1860) ends with the putatively happy marriage of Laura Fairlie and Walter Hartright, but it is Laura's failed first marriage to Sir Percival Glyde which provides the novel with its plot, not to mention the subplots concerning Count Fosco's marriage ("the rod of iron with which he rules [his wife] never appears in company—it is a private rod, and it is always kept upstairs" [244]), the failed marriage of Sir Percival's mother ("her husband had ill-used her, and had afterwards gone off with some other person" [550]), and the "dreadful scandal" and "miserable break-up in [the Catherick's'] household" (487). All of these failed unions suggest that Laura is more right than she knows when she tries to convince Marian that she is "so much better off as a single woman—unless—unless you are very fond of your husband" (235).[28] Laura here echoes the Queen's pronouncement, "I think unmarried people are very often very happy," and, like the Queen, she has trouble articulating the idea of a happy marriage. Just as the fact that a wife "is bodily and morally the husband's slave" "always sticks in" the Queen's "throat," Laura stutters when she tries to describe a scenario in which marriage is preferable to remaining single, and even when she manages to get her words out, it seems as if she is not really saying what she means.

Trollope's *He Knew He Was Right* also suggests quite vividly—and at length—that remaining single has very real advantages, for in this novel the miseries Louis Trevelyan inflicts on his long-suffering wife are protracted and cruel, much like Gilbert Osmond's treatment of his resigned wife, Isabel.[29] Trollope's novel tells the story of a proud and stiff-necked husband who is so offended by his wife's flirtation with their friend, Colonel Osborne, that he accuses her of improper conduct and will not retract his accusation. Guilty of unthinking flirtation, but by no means guilty of the behavior imputed to her by her husband, Emily Trevelyan leaves him, taking their little boy with her, and she lives apart from him for the remainder of the novel, reconciling with him only upon his deathbed, when he finally admits her innocence. *He Knew He Was Right* is an especially torturous version of the failed-marriage plot because while the failure of the Trevelyans' marriage is apparent almost from the outset of the novel, the reader is denied any resolution of this failed-marriage plot as the estranged couple maintains contact throughout the novel's 900 pages. In fact, they continually try to reconcile, and they never completely stop loving each other, although they never manage to rescue their marriage. Though their marriage is so clearly beyond repair, they can neither move past the incident that gives rise to the plot, nor can they put an end to their marriage in any way, as Helen manages to do when she leaves Arthur in *Tenant* or as Rochester does when he tries to marry Jane. The plotting of a failed marriage is not only central to the plot of *He Knew He Was Right*, then: it *is* the plot.

This failed-marriage plot revolves around the clash between what Christopher Herbert identifies as "the two antithetical ideals" governing the Victorians' conception of marriage: "the principle of male supremacy so deeply rooted in custom and in law" and "the great cult of Home" as preached by Ruskin and company. But as Herbert points out, instead of turning this into a melodramatic story of a tyrannous husband or developing the rake/dandy plot and allowing Emily to succumb to Colonel Osborne's less than honorable intentions, Trollope writes this plot in his "characteristic mode of restrained, finely detailed realism" (451, 456). Like Geraldine Jewsbury's matter-of-fact description of Alice's and Bryant's quotidian unhappiness in *The Half Sisters* (1848), Trollope eschews melodrama for realism, and he paints for his readers a painfully detailed picture of the dissolution and degeneration of the Trevelyans' marriage; it hurts to watch this marriage crumble over so many, many pages, and the details that contribute to its collapse are so picayune. That is, while Trevelyan is more right than Emily knows to be worried about Osborne's attentions (and intentions), and while Emily's relationship to Osborne is certainly innocent in her mind, it is not a matter of fidelity (or infidelity) or trust that is responsible for the failure of their marriage. Rather, Trevelyan is suspicious, Emily is offended, and they both become so dug into their respective positions that things go almost imperceptibly from bad to worse, to the extent that every trivial detail of their daily interactions ultimately contributes to the eventual stalemate that leads Trevelyan to kidnap their child, go mad, and finally, blessedly, die. Or as Henry James puts it, "touch is added to touch, one small, stupid, fatal aggravation to another; and as we gaze into the widening breach we wonder at the vulgar materials of which tragedy sometimes composes itself" ("Anthony Trollope" 1351). The "secret excess" that Bersani refers to is, in this case, an excess of detail, certainly; but, more to the point, it is the excessive incompatibility, not so much between Emily and her husband as between the two doctrines of Victorian marriage identified by Herbert, two competing versions of marriage that eventually explode in the novel's plot and in the Trevelyans' home.[30] This novel "animates," to use Luhmann's term, the codes by which husbands and wives were trained to behave in the nineteenth century: that is, Emily and Trevelyan act out the period's notions of proper spousal conduct, and the novel is thus an especially thoughtful and precise demonstration of the contradictions voiced by Mill and the Queen that define the vexing institution of marriage (Luhmann 11).[31]

As this brief survey of the domestic novel indicates, as early as the beginnings of the genre the novel has concerned itself with what happens to characters after they pledge their vows. This glimpse of the novel tradition also suggests the frequency and variety with which the novel yields a portrait of a problematic union. Yet the failed-marriage plot, as a plot, has received scant attention, especially in terms of our understanding of the Victorian novel as a cultural institution. At the beginning of this chapter I explored at length some of the reasons we have yet to move from an analysis of those novels that treat of marital demise to a consideration of the generic ramifications of that frequent theme, and now, before I turn to the legal history of marriage and divorce, I want to suggest one more reason we tend to privilege the courtship plot. The failure of marriage has been viewed with a certain kind of nervousness, both morally and methodologically. Morally, for many Victorians (and those that love them, as Eve Sedgwick might put it) this plot calls into question the widely held belief in the conservative role of the marriage plot and the conservative nature of the institution itself. As Mr Lillyvick, the newly-married and soon-to-be-abandoned husband in *Nicholas Nickleby* puts it, to cast suspicion on the sanctity of marriage is to aim "a blow at the whole framework of society" (403). And the nervousness that attaches to this plot in nineteenth-century culture has proven to be contagious in that that nervousness itself has played a formative, but largely overlooked, role in the novel's institutionalization. The frequent occurrences of the failed-marriage plot suggest the inadequacy of the myth of marriage as an institution that stabilizes society (in much the same way that the drastic changes in marriage law in the eighteenth and nineteenth centuries suggest that the institution is a construct and so manifestly a work in progress that it certainly should not be viewed as a moral or societal bulwark). While no one would question the existence of unhappy marriages or of marriages that fall apart, the tendency to assume the sanctity of the marriage bond and to insist that the courtship plot establishes closure for a novel form that claims to represent society in a realistic fashion bespeaks a strong concern with both the relationship of marriage and the culture which it is thought to shore up. The elevation of the failed-marriage plot to a category of its own would seriously jeopardize this view. Victorian novelists wrote failed-marriage plots, but critics—both Victorian and Victorianist—may (have) be(en) reluctant to admit them to the canon because they need to believe in the myth of marriage.[32]

In a similar fashion, the failed-marriage plot has been overlooked because of the tremendous importance of marriage as a metaphor. Indeed, for readers around 1950 it was the *locus classicus* of what literary meaning was striving to attain. Toward the beginning of Watt's chapter on *Pamela*, immediately after his pronouncement that "the great majority of novels written since *Pamela* have continued its basic pattern, and concentrated their main interest upon a courtship leading to marriage," Watt admits that the novel that sets that pattern for him does not, in fact, follow that pattern:

> *Pamela*, it is true, departs from the usual pattern in one important respect: even if we exclude Richardson's ill-advised continuation [*Pamela, Part II*], the narrative does not end with the marriage, but continues for some two hundred pages while every detail of the marriage ceremony and the resulting new conjugal pattern is worked out according to Richardson's exemplary specifications. (*Rise of the Novel* 149)

"The narrative does not end with the marriage." That last sentence is Watt, not me. Indeed, Watt goes on to explain that what follows the wedding is in fact the plotting of marriage ("every detail of ... the resulting new conjugal pattern is worked out"), although critics after, and in agreement with, Watt have insisted that marriage, especially a happy one, provides no narrative motion. This aspect of Watt's thesis, and, even more importantly, the fact that critics have, since 1957, tended to skip over this qualification in their eagerness to embrace the novel that ends at the altar, suggest that marriage and the stability of literary meaning have become metaphors for each other. That is, looking for the union of opposites is one of the ways in which we make sense of texts. It often seems that we cannot explicate a text without looking for the contraries it devotes its energies to bringing together. By the same token, when we start to think about how a text draws to a close, we start to think about the "marriage," literal or figurative, of opposed elements. In *The Well Wrought Urn*, Cleanth Brooks makes this association explicit, arguing about Donne's "The Canonization" that "for us today, Donne's imagination seems obsessed with the problem of unity; the sense in which the lovers become one—the sense in which the soul is united with God. Frequently, as we have seen, one type of union becomes a metaphor for the other" (18). Indeed, we often use the language of marriage when discussing literary meaning, even when we are not talking about matrimony; we use the verbs "wed" and "join" and "unite" to describe a kind of union, to talk about the nature of a paradox, to describe, as Coleridge put it, "the balance or reconciliation of opposite or discordant qualities" (qtd in Brooks 18). This "fusion," this "weld[ing] together [of] the discordant and the contradictory" is, more globally, "the effect of the imagination" and describes "the union which the creative imagination itself effects" (Brooks 19, 18).

Watt published *The Rise of the Novel* in the age of New Criticism, a school of interpretation that relies on paradox and antithesis, on the identification of contraries and opposed symbolic elements. He thus draws on the same kind of conceptual scheme articulated by Brooks and by Wimsatt and Beardsley. What is most telling about the connection between Watt's thesis and the New Criticism, though, is the way in which New Historicists and feminists, Marxists and deconstructionists, not to mention identity critics and formalists, have embraced this method of reading novels. Perhaps that strange fact of inheritance, if nothing else, is reason enough to distrust and resist the abstractions of the courtship paradigm.

Matrimonial Legislation in England: 1670–1923

Another incentive to resist Alexander Welsh's thesis that "in life and novels both, marriage is construed as a permanent relation" arises when we look at marriage as a matter of law (*The City of Dickens* 222). Even a cursory survey of British marriage and divorce law in the eighteenth and nineteenth centuries reveals that the contract, as a juridical practice, is multiplicitous and shifting. That is, legally marriage is not a stable entity, which is inducement, in and of itself, to distrust a critical position that implies that it is.[33] In the broad period that saw the rise and flourish of the novel, marriage was perceived as needing stabilization and, accordingly, the law turned its attention to codifying the institution, to defining what constitutes the beginning, establishment, and dissolution of a marriage. I will first sketch out some of the major pieces of matrimonial legislation enacted in that roughly two hundred-year period and then go back and fill in the details of that legal outline.

In 1670 the first divorce was granted in England, by private Act of Parliament, to a Lord Roos, on the grounds of his wife's adultery. In 1753 Lord Hardwicke's Marriage Act became law, putting an end to clandestine marriages and codifying the requirements for entering into a marriage. In 1801 a woman, Jane Addison, was first granted a divorce, again by private Act of Parliament, this time on the grounds of her husband's incestuous adultery with her sister. (Until the passage of the Divorce Act in 1857, only three other women successfully petitioned parliament for a private Act dissolving their marriages, and they all did so on the grounds of adultery aggravated by bigamy or incest.) The Marriage Act of 1836 enabled Britons to marry in a civil ceremony, while in 1857 they were granted the right to obtain a divorce without involving the Church. Various laws were passed between 1878 and 1895 which relaxed the requirements for obtaining a divorce and culminated in the Matrimonial Causes Act of 1923, which allowed women to sue for divorce on the same grounds as men: simple (as opposed to aggravated) adultery.

This outline not only reveals the sweeping legal reforms to the institution of marriage enacted in the eighteenth and nineteenth centuries, but it also highlights the shifting parallels between the history of the novel and the legal history of marriage and divorce. That literary development we call "the rise of the novel" corresponded with the greater policing of marriage articulated by Lord Hardwicke's Marriage Act, while the failed-marriage plot, which is my subject here, is paralleled by the story of divorce that begins with Lord Roos's privilege and ends with the relative clarity and equity of divorce law at the beginning of the twentieth century. Further, all the pieces of legislation enumerated above share a concern with the more extensive iteration of control over the institution of marriage and the way in which it was entered into and departed from. Even those acts of law that seem designed to make it easier to get married or divorced are actually methods by which marriage and divorce can be more easily classified and controlled. In other words, these Marriage and Divorce Acts set up ways for English society to tell the stories which lead into or out of wedlock; they supply it with narrative conventions. The perspective on law and narrative I am adopting here is shared by Niklas Luhmann, who observes that "the thematic choices and guiding principles informing literary, idealizing and mythicizing portrayals of love are not arbitrary, but rather represent reactions to the respective society and the trends for change within it" (20). The law is a set of social conventions, and it thus makes different sorts of plots available; it allows one to envision possible ways of plotting one's life (or a character's life). Indeed, the law often attempts to steer its subjects into one or another of these possible plots. Accordingly, in what follows, I want to suggest the extent to which the changing law of marriage and divorce affects and determines the potential narrative conventions of the English novel. Eighteenth- and nineteenth-century law, like eighteenth- and nineteenth-century novels, suggests how important it is that we attend to the failed-marriage plot as well as to the courtship plot.

At the beginning of the eighteenth century the standard procedure for marriage consisted of a ceremony in a church in the bride's parish, performed by an official clergyman, and preceded by the reading of banns or the purchase of a license. However, there were several other ways in which a legal marriage could be performed, the two most common being marriage by mutual contract (verbal or written) or a clandestine marriage. A clandestine marriage was legal since it was performed by an individual who at least represented himself as a clergyman, and it conformed to the ritual prescribed by the *Book of Common Prayer*. But it was a marriage that broke canon law in any one of a number of ways—chiefly because it was secret. It usually took place without the reading of banns or the purchase of a license, and it was seldom recorded in an official parish register. Clandestine marriages were an attractive alternative to the traditional church wedding because they were cheap and secret (this was an advantage because betrothed couples could thus circumvent any familial objections to the union), yet were still a valid form of the institution. They were perceived as a problem, however, because they allowed underage couples to be married without their parental (read, paternal) consent, and they provided a perfect opportunity for fortune-hunters and opportunists. Further, as the case that was largely responsible for the introduction of the bill that became the 1753 law (*Cochrane alias Kennedy* v. *Campbell*) suggests, clandestine marriages made it disturbingly easy to contract multiple marriages. As Erica Harth points out, the respondent's husband (now dead) "seems to have been a willing if not a happy bigamist" (127). But it is also important to point out that worries over clandestine marriage had as much to do with money as they did with morals. The case of *Cochrane alias Kennedy* v. *Campbell* was a dispute between the two putative widows over the money and property of their mutual husband. Harth also points to "recorded cases of clandestine marriages between heiresses and their footmen" and reminds us that "opponents viewed the bill as endorsing a type of class endogamy that would allow the aristocracy to strengthen its power by monopolizing England's new wealth" (127, 128). Reports of abducted, drugged, and besotted heiresses and runaway children thus abound in the pamphlets of the early eighteenth century protesting the shameful state of marriage law that allowed and condoned such atrocities.[34] Henry Fielding himself attempted to abduct an heiress in 1725, and in his 1742 novel *Joseph Andrews*, Mr Wilson assumes that Joseph has abducted Fanny, whom he takes to be "the daughter of some person of fashion" (195). Another, less spectacular, objection to clandestine marriages had to do with their unique legal status. While a clandestine marriage was a legal form of matrimony, it was often difficult to prove that a marriage had in fact taken place, due to the absence of witnesses or records. Thus, as David Lemmings points out, "the uncertainty of the law of marriage facilitated secret bigamy, whether intentional or unintentional, and the courts were in the invidious position of sometimes having to admit or even enforce legal rules which disinherited regularly married respectable wives and bastardized their children" (345).

In response to this confusion, Parliament passed the Marriage Act of 1753, an act which, according to Lemmings, "prescribed the law of marriage until 1822, and informed its substance much longer" in that it forbade clandestine marriages and required that all weddings adhere to the traditional church form described above (340). The act, officially entitled "An Act for the better preventing of clandestine Marriages," also required a parent or guardian's consent in order for those under the age of 21 to marry. Further, all marriages by verbal or written contract were nullified. Perhaps most importantly, the marriage was recorded in the parish register and signed by both bride and groom and at least two witnesses, as well as the officiating clergyman, and a copy of each register was sent to the bishop every year for safe keeping. Tampering with the register was a felony punishable by death. Viewed under the terms of Lord Hardwicke's Act, *The Woman in White*'s Sir Percival Glyde's forgery in 1827 of the parish records to make it appear that his parents had, in fact, been married (in 1803) resonates with all the sinister implications that Collins no doubt intended and makes it clear that this was, indeed, the action of a desperate man. Those performing clandestine marriages after the passage of this act were subject to transportation for 14 years.

Collins once again takes up Lord Hardwicke's Act and both subscribes to the fears over clandestine marriages and pokes fun at them in *Armadale* (1864–66). Allan Armadale, heir to the Armadale fortune, wants to marry Neelie Milroy, but since she is only 16 and her father has forbidden her to see Allan, they consider eloping. However, as the narrator confides

> there is a certain exceptional occasion in life—the occasion of marriage—on which even girls in their teens sometimes become capable (more or less hysterically) of looking at consequences. At the farewell moment of the interview on Saturday, Neelie's mind had suddenly precipitated itself into the future; and she had utterly confounded Allan by inquiring whether the contemplated elopement was an offence punishable by the Law? (442)

Her concerns are so grave that she insists that they "find out the law" (443). Consulting Blackstone, they learn that the only way they can successfully elope is to commit perjury, to swear, as Allan quotes from Blackstone, "that the consent of the person or persons whose consent is required, has been obtained, or that there is no person having authority to give such consent. The consent required by this Act is that of the father" (447). Collins's use of the law here is both ironic, in that Allan is the one with the money, and conservative, in that these lovers, bound as they are by the "cruel law" that prevents them from marrying, are determined not to "circumvent Blackstone" (447, 448).

While Lord Hardwicke's Act may have prevented Allan and Neelie from eloping in fiction, and while it decreased the number of clandestine marriages performed in England in fact, it also increased the business at Gretna Green. Indeed, Allan's first response when he learns that they cannot elope without committing perjury is that they "try the blacksmith at Gretna Green." "Lots of people in our situation have tried the blacksmith," he insists, "and found him quite as good as a clergyman" (447). Gretna Green is located on the border of Scotland and England, about 200 miles from London, and since Scotland had not followed England's example with respect to clandestine marriages, it was a popular place for weddings from 1753 until 1856, when a Gretna Green marriage was declared illegal for an English couple unless they had lived in Scotland for three weeks previous to their marriage. In *Pride and Prejudice*, Wickham seems to have reassured Lydia by suggesting they were going to Gretna Green when they run away together, but of course this was a false promise, and even if he had kept his word, it might not have been worth much, for the legal status of a Gretna Green marriage was uncertain between 1753 and 1856. According to Lawrence Stone, "the validity of a Gretna Green marriage was admitted by the ecclesiastical courts and the Court of Common Pleas, but denied by the Court of King's Bench" (133–4). That is, it was accepted by canon law and the court of equity, but not by common law. But perhaps the most serious flaw in the Marriage Act of 1753 was the fact that although Jews and Quakers were excluded from its requirements, no alternative measures had been established for Catholics and Nonconformists, leaving them with no legal alternative, except the questionable one of Gretna Green, to a traditional Church of England ceremony. This state of affairs was remedied with the passage of the 1836 Marriage Act which provided for marriage by a public registrar—a brief ceremony that was purely secular and most definitely legal. (It becomes clear that Richard and Ada, in *Bleak House* (1852–53), have taken advantage of this provision when Richard confesses to Esther that their marriage "was not a long-considered step. We went out one morning, and were married" [786].)

Like the attempt to clarify and control the law of marriage, the reform of divorce law in the mid-nineteenth century was as much an effort to streamline the confusing system of divorce at work in the country as it was to exert greater governmental control over the dissolution of a marriage.[35] Although divorce was, strictly speaking, illegal until 1857, the frequency with which the system was circumvented and divorces were obtained made for a paradoxical state of affairs in which a legal divorce could be obtained despite the law. True, before the Divorce Act of 1857, divorces were only granted by Private Act of Parliament and were tremendously expensive (£1,000 was a conservative estimate, if no opposition were encountered). Further, Parliament could only be petitioned after the claimant had brought his suit to the ecclesiastical court for a *divorce a mensa et thoro* (literally, a divorce from bed and board, a version of our legal separation) and to the common law courts, where he brought a charge of criminal conversation (adultery) against his wife's lover. As the common law procedure suggests, the only ground for divorce was adultery, and, as suggested by the case of Jane Addison, who had to prove her husband guilty of adultery and incest, the only kind of adultery perceived as a problem worthy of divorce was a wife's adultery. Indeed, a wife would have to prove her husband had committed aggravated adultery in order to sue for divorce until well into the twentieth century.

There were, though, men who could afford to divorce their adulterous wives (or who could afford to "prove" that their wives were adulterous), and there were a very few women who could afford to divorce their adulterous and incestuous/ bigamous husbands. Even men too poor or without the requisite unfaithful wives managed to extricate themselves from their marriages through various forms of self-divorce. As Lawrence Stone explains, "the middling and better sort" would draw up a private separation agreement, "negotiated between the two spouses and embodied in a deed of separation drawn up by a conveyancer. For the poor who possessed little or no property, the normal procedure was simply desertion or elopement" (141). While there is no negotiation and no third party involved, this is basically how Rawdon ends his marriage to Becky Sharp. More spectacular means were also sometimes employed; Stone relates that "husbands with a little property sometimes … ejected their wives and locked them out of the house" (141). And as Hardy's *The Mayor of Casterbridge* (1886) reflects, there also existed the extralegal "ritual of wife-sale, a custom unique to Britain and New England, by which a husband publicly sold to another man not only his wife but also all legal responsibility for her and her upkeep" (Stone 141).[36]

The increasing bureaucratization of marriage, as evidenced by the 1753 Act; a new, if reluctant, awareness of marriage as a secular matter, as evidenced by the 1836 Act; the fact that people were circumventing the system—legally and extralegally—and putting an end to their marriages; all combined with the government's desire to overhaul and streamline the legal system: all these shifts and anxieties paved the way for the formation of a new court of divorce which would combine the functions of the ecclesiastical court, the common law court, and Parliament, and thus turn divorce into a one-court process. The Divorce and Matrimonial Causes Act of 1857 was followed by a series of laws, among them the Matrimonial Causes Act of 1878, which added the husband's conviction of aggravated assault upon his wife to the grounds upon which a wife could seek a separation. Along with a separation, the wife would receive maintenance from her husband and custody of all her children under the age of ten.[37] Finally, the Matrimonial Causes Act of 1923 allowed wives, like husbands, to obtain a divorce on the grounds of their spouse's simple adultery.

The legal historian O.R. McGregor argues that the "main and only important purpose of the Act of 1857 was to make the civil system of divorce established by the House of Lords in 1697, more widely available" (18).[38] He is, in one sense, correct, since the grounds for divorce were not changed, nor was the sexual double standard abolished. Divorces were made slightly more affordable, given that only one court had to be appealed to, but the most significant of the bill's clauses in this respect was never put into practice—that clause, which permitted the divorce court to sit outside London, would have greatly reduced the cost, given that a trip to London for the plaintiff and witnesses, not to mention accommodations, would not be necessary.

The act did, however, represent a slight improvement in the state of divorce law. First, it made the dissolution of marriage, strictly speaking, legal. Because divorces had previously only been available by private dispensation from Parliament, they were not a part of English law. In other words, every time Parliament granted a *divorce a vinculo matrimonii* (literally, a divorce from the bonds of matrimony), they were setting the law aside—making an exception to the law—rather than acting within its framework. So the Divorce and Matrimonial Causes Act did represent an advance that was importantly, if only, semantic.[39] Further, the act provided for the protection of the future earnings and property of both divorced and separated wives, and it enumerated the grounds upon which a woman could sue for divorce (adultery aggravated by incest, bigamy, rape, sodomy, bestiality, cruelty, or desertion for two years). Granted, this last provision can be viewed in two ways. It can be seen as an advance in that a wife divorcing her husband was now on the books as a legal possibility, but it is also true that this provision limited her grounds for petitioning. Prior to 1857 a wife could bring a suit for whatever reason she wished. Precedent dictated that only aggravated adultery would suffice as grounds, but there was no limit set to the grievances she might bring forward. However, whether you view this aspect of the new law as a step forward or backward for women, it is clear that once again, as with the Marriage Act of 1753, the rules had been greatly clarified. In fact, the act as a whole clearly signals the codification of divorce, just as the act that preceded it by 100 years codified marriage. Private life thus became increasingly more policed and standardized;[40] all legal stories of marriage and divorce would now be told using the same language and the same narrative cues. And these legal stories would now also have a limited number of plots. A marriage could only be made in one of two ways, while a story of divorce could only have one origin: infidelity. Marriage and divorce are, after all, both legal institutions and markers of plot, explicit ways of codifying and of charting the relationship of men and women, and the novel, like the law, reveals the truth of the assumption that "proper attitudes and modes of behaviour could be codified" and that "we love and suffer according to cultural imperatives" (Luhmann 53, 4).

Allen Horstman, in *Victorian Divorce*, begins his chapter on the social effects of divorce reform by underlining the connections I am making here between the novelistic and the juridical versions of the failed-marriage plot:

> The Divorce Bill received the royal assent on 28th August, 1857. In that same year the three Dickens brothers, including the writer Charles, left their wives, and Marian Evans, known to us as George Eliot, moved in with G.H. Lewes, a married man. The wife of the writer and poet George Meredith went holidaying that hot summer in Wales with her lover, the painter Henry Wallis, and conceived a son. Though diaries and correspondence reveal remarkably little about discussions involving divorce, Victorians did take stock of marriage and their marriages. (113)

It is more than a little interesting that Horstman chooses to enumerate the indiscretions of novelists, that he tells a portion of the life stories of those whose lives were spent telling stories. And his claim that "Victorians did take stock of marriage" encourages us to think about the ways in which these three Victorians took stock of marriage in their own work. We immediately think of Eliot's portrait of a failed marriage in *Daniel Deronda*, and we just as quickly think of *Middlemarch*, with its narrator's insistence on marriage as "the home epic" and the several versions of that epic we get in that novel (the stories of Rosamond's and Lydgate's, and of Dorothea's and Causabon's's failed marriages, most obviously, but also the travails of Mrs Bulstrode and the interpolated story of Laure, the actress who murders her husband and pretends it was a stage accident).[41] Meredith's *Diana of the Crossways* (1885) also comes to mind: a novel that revisits the story of Caroline Norton, a Victorian who knew first-hand the embarrassment of an adultery trial and who worked to reform the laws of divorce, a woman to whom I will return in Chapter 3 in the context of the melodrama of failed marriage we find in her novels and essays. Perhaps most apropos of all is Meredith's novel-length sonnet sequence, *Modern Love*, which tells the story of a husband and wife whose marriage is coming to an end, and which Meredith wrote after the Welsh holiday to which Horstman refers became an elopement.

And then there's Dickens: putatively the most conservative of the three writers Horstman mentions, but the one most concerned, at least in his fictions, with the failings of the institution. In Chapters 2–5, I will focus on the failed-marriage plots in *Oliver Twist, Nicholas Nickleby, The Old Curiosity Shop, Dombey and Son, David Copperfield*, and *Hard Times*, but marital failure is interwoven into the plots of all his novels, from his first, *The Posthumous Papers of the Pickwick Club* (1836–37), in which we are told that "a wedding is a licensed subject to joke upon, but there really is no great joke in the matter after all," to his last completed novel, *Our Mutual Friend* (1864–65), in which we find what may be the most cynical look at the institution: that is, the sham marriage of the Lammles and their mercenary attempts to marry off Georgiana Podsnap (467).

Pickwick is especially notable in terms of this project, for in that novel we find a fictionalized account of the suit for criminal conversation George Norton brought against Lord Melbourne (which also furnished Meredith with his plot in *Diana of the Crossways*). Having reported the case for the *Morning Chronicle* in 1836, Dickens makes use of it in his first novel as the breach of promise suit *Bardell v. Pickwick*. *Pickwick* also includes two interpolated tales concerned with failed marriages: the Stroller's Tale, in which the dying, alcoholic husband confesses to the sustained cruelty with which he has treated his wife ("she must be an evil spirit—a devil! Hush! I know she is. If she had been a woman she would have died long ago. No woman could have borne what she has"), and the Convict's Return, a tragic story of family violence which tells of a woman's undying loyalty to her drunken brute of a husband. The Pickwickians are told that "people who passed the spot in the evening—sometimes at a late hour of the night—reported that they had heard the sounds of moans and sobs of a woman in distress, and the sound of blows: and more than once, when it was past midnight, the boy knocked softly at the door of a neighbour's house, whither he had been sent, to escape the drunken fury of his unnatural father" (108, 147–8). It is also in *Pickwick* that we find the story of the flirtatious Mrs Pott who, having been confronted with proof of her dalliance with Winkle, promptly threatens to leave her husband for having suggested such an insult to her character. "I'll be separated," she hysterically cries, and, indeed, she is a virtual divorcée when the Pickwickians next encounter her. The narrator tells us that "Mrs Pott, acting upon her often repeated threat of separation, had, in virtue of an arrangement negotiated by her brother, the Lieutenant, and concluded by Mr Pott, permanently retired with the faithful body-guard upon one moiety or half-part of [her husband's] annual income." Finally, consider the Wellerisms on the subject of the dreaded state of matrimony that abound throughout the novel, turns of phrase that include Sam's description of his newly-wedded father as "the wictim o'connubiality" and his father's recommended course of action should Sam ever be tempted to get married himself: "jist you shut yourself up in your own room, if you've got one, and pison yourself off hand … Pison yourself, Samivel, my boy, pison yourself, and you'll be glad on it arterwards" (321, 817, 355, 398).

Chapter 2 explores the monstrous marriages buried at the heart of the plots of Dickens's next three novels: *Oliver Twist, Nicholas Nickleby*, and *The Old Curiosity*

Shop. Similarly buried, and no less important in propelling and contexualizing the plot is the story of the hero's parents in *Barnaby Rudge* (1841), one of the saddest stories of a failed marriage in the novel tradition. Having murdered his master, Barnaby Rudge acquaints his pregnant wife with his crime; her shock leads to the birth of their half-witted son, also named Barnaby. Barnaby Senior flees, but reappears from time to time for money, protection and food—all of which his wife must supply him with, given that they are still married and that she does not want her son to be known as the child of a murderer. *Martin Chuzzlewit* (1843–44) also tells the story of a murderer—Jonas Chuzzlewit—and his failed marriage. Jonas marries Mercy because he loves her, but, once married, he seems only interested in exacting revenge for her insolence towards him during their courtship. And it is in the midst of that courtship that his crusty, suspicious grandfather reminds Mercy that "from your bridal hour to the day which sees you brought as low as these [graves], and laid in such a bed, there will be no appeal against him" (380). Old Martin Chuzzlewit is right, both in terms of the law of the day and in terms of the plot's resolution, for Mercy escapes from the hell that is her marriage only because Jonas kills himself. The novels that follow (*Dombey and Son*, *David Copperfield*, and *Hard Times*) receive the focus of my attention in Chapters 3–5; they reveal Dickens's continued interest in the question of marital failure; at mid-career, Dickens considers connubial disintegration and dis-ease with even more sustained attention.

Little Dorrit appeared in the midst of the renewed debate over the reform of the divorce law, and its final number appeared in June of 1857, just two months before divorce was legalized.[42] It is in this novel that we get, in addition to the failed-marriage plot of Fanny Dorrit and Edmund Sparkler and the extralegal separation of Arthur Clennam's parents, Affery Flintwich's remarkable assessment of her own marriage and the lack of agency she has as a passive victim: "Why, if it had been—a Smothering instead of a Wedding, … I couldn't have said a word" (79). Two years later, in *A Tale of Two Cities* (1859), Dickens presents us with another pathetic picture of failed marriage, though this marriage exists only in the besotted lover's imagination. As he confesses his love for her, Sydney Carton tells Lucie of the unhappiness that their union would have brought her, had she loved him enough to consent to be his wife:

> If it had been possible, Miss Manette, that you could have returned the love of the man you see before you—self-flung away, wasted, drunken, poor creature of misuse as you know him to be—he would have been conscious this day and hour, in spite of his happiness, that he would bring you to misery, bring you to sorrow and repentance, blight you, disgrace you, pull you down with him. I know very well that you can have no tenderness for me; I ask for none; I am even thankful that it cannot be. (180–81)

Similarly, in the last speech that Dickens imagines for him, Carton describes the happy domestic scene he leaves behind (and, indeed, makes available by his death) in a way that makes it clear not only that such a happy family could never be his, but also that it exists, as James Eli Adams points out, only "in the pleasures of imagination" (59): "I see the lives for which I lay down my life, peaceful, useful, prosperous and happy, in that England which I shall see no more. I see Her with a child upon her bosom, who bears my name" (404). Not only is his long soliloquy on the joys of the domestic one that Carton does not in fact speak ("if he had given utterance to his [last thoughts], and they were prophetic, they would have been these" [404]) and one that is introduced with a string of conditionals, but it is also, as Adams reminds us, a celebration of the domestic that "offers as much exemption as exclusion" (59), and it is an indication of "Dickens's tendency to present those [idyllic] spaces [of Victorian domesticity] as an increasingly overt realm of wish-fulfillment" (58). Like the relationship between the courtship plot that is so eager to celebrate marriage and the tensions that marriage so often yields, "Carton's desire is profoundly equivocal in its relation to the domesticity that marks its ostensible fulfillment" (Adams 58).

   That tendency to present domestic tranquility as the stuff of dreams is even more pronounced in *Great Expectations* (1860–61), a novel that denies Pip a happy ending with marriage to Dickens's beloved Estella, but, as his continued revision of that ending suggests, cannot quite cancel that ending, either. The original ending is, of course, quite clear. Estella has married the Shropshire doctor who once defended her from Drummle's violence, and her last meeting with Pip convinces him that "suffering had been stronger than Miss Havisham's teaching, and had given her a heart to understand what my heart used to be" (Calder 496). Estella is thus unavailable, and Pip has recovered from his infatuation with her. The published ending, however, reveals that Pip still has his dreams (and that Dickens allows him those dreams), for in this version Estella has not remarried. Despite Estella's last words in the published ending, "And will continue friends apart," Pip insists, in the last line of the novel, that he "saw no shadow of another parting from her" (493). Adding to our sense that this is what he hopes, rather than what will occur, is the fact that he does not give voice to his vision; he does not contradict Estella aloud, but rather confesses his view of the future to the reader in his capacity as narrator. Further, this line was only added in 1868; the last line of the final weekly part is the slightly more optimistic "I saw the shadow of no parting from her" (Calder 496). As Angus Calder suggests, "the later version hints at the buried meaning: ' … at this happy moment, I did not see the shadow of our subsequent parting looming over us'" (496). So while Dickens clearly establishes that they will not marry in the first ending, he suggests they do end up together in the first published ending, only to go back and revise that ending again, writing a conclusion that is, it would seem, deliberately unclear as to Pip and Estella's future together, but markedly clear that Pip is still operating in the realm of the imaginary, as opposed to the actual, when it comes to Estella. There is, of course, a difference between what seems to be Pip's fantasy and what are quite clearly Carton's "pleasures of imagination" in that Pip is deluding himself, while Carton is indulging in what is clearly a bout of fancy, but both endings reveal Dickens's uncertainty about the efficacy of marriage to ensure domestic happiness. In other words, *Great Expectations* does not end with a celebration of Biddy's and Joe's marriage, nor does *A Tale of Two Cities* end with an epithalamium to the Darnay family. Rather, these novels end with Pip's naïve insistence that he will not part from Estella and the narrator's projection of what Carton *would* have said (had he "given utterance") about the domestic happiness he will never enjoy—a happiness, it is important to stress, he can only frame as an imaginary scenario. They end, then, with projections of domestic happiness that are naïve, imaginary, and, in both cases, unarticulated.

More explicitly, the two endings of *Great Expectations*, both of which also concern Estella's marriage to the abusive Bentley Drummle, bespeak the existence of another failed-marriage plot at work beneath the surface of the narrative. In the last pages of the novel's published ending, Pip tells us that he had heard of Estella "as leading a most unhappy life, and as being separated from her husband, who had used her with great cruelty," which suggests that Estella is another of Dickens's heroines (along with Edith Dombey, Betsey Trotwood, and Lady Dedlock) who leaves her husband. And like the death of Jonas Chuzzlewit, the death of Drummle is described as a "release" for his wife (490, 491). Similarly, the Gargerys' marriage is detailed without reservation, and Joe's sufferings are so great that it seems Dickens felt compelled to give him a second chance at marital bliss with Biddy.

I have chosen to concentrate on the six novels from *Oliver Twist* to *Hard Times* (with a brief consideration of *Bleak House*) because they allow me to canvas Dickens's career from its early days to its midpoint (what many critics assess as its heyday) and because they reveal a variety of strategies Dickens employs in plotting the failure of marriage. I chose not to focus on novels post-*Hard Times* because, as I suggest in the first section of this chapter, novel critics have been willing to acknowledge the move away from a conventional marriage plot as early as 1863, while my aim in the case study section of this book is to uncover that plot in what may seem to be the work of an unlikely writer at what might seem to be an improbable or unpropitious time. Once divorce had been legalized, in other words, or once Dickens had (been) left (by) his wife, we might expect to see him take up the question of marital failure. My point is that he (and many other British novelists of the eighteenth and nineteenth centuries) made fictions out of domestic estrangement long before it was topical or personal.

In the chapters that follow, then, I undertake an avowedly revisionary reading of both the Victorian novel in general and Dickens's fiction in particular—a reading that takes Dickens as a case study of the failed-marriage plot, and an approach that moves beyond the Foucauldian readings of Dickens so popular since D.A. Miller's *The Novel and the Police* (1988). In my account, Dickens is neither the conservative agent of the patriarchy nor a kind of novelistic Bentham. Rather, the novels reveal his interest in the disintegration of marriage, the far-reaching and disastrous effects of the doctrine of coverture, and the comic, spectacular, and monstrous possibilities afforded by the failed-marriage plot.

Notes

1   Boone does identify *Wuthering Heights* as a novel that explores "marital conflict" "as an ongoing battle that can never be resolved given the patriarchal rules and oppositional roles by which society has locked partners in wedlock into place," but he notes its status "as something of an anomaly in the English tradition of the novel" and connects that status to its "unconventional attitudes toward love and marriage" (20, 151). My project is highly indebted to Boone's book, for he takes seriously the alternatives to the courtship plot he finds in Anglo-American fiction, and in his focus on the "tragic wedlock" plot, he anticipates my attention to the failed-marriage plot. However, he identifies the "countertradition" as a "small but subversive attack upon the evolving hegemony of the marriage tradition in Anglo-American fiction" and refers to the "narrative modes that have emerged from these gaps in the dominant discourse" as "the 'exceptions to the rule'" (2). I argue that the failed-marriage plot was a competing and complementary plot from the beginning of the novel's emergence in the eighteenth century and that marital separation is basic to the origins of the novel.

2   I am not arguing that critics have ignored these novels, but rather that the ramifications of their plots for our understanding of the genre have yet to be taken into account.

3   In this passage, Miller is explaining the logic of the novels of Jane Austen, but he begins his study with the more general claim that while "there is a wide spectrum of ways in which a novel may characterize the function of the nonnarratable," "in traditional fiction, marriage is a dominant form of this ne plus ultra" (3–4).

4   Heilbrun goes on to argue that once marriage does enter into a novel's plot, it is as a definitively failed institution, a claim she insists is "substantiated by the work of almost every major novelist writing after, say 1873, the year in which Hardy published *Far From the Madding Crowd*, and Butler began *The Way of All Flesh*" (175). In this respect, Heilbrun anticipates my argument about the failed-marriage plot, but the fact that she cannot identify this plot before 1873 suggests her allegiance to Watt and the similarity of her thesis to the arguments of Welsh, Poovey, and Boone.

5   One exemplary exception to this tendency is Claudia Johnson, who in "The Divine Miss Jane" suggests that "it is not novels but rather the professionalization of novel studies which deployed methods of reading that guaranteed certain outcomes and devalued others" (39). Johnson's goal is to remind us of the kinds of non-normative readings of Jane Austen that were so popular before Austen and the novel became a matter of professional study in the university, and in so doing she traces the path by which we came to privilege the courtship plot above all else in Austen's novels.

6   Similarly, Sharon Marcus's groundbreaking study of same-sex marriage in Victorian England, *Between Women*, Mary Jean Corbett's important study of incest law as it relates to marriage, *Family Likeness*, and Amy King's impressively contextualized work on sexualized courtship, *Bloom*, signal a still-lively interest in the courtship plot that culminates in marriage.

7   Individualism is also the subject of Watt's last published work, *Myths of Modern Individualism* (1996), in which he considers Don Quixote, Don Juan, Faust, and Robinson Crusoe as "powerful myths with a particular resonance for our individualist

society," myths that "derive from the transition from the social and intellectual system of the Middle Ages to the system dominated by modern individualist thought" (xiii, xvi). Watt's "working definition" of myth is "a traditional story that is exceptionally widely known throughout the culture, that is credited with a historical or quasi-historical belief, and that embodies or symbolizes some of the most basic values of a society" (xvi). This definition also suggests why Watt's thesis has had such staying power, I think, for it indicates that individualism is not only elemental, but also axiomatic.

8 Van Ghent's book actually predates *The Rise of the Novel* by four years. She plays a less frequently acknowledged role in solidifying hypotheses that would become discipline-defining and would come to be associated almost exclusively with Watt. Van Ghent provides a more formal vocabulary—that is, one specifically reflective of literary form—which later critics attach to Watt's concepts, making those concepts more portable and turning them into a professional idiom.

9 In terms of echoes, consider here Alexander Welsh's pronouncement in *The City of Dickens* that "courtship is the main action in most nineteenth-century English novels" (176). Welsh goes on to say, in a formulation that anticipates D.A. Miller's concept of the nonnarratable, that "marriage in conventional English novels is the event that regularly precludes further experience or change" (219). Welsh elaborates on this idea by suggesting that "novels imply that marriage is the most important epoch in life; they pretend that the years between coming of age and marriage are the whole of life; and therefore conceive of marriage as equivalent to death. Like *Waverly* itself, the hero and heroine, and a good many others, are consigned to rest forever. Nothing more happens in most English novels" (222).

10 I propose to build on their exposés by considering the ways in which theories of the domestic novel coerce the genre into fulfilling conventional expectations.

11 I am particularly struck by the fact that they uphold the novel's conservative approach to marriage even as they investigate individual instances of failed marriage.

12 This is, of course, the version of himself he created for his public (and some might argue, for himself, as well). In his handling of the failure of his marriage—that is, his refusal to allow Catherine to divorce him and his scapegoating of her as an inept mother who deserts her children—we see his concern with maintaining his reputation as a loving father and his insistence that he is a wronged husband. For a reading of Dickens's own failed marriage and its relation to the failed marriages he plots in his novels, see Chapter 3.

13 Luhmann goes on to explain that these differences "created different preconditions for their respective adaptability, specifically in the following context: only the semantics of *amour passion* was sufficiently complex ... to absorb the revaluation of sexuality that occurred in the eighteenth century. Despite having provided a preliminary basis for the integration of love and marriage, and under the same conditions as the French, the English were only able to come up with the Victorian malformation of sexual morality" (10).

14 Tony Tanner includes *Orley Farm* (1862), *One of Our Conquerors* (1891), and *Jude the Obscure* in his list of novels in which "adultery takes on a very special importance" (12, n.15). To this list I would add *The Woodlanders* (1887), *The Newcomes*, *Felix Holt*

(1866), and *Vanity Fair*. Indeed, Barbara Leckie argues that "adultery was never remote from middle-class concerns in Victorian England" and that "between 1857 and 1914 adultery was, in fact, everywhere in English print culture." Her project, to discover why "the discursive history of adultery has been overlooked, or rendered 'invisible,' in the English critical tradition," has much in common with my aims in drawing attention to the failed-marriage plot in the English novel (1).

15 *Middlemarch* anticipates this concluding pronouncement in the prolonged and detailed attention it pays to a multiplicity of marriages: to the successful unions of Celia and Sir James, Caleb and Susan Garth, Fred Vincy and Mary Garth, and even the relatively happy domestic life of Rosamond's parents. The novel also chronicles the failed marriages in Middlemarch: most notably the unequal and incompatible pairing of Dorothea and Causabon, but also the mismatch of Lydgate and Rosamond, and Featherstone's adulterous affair that produces Rigg.

16 Two rather sunny examples would be Fielding's *Amelia* (1752) and Richardson's *Pamela, Part II* (1741). Another very important example, though it is a poem, not a novel, would be Coventry Patmore's *The Angel in the House*. As Linda Hughes and Michael Lund remind us when they draw attention to the titles of the individual volumes of the poem—"The Bethrothal," "The Espousal," "Faithful for Ever," and "Victories of Love"—"victories of love are not won until long after marriage"; they point out that Patmore's poem "argued that true love is old love, that love, like people, grows up by growing old," and that Patmore "resisted closure and suggested that the story must continue if [Honoria and Frederick's] love was to reach a more distinct fulfillment" (20, 21).

17 Similarly, what Linda Peterson calls "the burdens of being a wife" are made clear at the outset of Margaret Oliphant's *Kirsteen* (1890) in the picture presented to us of Kirsteen's mother, "a powerless feminine figure reduced to silence and tears" (83, 82). Like the Austen novels I cite above, *Kirsteen* presents the cautionary tales of the heroine's sisters' marriages in order to "represent paths the heroine must avoid," while the story of Caroline Helstone's parents' failed marriage that forms the prehistory of Charlotte Brontë's *Shirley* (1849) introduces the courtship plots of its heroines as similarly perilous enterprises (Peterson 83). Caroline's mother warns her that "two people can never literally be as one: there is, perhaps, a possibility of content under peculiar circumstance, such as are seldom combined; but it is as well not to run the risk: you may make fatal mistakes" (Brontë 379). Her hesitant, grudging admission that "there is, perhaps, a possibility of content" suggests that she does not put much faith in that possibility, while her description of marriage as a "risk" anticipates Queen Victoria's assessment of it as a lottery.

In Gilbert Imlay's and Mary Wollstonecraft's *The Emigrants* (1793), the courtship of hero and heroine is presented in marked contrast to the stories of unhappily married women which surround it, and the courtship plot of the governess-heroine in Anne Brontë's *Agnes Grey* (1847) frames the story of her impetuous charge, Rosalie Murray, and the duplicitous, flirtatious courtship that leads to her unhappy marriage to the rake, Sir Thomas Ashby. Eliza Lynn Linton's *The Rebel of the Family* (1880) is similarly revealing in terms of the relationship between the courtship plot and the failed-marriage plot; Perdita (the heroine and the eponymous "rebel" of the family) is, like Jane Eyre, courted by a man married to a mad woman imprisoned but still alive, a man raising a daughter he assumes is not his own. While Perdita's plot, like Jane's, does end in marriage, it is a plot, again like Jane's, tainted by and entangled with the failure of marriage and the discontents of a union gone very, very wrong. Esther Lyon's plot in *Felix Holt* also ends in marriage, but her courtship plot must be read in the context of the adultery plot that surrounds it. Framed by the story of Mrs Transome's affair with the lawyer Jermyn, Esther's plot threatens to repeat that of Mrs Transome, though in rejecting the temptations of marriage to the rich, aristocratic Harold Transome, she thus distances herself from the world of arranged and mercenary marriages and guarantees herself a happy ending. We find a comical, though no less pointed, critique of mercenary marriages in *Our Mutual Friend*'s portrayal of the Lammles' sham marriage. Alfred and Sophronia marry because they each think the other has money. When they realize, on their honeymoon, that they were both wrong, they decide to join forces to prey on society for the financial support they believe is owed them; their machinations and the charade of their marriage run throughout Dickens's last completed novel, providing a cautionary counterpoint to the happy ending awarded to Bella Wilfer.

18 Barbara Leckie makes a similar point about the divorce court—that it "made vividly clear one of the central contradictions of bourgeois ideology: the gap between the promised happy marriage and the very difficult struggle that marriage so often was" (102).

19 Susan Ferrier's *Marriage* (1818) also reveals that to believe in the happily-ever-after of marriage is to subscribe to a foolish and romantic notion. Lady Juliana elopes simply because she is swept off her feet and charmed by the notion that she, in refusing the mercenary marriage her father has planned for her, occupies "the true position of a heroine: a handsome lover—an ambitious father—cruel fortune—unshaken constancy" (3). Ferrier's novel lays bare the naïveté of this assumption and is frankly a cautionary tale. In addition to depicting the misery of Lady Juliana's marriage (which, like Rawdon's and Becky's in *Vanity Fair*, ends in an informal separation), it treats the courtship plots of her twin daughters. One refuses to marry the rich husband her mother has chosen for her, while the other marries a very old aristocrat and finds herself "compelled to drag the chain by which, with her own will, she had bound herself for life to one she already despised and detested" (471). What is more, she leaves him after less than a year, eloping with her former lover, "vainly hoping to find peace and joy amid guilt and infamy" (475).

20 As Garrett Stewart remarks with respect to *Daniel Deronda*, "so strong are the structural conventions of the Victorian novel that almost any marriage occurring this early in a plot forebodes no good; the fact that it opens forward on to a narratable future suggests that there is something other to be said of it, something more specific, restless, troubled, than a formulaic 'happily ever after'" ("Beckoning Death" 71).

21 There are, to be sure, a number of other ways in which the novel suggests that relationships between husbands and wives provide it with its plots; one is to plot loveless marriages that become companionate and affectionate unions. *The Woman in White*'s Marian Halcombe insists that this is "the position of hundreds of other women, who marry men without being greatly attracted to them or greatly repelled by them, and who learn to love them (when they don't learn to hate!) after marriage, instead

of before" (97). In Dinah Mulock Craik's *Agatha's Husband* (1853), Emily Eden's *The Semi-Attached Couple* (1860), and throughout Trollope's Palliser series, in the extended courtship and marriage plot of Lady Glencora and Plantagenet Palliser, husbands and wives "learn to love" each other, and their marriages are the focus of these novels' plots.

22   In the rake/dandy plot, the failure of marriage is marked by adultery (or by such a narrow escape from actual sexual infidelity that the intention damns the heroine as much as the deed), while the Gothic bigamy plot takes that infidelity one step further by (falsely) codifying it and, as P.D. Edwards argues, sanitizing it in the form of marriage, albeit an illegal one. The bigamy plot thus reveals a culture's awareness of the frequent failure of marriage even as it subscribes to matrimony by plotting another marriage for the hero or heroine while they are still enmeshed in one so obviously faulty. It could be argued that the bigamy plot shows how to maneuver around a failed first marriage so that a new, more perfect, union might be effected, and that the bigamy plot is both optimistic (in that it reveals an unshakeable belief in marriage) and radical (in that it poses an extralegal solution to the problem of a failed marriage). Unlike the second-chance plot, which similarly replaces one spouse with another, the bigamy plot suggests that (re)marriage is so important and that the suitor is so eager to (re)marry that it is either impossible or unnecessary to wait for death (or even the delay of a divorce) to end one marriage before plotting a new one. On the other hand, Karen Chase and Michael Levenson argue that "within a culture still struggling to represent the change, marriage after divorce remains a form of bigamy. In the uncertain new world of the Matrimonial Causes Act, love for a second spouse, while the first spouse still lived, was bound to seem an infidelity. In this respect, the bigamy novels of the sixties are all divorce novels, which is to say, novels about the failure of divorce to achieve a true separation" (203). While the bigamy plots of sensation novels often suggest that the failure of marriage is scandalous and spectacular and that it has more to do with the wicked adulteress or the greedy and profligate fortune-seeker that threatens the sacred domestic sphere than it does with the institution thought to shore up the domestic, novels that concentrate on the impoverished legal status of wives and on problems with marriage law more generally suggest that the failure of the contract results from systemic, institutional flaws. Paralleling Mill's argument in *The Subjection*, these novels suggest that the failure of marriage results from the inequities that are a part of the law itself and show how that structural imbalance inevitably leads to the matrimonial cruelty and violence inherent in a patriarchal system.

23   As Deborah Denenholz Morse argues in her essay on *Tenant*, "Brontë is concerned with truthfully depicting the injustices of patriarchal culture that are encoded in the very laws of the land. Her book provides the evidence that a married woman could not give in a court of law" (104).

24   Lisa Surridge argues that the novel "criticizes marital coverture as an underlying cause of domestic assault and abuse, and compares women to domestic animals abused by their owners" (73).

25   Before 1857 her only options were, as Maeve Doggett enumerates them, "just to put up with [her husband's abuse], and this is probably what the majority of wives did."

Or she could "pray the peace against him," but after exhibiting articles of peace against him, "the court would expect her to accompany him home." She could also pursue a criminal prosecution, though this not only cost money she likely did not have, but also required her to fly in the face of received gender politics. As Doggett puts it, "the higher courts seemed to exude an aura of disapproval when wives asked for more than the customary security of the peace" (30). Indeed, Doggett finds that "a wife's only real hope was to petition the ecclesiastical courts for a separation *a mensa et thoro* on the grounds of cruelty" (31). The advantage to this remedy was that she could live apart from her husband, but they were only legally separated, not divorced, and "all the common law disabilities attendant on wifehood remained" (31). Perhaps even more daunting was the fact that, as A. James Hammerton points out, even defining what constituted legal cruelty was a complicated matter; see his *Cruelty and Companionship*, especially 120. Two recent studies are also well worth consulting: Elizabeth Foyster's *Marital Violence: An English Family History* and Martin Weiner's *Men of Blood: Violence, Manliness and Criminal Justice in Victorian England*.

26 Morse argues that Gilbert thus "writes his support of married women under English law. He, like Brontë herself, implicitly questions the legitimacy of laws that usurp women's rights to custody of their children in the face of mistreatment by reprobate fathers, that assign all the wife's earnings to the husband, that give the husband legal rights to the body of his wife, even if he abuses her" (105).

27 That frame narrative is so traditional that it begins in a manner that brings *Pride and Prejudice* irresistibly to mind. In the novel's first chapter, Rose (Gilbert's sister) is eager to impart "an important piece of news": "You know it was reported a month ago, that some body was going to take Wildfell Hall—and—what do you think? It has actually been inhabited above a week!" (11). Like Mrs Bennet's "Netherfield Hall is let at last," the news heralds not only the arrival of an eagerly awaited tenant, but it also leads the reader to expect (correctly) that the advent of this tenant will, like Bingley's appearance in Austen's novel, inaugurate a courtship plot for one of the novel's characters (1).

28 For an argument that emphasizes the class aspect of the failed-marriage plot in Collins's novel, see Marlene Tromp's "Brutality and Propriety: Wilkie Collins's *The Woman in White* and the Divorce Act of 1857" in her *The Private Rod* (a title she takes from Collins's novel). Tromp argues that the novel "moves violence out of the working class of Dickens's fiction and Parliament's laws" and thus performs an "implicit critique" of the Divorce Act (17).

29 *The Portrait of a Lady* (1881) is, of course, one of the most understated and chilling accounts of a failed marriage. James's portrait of Gilbert Osmond reveals one more way in which marriage makes men monsters, yet Isabel believes that "marriage meant that a woman should cleave to the man with whom, uttering tremendous vows, she had stood at the altar" (575). That the vows of marriage are "tremendous," (i.e. immense, vast, substantial, and considerable) is demonstrated not only by Isabel's belief that "if I were afraid of my husband, that would be simply my duty. That's what women are expected to be," but also by the fact that although she finds him to be "unjust," "malignant" in his opposition to her wishes, and skilled at "spoiling everything for her that he looked at," she believes she must "accept" what she calls the "mistake" of her marriage and

endure her "horrible life" (537, 570, 455, 435, 465). Although "she was morally certain now that this feeling of hatred, which at first had been a refuge and a refreshment, had become the occupation and comfort of his life," she returns to her husband and to that "very straight path" (464, 628). In "'A Strange Opposition': *The Portrait of a Lady* and the Divorce Debates," Melissa Ganz argues while "the novel insists upon the sanctity of the conjugal bond, it highlights the costs of remaining in a miserable marriage and it reaches toward a remedy for Isabel. At many moments the novel imagines the possibility—indeed, desirability—of dissolving the conjugal tie" (157).

30 See also Kathy Alexis Psomiades's recent essay on the novel's connection to Victorian liberalism. Psomiades argues that the novel "uses the problematics of power and rule in relations of marriage and kinship to address larger questions of what it means to govern and be governed, and of how to allow for and yet contain the changes the progressive logic of liberalism would seem to demand" (32). To Herbert's argument, she adds "that the story of the tyrannical husband is not just a story that acts to manage tyranny in marriage, but one that also acts to manage the larger liberal fiction in which tyranny as liberalism's other, is always somehow disappearing and hanging on. It is not just a 'literary institution,' but also one of the institutions of liberal social theory" (36).

31 A. James Hammerton reminds us that "during the 1860s, in the shadow of the new Divorce Act, and in tune with so many of the press reports of the new court's proceedings, novelists devoted an increasing amount of attention to errant husbands. ... The fictional characters invariably offended against the norms of companionate marriage by carrying their desire for mastery over their wives to extremes." And he points to He Knew He Was Right as the novel in which "these themes were played out in most detail for a popular audience" (Cruelty and Companionship 153). Similarly, Lisa Surridge argues that "though the novel's archconservative character Miss Stanbury deplores them, the contemporary issues of 'divorce bills and women's rights, and penny papers' (HK 140) dominate the novel" (166).

32 I phrase this sentiment under erasure in large part because of the discussion on the Victoria list-serv in August 2008 about the canonical and the non-canonical and the novels we teach in Victorian literature classes. As that thread revealed, the notion of the canonical Victorian novel has changed in marked ways: from Leavis's *Great Tradition* to the quintet Dickens, Brontë, Eliot, Thackeray, and Trollope so popular in the 1960s and 1970s, to the jettisoning of Thackeray and the enshrinement of the sensation novel (Collins and Braddon most often) in the syllabus around the turn into the 21st century.

It is tempting to speculate that Thackeray's relative unpopularity might also have something to do with our tendency to read over and by the failed-marriage plot. Hughes and Lund are inspired by their study of serial reviews of *The Newcomes* to argue that in that novel "the troubled unions ... outnumber the happy ones" and that "in nineteenth-century England 'homely tyranny'—as Mrs. Mackenzie's reign over Clara's household is characterized—is more common than the 'happy home' once imagined by the Colonel for Ethel and Clive." Similarly, they cite the narrator's rhetorical question, "Is life all over when Jenny and Jessamy are married; and are there no subsequent trials, griefs, wars, bitter heart-pangs, dreadful temptations, defeats, remorses, sufferings to bear, and dangers to overcome?" and come to the conclusion that, "as with *The Angel in the House*, then, the real subject of *The Newcomes* is domestic life beyond courtship, where daily mundane cares weigh down the dreams of romantic youth." They even go a step further and assert that: "the pressure of 'what you have daily to bear' [the phrase is the narrator's] is the great subject of this work, one which, according to the novel, dominated English national life in [the narrator's] time: 'If you were acquainted with the history of every family in your street, don't you know that in two or three of the houses there such tragedies have been playing? The fate under which man or woman falls, blows of domestic tyranny, heartless desertion, weight of domestic care too heavy to bear—are not blows such as these constantly striking people down?'" (45, 51, 52).

This last quotation from Thackeray suggests that the Victorians were well aware of the failed-marriage plots that littered the pages of the narratives they read, and Hughes and Lund are alive to this possibility. They not only cite Edward Burne-Jones's description of "unhappy wedded life" as "the very heart and core of social disease" (in his 1856 "Essay on *The Newcomes*"), but they also quote from a particularly cynical 1869 serial review of *The Ring and the Book*: "If your wife has run away from you (which is not improbable in these days), you will … see in Count Guido's crimes a natural act of punishment; if you are a lady, and consider that your husband does not pay you sufficient attention (which is at least possible in these days), you will claim Pompilia's conduct quite justifiable" (91). Whether it is due to their emphasis on contemporary reviews, the fact that they explore poetry and nonfictional prose, as well as novels, or their sustained analysis of Thackeray (or the combined influence of all three factors), I want to highlight the fact that, in their work on Victorian periodicals, they are the rare critics who embrace the failed-marriage plot as a fundamental characteristic of the literature of the period.

33 In the same vein, but in the service of her argument about same-sex marriages in Victorian England, Sharon Marcus refers to the institution of marriage as "plastic." Noting, as I do here, that "marriage as an institution" "was mutating in the Victorian present, inspiring competing visions of what it had been in the past and might be in the future," she argues that "Victorian debates about divorce and marriage indicate a general awareness of the plasticity of marriage" (5, 227).

34 See Erica Harth's "The Virtue of Love" and Katherine Sobba Green's "The Heroine's Blazon and Hardwicke's Marriage Act" for references to the pamphlets against clandestine marriage. It is also worth noting that stories of abducted heiresses dominated the debates over the bill. See Christopher Lasch, "The Suppression of Clandestine Marriage in England," especially 98–100 and notes 20–25.

35 This is not to say that the debates over clandestine marriage and divorce were not fraught with class and gender prejudice, enormously complicated, and prey to political interests far removed from the actual issues at hand, but my concern here is to draw attention to an overarching pattern in matrimonial legislation, not to provide a complete and comprehensive account of the intricate and imbricated history of marriage law in the last two centuries.

36 Samuel Menefee finds that while the wife sale depicted in Hardy's novel "shocked Victorian sensibilities," "wife-selling *was* an established British institution. Wife sales were popularly believed to be a legal and valid form of divorce. The husband, by

transferring his wife to a purchaser, considered himself freed from responsibility for the woman." He goes on to explain that "such conjugal sales were often pre-arranged, taking place at market or in a pub in order to publicize or validate the exchange" and that "wife-selling occurred throughout the British Isles, perhaps as early as 1073, with scattered cases as late as the twentieth century," though he notes that "many writers trace the institution's decline" after the passage of the Divorce Act in 1857 (1, 2, 3).

37   The Matrimonial Causes Act of 1884 established that a spouse's refusal to obey an order for the restitution of conjugal rights would be considered desertion, and the other spouse could then obtain a separation immediately, rather than waiting for two years. Lee Holcombe points out that the act of 1884 also established "that if the decree was obtained by the wife and the husband committed adultery after their separation, she could petition for divorce on the ground of his adultery coupled with desertion, even though the desertion might not be of two years' duration" (105). The Summary Jurisdiction (Married Women) Act of 1895 extended the definition of cruelty upon which a wife could obtain a separation and added imprisonment for over two months as additional grounds for separation. The Licensing Act of 1902 added habitual drunkenness as grounds for separation for both spouses.

38   McGregor cites 1697 as the year in which civil divorce was established because that was the year the Earl of Macclesfield obtained his divorce, but I follow Allen Horstman and Lawrence Stone in their identification of 1670 as the year in which parliament first granted a divorce, to Lord Roos. McGregor makes no mention of Roos.

39   To say a change is semantic is not, as Niklas Luhmann reminds us, to belittle it, either. Luhmann argues that semantics "describe how [motives] can exist and how they are to be presented and comprehended. Motives are themselves a product of the evolution of generalized symbolic communicative media, i.e. an artefact of socio-cultural evolution." He goes on to argue, in a passage that suggests quite explicitly how intertwined the legalization of divorce and the failed-marriage plot are, that "taking a chance on love and the correspondingly complicated, demanding reorientation of everyday life is only possible if one has cultural traditions, literary texts, convincingly evocative linguistic patterns and situational images—in short, if one can fall back on a timeworn structure of semantics" (39). Luhmann's argument here is especially important because he suggests the ways in which literature and the law inform each other; literary texts and cultural traditions (novels and the law of divorce) are both semantic structures, and both are examples of the kinds of structures that need to be in place in order for the "motive" that gives rise to courtship or divorce to exist, to be articulated, and to be understood.

40   As Barbara Leckie puts it, the law "relaxed the regulation relating to divorce and, at the same time, subjected marital sexuality to an exacting surveillance" (67).

41   Kate Lawson and Lynn Shakinovsky begin their analysis of domestic violence in "Janet's Repentance" by reminding us that "among the enduring and repeated topics addressed by George Eliot's fiction is the question of what makes, and in some cases, breaks a marriage; the other two tales in *Scenes of Clerical Life*, 'The Lifted Veil,' *Silas Marner, Felix Holt, Romola, Middlemarch*, and *Daniel Deronda* all address this problem. Eliot's interest in marital violence in 'Janet's Repentance' should thus not be

viewed in isolation, but as part of her larger concern with destructive marriages as a whole" (64).

42 The Divorce Bill was first introduced in parliament in 1854, as the weekly numbers of *Hard Times* were appearing in *Household Words*, but was withdrawn less than a month later. It was reintroduced in 1856 with the same basic purposes as the initial bill, but between July 1854, when Lord Chancellor Cranworth withdrew the bill, and May 1856, when he reintroduced it, several things had occurred which radically altered the character of the debates that ensued over the 1856 bill. Caroline Norton wrote and privately published a letter to Queen Victoria on Cranworth's 1854 bill, Barbara Leigh Smith and a group of protofeminists, who came to be known as the Langham Place Group, banded together to work for married women's property rights, and the Law Amendment Society, a group of Whig lawyers organized in 1844, directed their attention toward the bill and, together with Smith's group, drafted a petition to Parliament regarding the rights of married women to hold property and income in their own names. These three parties had their own agendas, of course, but the effect of their quasi-simultaneous efforts was, as Lawrence Stone accurately notes, "to convert the bill from a purely administrative reorganization of the courts to a significant change in the laws governing divorce" (373). It is at this point that the debate over the bill takes on what we would call a feminist character; as Mary Poovey points out, the passage of this bill as the Matrimonial Causes Act of 1857 "was the first major piece of British legislation to focus attention on the anomalous position of married women under the law" (*Uneven Developments* 51). By delaying the bill for two years, the government thus inadvertently committed itself to a re-examination of the principle of coverture, and subjects which were not at issue two years before—the right of a woman to sue for divorce on the same grounds as a man, to own property, and to earn income in her own name—came to the fore. These debates surrounded the publication of *Little Dorrit*.

Chapter 2
Monstrous Marriage in Early Dickens

The marriages that set the plots of early Dickens novels in motion are monstrous, rather horrifying visions of incompatible parts. To refer to marriage in a Victorian novel as monstrous is perhaps surprising, even in the context of a study of the failed-marriage plot. To refer to the sacred institution in a Dickens novel in such a manner may seem to border on heresy. After all, Dickens is the self-appointed novelist of hearth and home. But, despite the apparently conservative nature of his domestic plots and our vague sense that most marriages in Dickens are as happy as David and Agnes's, Esther and Allan Woodcourt's, Biddy and Joe's, it is in fact true that Dickens devotes much of his narrative energy to the plotting of marriages that have very little in common with the happily-ever-afters he rewards those couples. Indeed, marriages in Dickens's first three plotted novels—*Oliver Twist*, *Nicholas Nickleby*, and *The Old Curiosity Shop*—are monstrous in several senses of the word. First, they are composed of ill-assorted parts (like the harpy or the Sphinx), made up of a man and woman who are so ill-matched that their union is as freakish and aberrant as the mythological creatures they metaphorically resemble. Marriages in early Dickens are also like monsters in that they are made to seem marginal to the main plot as if they were a shameful secret, much like the Minotaur at the center of the maze which Minos has Daedalus construct to hide the shame of his wife's infidelity. Finally, marriages are monstrous in early Dickens in that they function as warnings to the other characters, especially those who are about to enter into the institution of marriage. As Chris Baldick reminds us in his study of the myth of the monster in the nineteenth century, the word "monster" comes from the Latin *monstrare*, the English "demonstrate." A monster "reveal[s] visibly the results of vice, folly, and unreason, as a warning to erring humanity" (10). Or as Marie-Hélène Huet puts it, "monstrosity always reveals a truth" (128).

This chapter, then, uncovers the monstrous marriage at the heart of each of these novels, exposing it for the mismatch of parts that it is, taking it seriously as a warning about the nature of matrimony, and revealing the way in which this marriage sets the novel's plot in motion even as it is marginalized and disowned by that plot. Because the early Dickens novel is generally considered to be poorly plotted—to be, as Hilary Schor so succinctly puts it, "a mess"—this last aspect of the failed-marriage plot in early Dickens is especially important, for it suggests that Dickens's characteristic interest in marriage and its discontents was, at least early in his career, a kind of guilty secret (much like the shameful story of his childhood that he could never quite tell and also never stop telling[1]) that threatened to derail his novels and sabotage that aspect of his fiction—his careful, dense, and intricate plotting—that would become his hallmark (Hilary Schor 19).

How Monstrous Marriages Drive Dickens's Plots

In *Oliver Twist*, the story of the hero seems unconnected to and unsullied by the failure of marriage. While he is an illegitimate child, and while, as Schor reminds us, "the novel obsessively returns to the moment of Oliver's birth," neither his illegitimacy nor the novel's overwhelming interest in his birth seems to have anything to do with the failure or the monstrosity of marriage (28). We might even say that Oliver's illegitimacy means that neither his plot nor his mother's has anything to do with marriage at all. Given that he was born out of wedlock, we must conclude that his story begins not with the failure of marriage, but rather with what we might call the failure of courtship, for that is the plot that has been short-circuited. But the novel is not really interested in the derailment of that plot either; the novel's concern with the facts of Oliver's birth has more to do with solving the mystery of his identity—figuring out who his parents are—than with uncovering the circumstances that would account for his illegitimacy—learning how it is that Rose Maylie's sister could have sunk so low as to give birth to an illegitimate child in the poorhouse. And while the mystery of his parentage is one the reader soon solves, it is nevertheless one the novel hovers over obsessively, almost as if it takes a kind of delight in delaying the revelation that will save its hero. In fact, it is in delaying the revelation that Oliver is the son of Mr Brownlow's oldest friend that the novel betrays its commitment to keeping the monstrous marriage that fuels the plot of *Oliver Twist* well out of sight.

If at this point my reader is confused, if my allusions to the monstrous marriage at the heart of *Oliver Twist* seem deliberately obscure, it is because Dickens has kept that marriage so well hidden. Careful readers of *Twist* will remember that Oliver is the love-child of Edwin Leeford and Agnes Fleming, and the half-brother of Edward Leeford, alias Monks, the villain who tries to rob Oliver of his identity and his inheritance. But as this review of Oliver's family tree suggests, someone and something has been left out. Why is it that Edwin Leeford will not marry Agnes? Who is Monks's mother? The answer to both questions leads us to the failed marriage at the center of the novel—the marriage of Monks's parents that prevents Edwin from marrying Agnes—just as it helps us trace the connection between that marriage and the novel's obsessive desire to rescue Oliver.

It is the marriage of Monks's parents—that is, the marriage of Oliver's father and his wife, a woman by no means to be confused with Oliver's mother—that is at the heart of *Oliver Twist* and that sets Oliver's progress from parish boy to gentleman in motion. Mr Brownlow describes this union to Monks (whom he calls its "sole and most unnatural issue") as "the wretched marriage, into which family pride and the most sordid and narrowest of all ambition, forced your unhappy father when a mere boy" (435). He goes on to detail "the misery, the slow torture, the protracted anguish of that ill-assorted union" and to describe "how listlessly and wearily each of that wretched pair dragged on their heavy chain through a world that was poisoned to them both" (435). And, finally, he tells Monks how the marriage ended:

> how cold formalities were succeeded by open taunts; how indifference gave place to dislike, dislike to hate, and hate to loathing, until at last they wrenched the clanking bond asunder, and retiring a wide space apart, carried each a galling fragment, of which nothing but death could break the rivets, to hide it in new society beneath the gayest looks they could assume. (435)

His marriage is, then, a marriage of convenience, an alliance the young Edwin ("a mere boy") is forced into by his grasping family. It seems to have everything to do with financial status and social ambition and nothing to do with love. It is arranged in accordance with the parents' wishes rather than the desires of husband or wife. Such an arrangement was, in fact, guaranteed by the state of marriage law at the time, codified by the Marriage Act of 1753. This act, officially entitled "An Act for the better preventing of clandestine Marriages," required a parent's or guardian's consent in order for those under the age of 21 to marry. It was, as I discuss in Chapter 1, designed to protect heiresses from being abducted into clandestine marriages and to prevent minors from eloping. But it also meant that parents could exercise their own desires in arranging marriages for their children. As Ruth Yeazell points out, "when marriages are made by the authority of fathers, 'it is not the persons who are married; it is rank and wealth'" (*Fictions of Modesty* 38).[2]

Brownlow's description of this mercenary marriage also calls attention to its monstrosity: the union of the young Leefords is "ill-assorted," and they endure matrimony much as the souls in Dante's *Inferno* endure life in hell. They are consigned to "a world that was poisoned to them both" and to the endless and painful labor of bearing the burden of their marriage, of pulling "their heavy chain" through that poisoned world. What's more, this is a chain that can only be broken by death. That is, while they do manage to "wrench the clanking bond asunder," they each must carry "a galling fragment" of that chain—a fragment that serves as a constant reminder that they are linked to each other "until death do [them] part" (435). Again, this is an historically accurate description of the state of marriage law in the late 1830s. As I outline in Chapter 1, until 1857 obtaining a divorce involved petitioning three courts, spending an overwhelming amount of money, and losing your reputation. Even once divorce was legalized, 20 years after the publication of *Twist*, it was only available on the grounds of a wife's adultery or a husband's aggravated adultery, neither of which seems to apply in the Leefords' case. So their marriage is not only monstrous, but it is also permanent and binding. Or as Quilp would put it, they are "tied for life," and "the knot's tied hard and fast" (228).

Telling the story of their separation by means of the same metaphor he used to describe their marriage, Brownlow tells Monks that his mother managed successfully (and easily, he implies) to forget the "galling fragment" of the marriage bond she carried with her. However, this remnant "rusted and cankered at [his] father's heart for years" (435). Unlike Monks's shallow and unfeeling mother who, "wholly given up to continental frivolities, had utterly forgotten [her] young husband," his father, "his prospects blighted," stayed at home. Another way to put this would be to say that his father is allowed to remain in England, while his mother is banished from the country. Like Little Em'ly, who is sent to Australia after Steerforth ruins her, and Edith Dombey, who is consigned to the margins of the novel and the south of Italy after she compromises her character with Carker, Monks's mother becomes an expatriate and a woman with a past. Monks's father, on the other hand, stays safe at home.

However, in this case, home is not so safe. For as Brownlow reveals to Monks, at home in England, Edwin makes some new friends: namely, a widower with two daughters. Here is where the story gets complicated. While Brownlow tries to turn this into a story of the heartless wife and the sorrowing husband, of the evil woman and the wholly innocent man, he simply cannot. He tries to besmirch Mrs Leeford's character, but all he can say is that she was "wholly given up to continental frivolities." By the same token, when he tries to enshrine Mr Leeford, comparing him to his saintly dead sister (Brownlow's fiancée, who died on what was to have been their wedding day), he has no choice but to admit that the married Mr Leeford, one year after separating from his wife, becomes engaged to another woman. And this other women is no flirt, no cunning female out to entrap a man, but rather "a guileless girl" who feels for Leeford her "first, true, ardent, only passion" (436). Monks's response to all these revelations is one of restless impatience. "Your tale is of the longest," he says to Brownlow (436). But in fact it is not, and its brevity has much to do with the fact that most readers forget it. That is, while this is quite a story—sensational, tragic, shameful—and while it seems hard to believe that any reader could overlook it or its ramifications for the plot of *Oliver Twist*, the fact that it is told in less than two pages, 40 pages from the end of the novel, and at a point in the novel where the reader is more interested in the fate of Sikes (who has just killed Nancy) and Fagin (who is in jail awaiting trial) than in a story about two characters she does not even know virtually guarantees that the reader will read it quickly, impatiently, and carelessly. In the previous paragraphs I have tried to resist that kind of reading, taking up every detail Brownlow relates and paying close attention to the failed-marriage plot and the shameful courtship plot that are thus revealed. I want to continue that mode of analysis a bit longer, for in the subsequent pages of this pivotal chapter we are given even more telling details about the Leefords' marriage.

For instance, we learn that Mrs Leeford was ten years older than her husband, that Edwin was nineteen when he married, that "his father ordered him to marry," and that the goal of the marriage was "to strengthen" the "interest and importance" of a rich relation of the Leefords (436, 437). We also learn that the last time Brownlow saw Edwin Leeford, he was overwhelmed with guilt for having so dishonored the widower's daughter, and that he was planning to turn all his property into ready money, settle a portion of that money on Monks and his mother, and then leave the country with his new love. But before he can put this dishonorable plan into action, he dies. At first we are led to believe that he dies without a will and that the entirety of his property was thus left to his wife and his son by default. However, a page later, we find Brownlow insisting that there was in fact a will, that Monks's mother destroyed it because "it contained a reference to some child likely to be the result of this sad connexion," that Monks's mother passed on the secret of this child to Monks before she died, and that Monks, upon "accidentally encounter[ing]" this child some years later, was struck by the resemblance and thus motivated to do some detective work of his own (436). All this already seems a little contrived and ad hoc, but there is still more.

Monks goes to what Brownlow calls "the place of [Oliver's] birth," a reference that is so opaque as to be downright mystifying since the fate of the seduced widower's daughter (who has yet to be given a name) has been left up in the air. (A page earlier we learned that after Leeford died, Brownlow went to visit her, determined to take care of her for the sake of his dead friend, only to find that the family had disappeared, in the middle of the night no less, a week before.) Monks goes to Oliver's birthplace, wherever that might be and however he might have discovered it (Brownlow implies that this information was in Leeford's will and passed on to Monks by his mother, but figuring this out takes some rereading and not an inconsiderable amount of reading between the lines), discovers "proofs of his birth and parentage," and destroys them. Brownlow knows these details because Nancy has reported to him that she has overheard Monks giving Fagin this information.

The novel would thus have us believe that it is the product of that failed marriage that poses the greatest threat to Oliver, and also that it is the failed marriage of Oliver's father which leads him to seduce Oliver's mother. It is, in fact, the failure of marriage that brings Oliver into being, just as it is the failure of marriage that situates him in such a way as to set in motion the novel's plot. As Catherine Waters reminds us, "it is Oliver's illegitimacy which causes his initial plight and subsequent misadventures" (32). And the convoluted and elliptical way in which the novel is plotted asks us to believe that it is the failure of marriage (not his parents' failure to marry. but rather the disaster of the Leefords' marriage) that is responsible for his illegitimacy. That is, we are asked to blame Monks's mother, rather than Oliver's parents, for their adulterous affair and its shameful result. More generally, we are asked to blame the conventions and the codification of marriage (represented by the 1753 Act), which allow parents to force their children into loveless marriages and prevent these children from escaping from those bonds, for the circumstances of Oliver's birth and upbringing.

This is quite a burden to put on a failed marriage. Like the disastrous and far-reaching effects of the failed marriages at the heart of *Nicholas Nickleby* and *The Old Curiosity Shop*, which I take up below, Dickens's plot asks us to accept that the failure of marriage has enormously powerful consequences, that this relationship, when it fails, has the power to change a character's personality, as it does in the case of Edwin Leeford, who is described as both saintly and, ultimately, as a seducer. Steven Marcus insists that his "guilt is not in any event made to seem very grave" and that in fact "the immaculateness of Oliver's character suggests as immaculate as possible a conception. It entirely acquits the characters of his parents" (*Dickens from Pickwick to Dombey* 85, 86). Similarly, J. Hillis Miller insists that Oliver is "a good boy, the son of a gentleman" (*Charles Dickens* 43). Yet the details of the plot reveal that while he is indeed a good boy, he is only the bastard son of a man who is hardly a model of gentlemanly behavior. Or as Homer Brown argues about another famous fictional bastard, "everyone is so excited by the discovery of Tom [Jones]'s good birth that they forget it is still a bad birth— that is, illegitimate" (83). Like the discovery of Tom Jones's identity, then, the discovery of who Oliver really is does not reveal a legitimate identity.

Marcus and Miller are not wrong in their assessment of Oliver's purity or of the way in which the novel absolves his parents of their sin. The novel does indeed try to have it both ways: to present us with a bastard who is more legitimate than his half-brother, with an unmarried adulterous couple who are purer than the couple that is legally married. This inherent contradiction reveals yet another way in which the novel encourages us to ignore the details and the consequence of the failed marriage it buries so deeply within its confusing and confused plot. For in presenting us with a Bunyanesque story of progress, the novel wants us to believe that it is uncovering the noble nature of Oliver's true identity. Yet it is really engaged in covering over the sordid details of his conception and the shameful story of his father's affair with his mother. What looks like a revelation is really an evasion. Rather than telling the truth about Oliver's parentage, the novel concentrates on scapegoating Monks and his mother. As Marcus points out, "it is upon Monks, the lawful son and rightful heir, that the legacy of sin and malevolence devolves" (*Dickens from Pickwick to Dombey* 85). He is guilty of plotting his half-brother's downfall, just as his mother is blamed for Agnes's fall.

The whole of the novel is, in fact, an attempt to work out and correct the marital failure at the heart of the story, its causal center and motivating force. By trying so hard to whitewash the circumstances of Oliver's conception and the characters of his parents, by redeeming the stain that Agnes's sin left on her sister Rose and celebrating the marriage of Rose and Henry Maylie as the triumph of pure and virtuous love, and by closing with a scene of perfect domestic harmony, *Oliver Twist* dedicates itself to repairing the damage wrought by the failure of marriage that lies at its core. The novel is an atonement for the sin that sets it in motion; its plot revolves around making that sin disappear—both by making up for it and by obscuring it.

The failed marriage at the heart of *Nicholas Nickleby* is similarly, if perhaps not so deeply and defensively, obscured. Like the Leefords' marriage, Ralph Nickleby's failed marriage is both buried—in that we do not learn about it until Chapter 60, five chapters from the end of the novel—and embedded—in the sense that we learn about it immediately after Smike dies and when we are anxious to see Nicholas and Kate overcome their overscrupulous consciences and marry their true loves. Like the story of failed marriage in *Twist*, this story is presented to us when our attention is concentrated on pivotal moments in the lives of characters to whom we have become quite attached. Furthermore, this story is only told in order to explain that Smike is Ralph's son; it is provided only as a context for the more important revelation of Smike's parentage and of the history of his life before Nicholas rescued him. Coming as it does immediately after his death, it serves as a kind of eulogy, and thus its effect is to increase our sympathy for what he suffered and to underscore the cruelty visited upon him for most of his short life. Similarly, this story is told in the context of breaking the news to Ralph; it is presented as a story of loss and of accusation—a story of abandoned children and heartless fathers—rather than a story about the failure of marriage.

Like the failed marriage of the Leefords that has the power to turn the upright Edwin into a seducer and a would-be bigamist, the failed marriage of the Ralph Nicklebys is presented as an event that has far-reaching consequences. *Nickleby* asks us to believe that it is the failure of this marriage that is responsible for Ralph's misanthropy in general and his cruelty toward his nephew, Nicholas, in particular. That is, just as *Twist* scapegoats Monks's mother, *Nickleby* targets Ralph. While we might be tempted to argue, as John Bowen does, that the blame lies with Nicholas's father "who in speculating loses his patrimony, breaks his heart and impels the action of the novel," the novel instead wants us to believe that Ralph, not his brother, is the responsible party, that Ralph is more culpable for not helping his dead brother's family and thus forcing Nicholas to support them than Nicholas's father is for ruining his family and then dying, leaving them to fend for themselves (Bowen 158). Accordingly, we find Ralph at every twist and turn in the plot. Whenever something goes wrong or Nicholas and his sister are in danger, Ralph is to blame. Instead of the story of a boy prematurely promoted to manhood and too early saddled with the responsibility of supporting his family, we have the story of a cruelly warped man who has been so soured by the failure of his marriage that he malevolently refuses to help his nearest kin.

It is implied throughout the novel that Ralph is the monster at the heart of the plot, that his poisoned nature is to blame for everything that happens to Nicholas. This link is made explicit when the narrator relates to us Ralph's musings before he kills himself; this moment is especially telling, for herein Ralph also reveals his own suspicion that his marriage is to blame for turning him against his nephew. After learning of Smike's death, Ralph goes home to his empty house and thinks about the wreck that has been made of all his plots and plans, ending with the fact that he has unwittingly been the agent of his own child's death. This thought gives rise to a string of fantasies about the comfort he and Smike could have been to each other and the happiness that might have been his. He thus becomes convinced that "his wife's flight had had some share in making him the morose, hard man he was. He seemed to remember a time when he was not quite so rough and obdurate, and almost thought that he had first hated Nicholas because he was young and gallant, and perhaps like the stripling who had brought dishonour and loss of fortune on his head" (904). The stripling Ralph refers to is the man that his wife left him for, "a younger man" and one who not only costs Ralph his wife, but also the fortune for which he married her.

Like the marriage Edwin Leeford is forced into, Ralph's marriage is a mercenary one. In a plot that has much in common with the one Frederick Trent tries to hatch between Dick Swiveller and his sister Nell in order to gain his grandfather's supposed fortune, Ralph marries the sister of one of his "rough fox-hunting, hard-drinking" friends. This friend "had run through his own fortune, and wanted to squander away that of his sister" (888). But this plot is more complicated and back-stabbing than the one Fred suggests to Dick, for while Dick half-heartedly agrees to give up his attachment to Sophy Wackles and go along with Fred's plan, Ralph goes behind his friend's back and marries the sister secretly, hoping to keep all her property for himself. Unlike Leeford, Ralph chooses to marry for money, and he keeps his marriage a secret for the same reason: "for a clause in [his wife's] father's will declared that if she married without her brother's consent, the property … should pass away altogether to another branch of the family." The fact that this brother's consent is only available for a price ("the brother would give no consent that the sister didn't buy and pay for handsomely") further highlights the mercenary nature of this marriage, just as it explains Ralph's double-dealing ("Mr Nickleby would consent to no such sacrifice"). Thus, Ralph insists that they keep their marriage a secret until the brother dies so that he can have all his wife's fortune. They keep this secret for seven years, during which time they have a child that they "put out to nurse a long way off" in order to avoid suspicion, and during which time their marriage deteriorates (888). They live apart, quarrel violently when they are together, and finally Ralph's wife leaves him for "the stripling" he imagines Nicholas to resemble.

Nickleby, then, like *Twist*, is presented to us as a novel whose plot originates in the failure of marriage, but whereas we are led to believe that in *Twist* the failure of marriage sets the plot in motion, *Nickleby* not only insists that the failure of a mercenary marriage inaugurates its plot, but it also is the plot. For the episodic adventures of *Nicholas Nickleby* are all associated with mercenary marriages. From the novel's opening paragraph—which purports to celebrate the marriage for love of Nicholas's grandfather, only to be followed by the narrator's reflection on the haplessness and hopelessness of such an arrangement—to Nicholas's exposure to the shared greed that makes such a mockery of the Squeers's marriage, the ambition that marks Mr Kenwigs's marriage, and the mercenary marriages of Mr Lillyvick and Henrietta Petowker and of the Mantalinis, not to mention the mercenary courtships Ralph plots for Kate and Madeline, the novel is a portrait gallery of mercenary marriages, of marriages which advertise their failure to Nicholas and Kate so that they can profit from their negative examples and marry wisely and happily.

This reading of *Nickleby* as a novel of mercenary marriage may seem to fly in the face of its ending—an ending that reminds us of a Shakespearean comedy in that everyone is paired up in the final scene: Nicholas and Madeline Bray, Kate and Frank Cheeryble, Tim Linkinwater and Miss La Creevy. This reading may also seem to ignore all the positive depictions of marriage to which Dickens treats us in this novel: Tilda and John, Nicholas's parents and grandparents, the Crummles. It is also true that the mercenary marriages in *Nickleby* almost always fail (Ralph's wife leaves him, Henrietta Petowker leaves Mr Lillyvick, and Mrs Mantalini leaves her husband), just as Ralph's villainous attempts to make mercenary matches (Kate with Lord Verisopht, Madeline with Arthur Gride) are inevitably foiled.

Yet it is precisely these facts that lead me to assert that this novel is about marriage and its discontents, and that it is plotted, like *Twist*, in a manner that seeks to shrug off its association with and its origination in the failure of marriage. In *Nickleby*, the proliferation of mercenary courtships and marriages that fail serves as a covert technique by which to illustrate the problems inherent in the social form. Because it is only those marriages entered into for unworthy motives that fail (and because we are given multiple examples of happy marriages), the novel seems to pose no real threat to the institution of marriage. The fact that so many wives leave their husbands can be read as an indictment not of marriage, but of mercenary marriage. By the same token, the failure of marriage that greets Nicholas and Kate at every turn, the unhappy couples and threatening seducers that Dickens strews along their paths, can be read as negative examples, as cautionary tales for their own courtships and eventual happy marriages. Such a reading helps us see what is at stake in the counterpoint the novel establishes between mercenary marriage and marriage for love. For example, Kate and Nicholas struggle against the fairy-tale ending which Dickens has so clearly designed for them. The reader is aware early on that Nicholas is destined to marry Madeline and that Kate is to marry Frank. But Kate and Nicholas constantly insist to each other that they cannot marry the ones they love because their motives might be misconstrued. Kate calls Frank's love for her a "disinterested love" because she is poor (894). Because he is rich, she is convinced she must do what is "right and honourable" and refuse him (895). By the same token, Nicholas thinks it would be "base of [him] to take advantage of the circumstances" and propose to Madeline (895). Thus he imposes on himself an "anxious and careful sense of duty" and resolves to stay as far away as possible from Madeline (895). Nicholas and Kate know they love Madeline and Frank honorably and disinterestedly, and they know they are so loved in return. But because Madeline and Frank are rich, while they are poor, they are convinced that to marry for love would actually be to marry for money. The difference between marrying for money and marrying money is one they cannot admit, for their experience has shown them so many instances where one is rationalized as the other. Because most men in the novel can only be persuaded to marry because of the financial benefits they will enjoy from their wives (and because, as in *The Old Curiosity Shop*, there are so many confirmed bachelors), and because calculating characters like Lillyvick and Gride are reluctant to marry even when guaranteed significant financial compensation, it comes to seem that marriage is only to be entered into for economic reasons, and perhaps not even then. Thus the selfless and loving marriages of Nicholas and Frank (and of Tim Linkinwater) can be celebrated, idealized, and valorized as extraordinary unions of wedded bliss. It is, in fact, the fairy-tale nature of the ending that highlights the hard facts of marriage in general. It is only our conditioned mode of reading—our assumption that the happily-ever-after of marriage is at the heart of all domestic fiction—which blinds us to the way in which *Nicholas Nickleby*'s plot is initiated by, and revolves around, the failure of marriage, and the way in which it suggests that marital failure, not success, is what typifies the institution.

In much the same way as *Twist* attempts to work out and correct the failure of marriage that generates its plot, then, *Nickleby* ends with Tim Linkinwater's epithalamium—"Let's be a comfortable couple"—and with a tableau that has much in common with the scene of domestic security at the end of *Twist* (916). Both *Twist* and *Nickleby* do end in marriage, and the marriages that mark the end of these novels do suggest that the worlds of these novels have thus been stabilized. In working so hard to get its hero and heroine happily married, *Nickleby* seeks to shore up the convention it has destabilized, just as *Twist* tries to undo the damage done by Monks's parents.

The larger pattern I am pointing to here has to do with the relationship between the failed mercenary marriages that function as warnings and the way in which, as Bowen points out, "at the level of explicit ideology, the novel celebrates the domestic virtues in the closures of Nicholas's marriage to Madeline, Kate's to Frank Cheeryble, and Miss La Creevy's to Tim Linkinwater" (154). On the one hand, *Nickleby* is full of wives who leave their husbands. On the other, it ends with not one, but three, marriages. This is, of course, a pattern we will see throughout Dickens's subsequent novels, wherein what Catherine Waters calls "families made memorable by their grotesque failure to exemplify the domestic ideal" are juxtaposed against families that illustrate that ideal and idyllic state of domestic bliss (27). As Waters points out, Dickens's novels are full of "fractured families," yet they also almost always end "with the recovery of an apparently timeless realm that is sheltered from the vicissitudes of economic and social life … a realm in which the values of the middle-class family are generalized as transcendent ideals" (37). I want to dedicate the rest of this chapter to an analysis of that counterpoint, and I want to do so by concentrating on a novel that makes that pattern of contrast especially clear, relying as it does on the politics of display. The pages that follow perform a detailed reading of marriage in *The Old Curiosity Shop*, focusing on how the comic and grotesque displays of the institution both conceal and reveal a story of marital skepticism.

Jasper Packlemerton, Victorian Freak

Bad marriages in *The Old Curiosity Shop* are literal monstrosities; the metaphor becomes an actuality here, with marriages that are as physically grotesque as they are abnormally incompatible. Good marriages are just as unusual in *The Old*

Curiosity Shop. They are literally curiosities in that they are, to quote the *OED*, "odd, rare, strange, novel." Appropriately enough, both the monstrosities and the curiosities, both the unhappy and the happy couples are put on display in a kind of freak show or curio cabinet, respectively. The happy couples—Kit and Barbara, the Garlands, both Senior and Junior, Dick and the Marchioness—are not only comic characters, but also miniatures, perfectly posed little figures of preciousness or strangely appealing quirkiness. They are made much of as specimens or rarities. By the same token, unhappy marriages are exhibited in a kind of freak show. Consider how the women of the neighborhood congregate in the Quilps' parlor to gawk over "pretty little, mild-spoken, blue-eyed" Mrs Quilp and her "strange infatuation" for her misshapen and equally misanthropic husband (73). Or for a more literal example of this kind of display, consider Jasper Packlemerton, the freak that gives this section its title. Jasper Packlemerton is a serial killer and a serial husband. He is a curiosity in that he is one of the figures in Mrs Jarley's waxworks, and he is a monster in that he merits his place in the waxworks for having tickled his fourteen wives to death. That their deaths are no laughing matter is suggested by the story Mrs Jarley teaches Nell to tell about this freak of a husband:

> on being brought to the scaffold and asked if he was sorry for what he had done, he replied yes, he was sorry for having let 'em off so easy, and hoped all Christian husbands would pardon him the offence. Let this be a warning to all young ladies to be particular in the character of the gentlemen of their choice. (285)

The fact that this warning could serve as the moral of all the novel's stories of marriage leads me to nominate Jasper Packlemerton as the emblematic freak of *The Old Curiosity Shop*.

Although, then, *The Old Curiosity Shop* is populated by monsters and freaks and curiosities—Dickens in this novel gives physical form to the mismatch that is marriage—I want to concentrate on Jasper Packlemerton, to take his story as a cautionary tale. I want to argue that the real monster, the most chilling freak of nature in *The Old Curiosity Shop* is not so much Quilp, or the waxworks, or any of the performers we see at the Jolly Sandboys (the giant, the "little lady without legs or arms," Sweet William, who puts "leaden lozenges into his eyes and brings[s] them out at his mouth"), but rather the institution of marriage (203). Such a reading will not only enable us to discover what is perhaps the most monstrous marriage of all, but it will also help us see that, like the marriage of Monks's parents that sets up the plot of *Twist* and the secret and unhappy marriage of Smike's parents that gives rise to *Nickleby*'s plot, it is this miserable marriage that sets the plot of *Curiosity Shop* in motion and provides the novel with its narrative energy.

This marriage is the wretched union of Nell's parents, a marriage the novel asks us to believe is so miserable that it warps Nell's grandfather's mind and turns him into a miser desperate enough to steal from his own granddaughter, to endanger her life and her virtue, and to fall prey to Quilp. In a pattern that should be familiar by now, few readers even remember Nell's mother's marriage, much less the fact that it is crucial in making any sense of the plot. But this kind of forgetfulness has everything to do with the monstrosity of marriage, with the fact that we refuse to take seriously the tragic consequences of a failed marriage and instead blame Nell's plight on Quilp, a monster we can more easily countenance. Rather than acknowledge the far-reaching and ultimately fatal consequences of Nell's parents' marriage, rather than link the reason Nell and her grandfather have to leave their home and the events that account for Quilp's hold over them to that marriage, we let Quilp shoulder all the blame, as we turn the novel into a familiar story of threatened innocence and overwhelming greed.[3] Like the story of the victimized Edwin Leeford and the pathetically mistreated Smike, the story of Quilp's grotesque evil and of Nell's threatened purity distracts us from the story of failed marriage that early Dickens novels give us with one hand and simultaneously obscure with the other.

It is true that, like the buried stories of failed marriage in *Twist* and *Nickleby*, the story of Nell's mother's marriage is not told until late in the novel, and it is also true that we are given few details about this marriage, and that this story is presented as one of only marginal significance, of interest to the single gentleman more than anyone else. But when we learn about the marriage of Nell's mother, we also learn why her grandfather is so obsessed with money and how and why Quilp can exercise such terrifying control over her grandfather. In Chapter 69 we are given the prehistory of the novel: we learn that the single gentleman who has been so tirelessly searching for Nell and her grandfather is actually her great-uncle, her grandfather's long-lost brother, and we hear—finally—the grandfather's story, which unravels the connection between his love for Nell and his miserliness, explaining both Nell's iconic status in his heart and his obsession with money. Here, then, is that story.

Nell's grandfather and the single gentleman are in love with the same woman, but when he discovers their rivalry, the single gentleman leaves the country so as not to compete with his older brother. The older brother marries this "Good Angel," who then dies in giving birth to their daughter (637). That daughter is her mother all over again, and thus her father loves her both for her own sake and for the sake of her dead mother. The story of her life is told succinctly: "She grew to womanhood, and gave her heart to one who could not know its worth." Her father is thus condemned to watch "the misery which followed this union" and also to suffer from the poverty her husband brings upon them all (637). Broken-hearted and beggared, he is left, 12 years later, with his two orphaned grandchildren: a boy who is the image of his cruel, improvident father and who soon abandons what is left of his family; and a girl who is the image of her mother and her grandmother. Left alone with this little girl, whom he loves with all the love he had for "the two dead people who had been nearest and dearest to his heart," and who serves as a constant reminder of her mother's sufferings, he falls prey to the obsession that will dictate the course of his life and bring him under Quilp's power (638). That is, he can think of nothing but the "gloomy dread of poverty and want," not as it might affect him, but insofar as it might touch Nell, the image of everything he holds dear. This fear was a "spectre in his house, and haunted him night and day" (638).

With the revelation of this story, everything snaps into place: Nell's status in the novel in general, and in her grandfather's heart in particular, as an otherworldly angel; her grandfather's sickening greed; and the hold Quilp has over him; not to mention the logic behind the proliferation of bachelors and the barely disguised hysteria with which even the happiest of marriages is depicted in this novel. We are told that it is precisely because he had to stand by and see the "misery" of his daughter's marriage from day to day, because he was powerless to prevent "her ill-usage and unhappiness," because Nell's face reminds him "of all the suffering he had watched and known, and all his child had undergone" that he loses his wits and becomes a man so obsessed with money that he will even steal from Nell in his pathetic attempt to protect her (637–8). Watching "the struggles of their daily life, too mean and pitiful to tell, but dreadful to endure" has, we are given to believe, broken his spirit and warped his mind (637). Having to witness the failure of marriage up close and day-to-day has created a monomaniac and a plot of monomania. In short, the marriage of Nell's mother and father has put the plot of *The Old Curiosity Shop*, surely one of the most perverse and violent of Dickens's novels, into motion.

Yet the failure of marriage functions as something of a mystery in this novel, just as it does in *Twist* and *Nickleby*. Not only does the revelation of the failed marriage that is at the heart of the plot come late in the narrative,[4] but it is also information that is only revealed after a long investigation into what seems to be an entirely unrelated mystery. Mr Brownlow will only reveal the shameful secret of Oliver's parentage when it is necessary to establish Oliver's claim to his father's property, and Monks will only reveal what he knows of the story when compelled by the force of the law. Similarly, Brooker, Ralph Nickleby's former confidential clerk, only reveals the sordid circumstances of Ralph's early marriage in an attempt to get revenge on the employer who had him transported for fraud. The single gentleman, after chapters and chapters of searching for Nell and her grandfather and mysteriously protecting his identity, tells the story of Nell's mother's marriage only to the benevolent Mr Garland and only when it seems certain that he has discovered his great-niece and his long-lost brother. Such information, in other words, does not come easily or without a price. But the most curious thing about the failure of marriage at the heart of these plots is that its revelation does not have the spectacular effect we usually associate with full disclosure. While we may be surprised to learn that Nell's grandfather and the single gentleman are brothers, just as we are surprised when we realize that Oliver and Monks are half-brothers and that Smike and Nicholas are cousins, none of these revelations hits us like a bombshell. Even more to the point, while we may be surprised by the degrees of consanguinity the plots have been hiding, the real secret at the heart of these novels has to do not with filial or fraternal relations, but with the failure of matrimonial relations. Yet the failure of marriage neither comes as much of surprise nor has much of an impact on our sense or our memory of these novels.

In order to understand why this is so in the case of *The Old Curiosity Shop*—why and how the monster at the heart of this novel remains so effectively hidden—I turn to what the novel so brazenly puts on display: to the monstrous and curious marriages I describe at the beginning of this section, and to the displays of marriage we get throughout the novel in the shape of the Punch and Judy show and the traveling waxworks. I turn, then, to what the novel so desperately wants to show us and to what Dickens uses to distract us from the failed marriage of Nell's nameless parents, to keep us from attending to its significance—for Nell and for the novel.

Both the rarity, the curiosity, of the happy marriages and the monstrosity of the unhappy ones suggest that marriage is an unnatural state of affairs in *The Old Curiosity Shop*. For instance, the fact that the narrator feels compelled to make it clear that Kit's and Barbara's story does end in matrimony suggests that such a happy ending is not to be counted upon. And while he gives us this news in a series of rhetorical questions—questions that insist the answers go without saying—the answers to these questions suggest they are more grammatical than rhetorical, that there is more than one possible answer: "Did Kit live a single man all his days, or did he marry? Of course he married, and who should be his wife but Barbara?" (671). That Kit might indeed "live a single man all his days" is very much a possibility in this novel so overrun with bachelors. And to the question "who should be his wife but Barbara?" we might answer: "Little Nell, if she hadn't died." This is certainly Barbara's fear. In trying to present their marriage as a foregone conclusion, the narrator both betrays his anxiety about the outcome of their courtship, even as he insists that these sorts of things always work out just as they are supposed to.

The narrator's description of the Garland's cottage suggests that their marriage is, like Kit's and Barbara's, unnaturally serendipitous, that it too represents an almost unbelievable kind of happily-ever-after:

> To be sure, it was a beautiful little cottage, with a thatched roof and little spires at the gable ends, and pieces of stained glass in some of the windows, almost as large as pocket-books. On one side of the house was a little stable, just the size for the pony, with a little room over it, just the size for Kit. White curtains were fluttering, and birds, in cages that looked as bright as if they were made of gold, were singing at the windows; plants were arranged on either side of the path, and clustered about the door; and the garden was bright with flowers in full bloom, which shed a sweet odour all round, and had a charming and elegant appearance. Everything, within the house and without, seemed to be the perfection of neatness and order. In the garden, there was not a weed to be seen, and to judge from some dapper gardening-tools, a basket, and a pair of gloves which were lying in one of the walks, old Mr Garland had been at work in it that very morning. (232–3)

This is a cottage straight out of Goldilocks and the Three Bears, a cottage where everything is "just the [right] size" and even the mess that Mr Garland has left in the garden is pleasing to the eye. Or perhaps this is more Martha Stewart than Goldilocks; those "dapper gardening tools," the white curtains, and the "pieces of stained glass in some of the windows" suggest the sustained effort that goes into the appearance of easy charm that is her trademark. Like Martha Stewart's creations, too, the Garlands' cottage is unnatural. No weeds, "the perfection of neatness and order"—we disbelieve the picture as too good to be true even as we enjoy it. This is precisely Kit's reaction to the house and to his new life with the Garlands, and it is also our reaction to their cheerful benevolence and their unfailingly cheerful state of mind. So while their marriage (indeed, their life) is undoubtedly happy, it is too much so for us to take seriously. They are Kit's fairy godparents, characters from an entirely different genre, and while we enjoy the charming picture they present, we do not make any connection between it and the other more sordid and realistic plots of *Curiosity Shop*. The Garlands are so picturesque that we immediately discount them, even as we admire them and all that belongs to them.

The fairy-tale continues into the next generation and the happy marriage of the junior Mr and Mrs Garland. When young Abel Garland enters into a business partnership, his parents host a party in celebration of the event, a Cinderella-like affair that sets in motion another fairy-tale story of true love:

> Unto this ball there happened to be invited the most bashful young lady that was ever seen, with whom Mr Abel happened to fall in love. *How* it happened, or how they found it out, or which of them first communicated the discovery to the other, nobody knows. But certain it is that in course of time they were married; and equally certain it is that they were the happiest of the happy; and no less certain it is that they deserved to be so. (666–7)

The proliferation of absolutes in the narrator's depiction of this marriage ("the most bashful young lady that was ever seen"; "the happiest of the happy") not only suggests the state of perfection Abel and his bashful wife share with the senior Garlands, but these descriptions also seem like captions or titles, as if young Mrs Garland were an exhibit in a circus, alongside the fat lady and the world's tallest boy. These are the storybook versions of the freaks Nell meets at the Jolly Sandboys, just as their marriage is the antithesis of that of Daniel and Betsy Quilp. That the young Garlands deserve to be put on display is underscored by the way in which the narrator announces the rather unsurprising fact that they not only marry, but also have children: "And it is pleasant to write down that they reared a family; because any propagation of goodness and benevolence is no small addition to the aristocracy of nature, and no small subject of rejoicing for mankind at large" (667). The raising of a family, while certainly not an unusual occurrence (especially not in Dickens) is here celebrated as "no small subject for rejoicing"; having children is valorized as the "propagation of goodness and benevolence" and a sizeable contribution to "the aristocracy of nature." This is no ordinary marriage, and the Garlands are no mere happy family. They are extolled as public benefactors and national heroes.

After all this hyperbole, the happy ending rewarded to Dick and the Marchioness seems positively down-to-earth:

> Sophronia was ever a most cheerful, affectionate, and provident wife to him; and Dick (excepting for an occasional outbreak with Mr Chuckster, which she had the good sense rather to encourage than oppose) was to her an attached and domesticated husband. And they played many hundred thousand games of cribbage together. And let it be added to Dick's honour, that, though we have called her Sophronia, he called her the Marchioness from first to last. (669)

The parenthetical admission that Dick still swivels on occasion comes as something of a relief, just as the not insignificant detail of their cribbage games suggests a realistic daily-ness about their marriage. And, happily, Dick honors his wife. She is neither the stereotypical angel of his house nor the domineering queen of his castle. Rather, she is the Marchioness of his heart. But even here, the absolutes claim our attention. The Marchioness "was ever a most cheerful, affectionate, and provident wife," while her husband honors her with her royal title "from first to last." What is more, the Swiveller has been "domesticated."

All of these marriages, then, like the happy marriages that mark the end of *Nickleby*, are brought out for display, put on parade, marveled over and remarked upon as if they were each as miraculous and unusual a state of affairs as you could ever hope to come across. They are like *tchotchkes* in a curio cabinet, almost unbelievably adorable matched pairs of knick-knacks. They are little, they make you smile, and they are not meant to be taken seriously. It is, in fact, no accident that all of these couples are small in stature.[5] It is also important to recognize that they are not dwarves, like Quilp, but miniatures or midgets. As Susan Stewart makes clear in *On Longing*, "the contrast between dwarf and midget, between the grotesque and the model" is crucial. "The dwarf," she reminds us, in a passage that seems to be written explicitly about *The Old Curiosity Shop*, "is assigned to the domain of the grotesque and the underworld, the midget to the world of the fairy— a world of the natural, not in nature's gigantic aspects, but in its attention to the perfection of detail" (111).[6] Stewart's concept of the "miniature" is an especially accurate term for the world that contains the baby cottage of the Garlands, with its kitchen that looks like it belongs in a toy-shop, the diminutive Marchioness, and coy little Barbara. It is a realm Stewart associates with the model, a connection Dickens also makes when he displays these happy little marriages as curios or rarities. According to Stewart, "the miniature always tends toward tableau rather than towards narrative, towards silence and spatial boundaries" (66). By virtue of its size, the miniature is something on display, something that fascinates us and holds our gaze. We are transfixed by the tiny picture of perfection we see in the Garlands' cottage and by Barbara's demure prettiness, ensconced as it is in the dollhouse kitchen, just as we are charmed by the Marchioness's small form and by the curiously appealing picture she makes when Dick first sees her—"Dick leant over the table and descried a small slipshod girl in a dirty coarse apron and bib, which left nothing visible of her but her face and feet. She might as well have been dressed in a violin-case" (332). But because we look upon these characters as objects on display rather than as characters that participate in and propel the plot, as "tableau" instead of "narrative," we unconsciously distance ourselves from them and refuse them the kind of status we grant other fictional characters. Because they are so small, they afford us what Stewart calls "a transcendent and simultaneous view," yet it is this bird's-eye view that "traps [us] outside the possibility of a lived reality of the miniature" (66). Unlike those plots we find "absorbing," those novels that, to borrow Richard Brodhead's intuitively accurate terms, we "get into," that "open up a world-within-a-world with the power to enclose the reader within [their] projected horizons," unlike the kind of reading that is a "going-out of oneself into intersubjective space," our response to these characters would be more accurately described as looking or viewing (46).

Our reading of the miniature is not participatory but detached; we do not enter into it as we do when we "read for the plot," as Peter Brooks would put it. We are more like shoppers or tourists than Brooks's plot-obsessed novel readers. That kind of engaged reading is highly participatory; Brooks describes it as "a form of desire that carries us forward, onward, through the text." The miniature does not "arouse and make use of [the reader's] desire" (*Reading for the Plot* 37), but rather presents us with what Susan Stewart calls "a world of arrested time" (67). Stewart associates this "stillness" with the structure of fantasy, and the precise nature of that fantasy is, like those pictures of marital bliss I have collected from *Curiosity Shop*, one of domestic tranquility. Similarly, Andrew Miller argues that "the representation of the miniature … creates an imaginary space away from fragmenting urban environments in which one feels 'more at home'" (138). Like the little fortified Walworth of *Great Expectations*, where Wemmick feels most at home, the "miniature world [tends] to present domesticated space as a model of order, proportion, and balance … a diminutive and thereby manipulable, version of experience, a version which is domesticated and protected from contamination" (Stewart 68–9).

We have only to think about the other version of smallness—the dwarf, the grotesque—to understand the importance of the protection afforded by the tableau and to be reminded of precisely what threatens to contaminate the happy domesticity of these little couples. For while they are all, ultimately, protected and even somewhat removed from the novel's other, more immediate and "absorbing" plots, that is not to say that these pictures of marital bliss are not threatened or that the world of the novel does not, from time to time, penetrate the boundaries of their picturesque existence. Daniel Quilp represents, both literally and figuratively, the dangers that threaten the peace of the Garlands, the Nubbles, and the Swivellers. Literally, Quilp imprisons Kit and tries to use Dick to entrap Nell. Figuratively, the monstrosity of his marriage contaminates the portrayal of the other, determinedly happy marriages the novel depicts, creating a tension, which the novel never resolves in anything but a provisional fashion, between the fictitiousness of happy marriage and the grotesquerie of marital failure. The one can be seen to drive the other almost completely out of sight. Thus we find it hard to consider the marriage of the miniatures alongside that of the dwarf. We find it almost unfathomable that the relationship between Betsy and Daniel Quilp belongs in the same category as that of Kit and Barbara. Yet thinking about them together enables us to see that marriage in *Curiosity Shop*—whether happy or unhappy, a pretty little picture or an appalling sight—is not only an unnatural state of affairs, but also one that the novel is invested in displaying to its readers in all its different forms.

A sinister version of Beauty and the Beast, the Quilps' marriage is both a fairy-tale gone wrong and a rather literal monstrosity, composed as it is of a couple ill-matched both in temperament and appearance. This monstrosity functions as a warning or a demonstration not only because Quilp is so cruel to his wife that her mother and all her friends encourage her to rebel, but also because the narrator encourages us to believe that Mrs Quilp "performed a sound practical penance for her folly [in marrying the dwarf] every day of her life" (73). This action brings to mind the ritual lamentations of *David Copperfield*'s Mrs Micawber, another wife who meditates on her marriage on a daily basis. But whereas Mrs Micawber revisits her marriage vows and comes to the conclusion that she cannot leave her husband, turning that realization into a *faux* pledge of allegiance to her husband ("I will not desert Mr Micawber!"), Mrs Quilp actually does the opposite. That is, while Emma Micawber wants to leave her husband and only insists that she will not because she cannot, Betsy Quilp does not want to leave her husband and is continually threatened by women who insist that she must.

She thus has more in common with another Betsy, also in *Copperfield:* David's great-aunt Betsey Trotwood, a woman who leaves her husband because of his cruelty but never stops loving him, who is by his side at his deathbed, and who remains a faithful, generous, loving (ex)wife throughout the novel.[7] Like Betsey Trotwood, Betsy Quilp inexplicably loves her abusive husband. When we first meet Mr Quilp, he tells us that this is the case: "obedient, timid, loving Mrs Quilp ... will be anxious and know not a moment's peace till I return. I know she's always in that condition when I'm away" (68–9). Of course, we do not believe him. But in this case we are wrong to mistrust the dwarf, for when he returns to her after he has been presumed dead, she is, much to our surprise, genuinely relieved to see him, though the narrator still has difficulty accepting her devotion: "In truth Mrs Quilp did seem a great deal more glad to behold her lord than might have been suspected, and did evince a degree of interest in his safety which, all things considered, was rather unaccountable" (463). The narrator has not considered exactly everything, though, nor is Mrs Quilp's attachment to her husband really "unaccountable." She accounts for it herself the very first time we meet her. In that first scene, when her mother and all her friends are encouraging her to stand up to Quilp, to resist his control, and as they pity her for being married to such a tyrant, she sets them all straight:

"It's all very fine to talk," said Mrs Quilp with much simplicity, "but I know that if I was to die to-morrow, Quilp could marry anybody he pleased—now that he could, I know! … Quilp has such a way with him when he likes, that the best-looking woman here couldn't refuse him if I was dead, and she was free, and he chose to make love to her. Come!" (75–6)

This declaration surely points to the most perverse way in which the Quilps' marriage is unnatural and unusual, to the clearly sexual nature of their relationship and to Quilp's "unaccountable" but irresistible ("the best-looking woman here couldn't refuse him") sex appeal. Again, the Betsys have this in common, for as Betsey Trotwood admits to David, her attraction to her husband was largely sexual, and it is an attraction she still feels: "'he was a fine-looking man when I married him,' said my aunt, with an echo of her old pride and admiration in her tone" (562).

At this point it sounds very much like I am arguing that a marriage based on sexual attraction is unnatural and unusual, and while it is tempting to argue that in Dickens those who marry for sex are always suspect (think of the Mantalinis, of David's unmistakable but disastrous sexual attraction to Dora, or of Pet Meagles and Henry Gowan in *Little Dorrit*), my point here is both more complex and perhaps more perverse. All of Betsy Quilp's friends "bridle up" when she insists on their susceptibility to Quilp's attractions (76). They immediately spring to the defensive, "as much as to say, 'I know you mean me. Let him try—that's all'" (76). But they also become strangely jealous. When a widow insists that she "should stab him if he hinted at it," Mrs Quilp's friends are, oddly enough, more enraged by the widow's threat than they are by Betsy's assertion of Quilp's charms: "for some hidden reason they were all angry with the widow, and each lady whispered in her neighbour's ear that it was very plain the said widow thought herself the person referred to, and what a puss she was!" (76). Three elements of this reaction seem important: first, the fact that the woman resented by all the others is a widow (and thus more available to Quilp than they are); second, that she sets herself above them and insists on a higher—and more violent—degree of resentment; and, third, that the ladies call the widow "a puss" for thinking that Quilp would be any more attracted to her than to the rest of them. When combined with her availability, the fact that she wants to stab Quilp is suggestive. When we go on to consider what it means that the other women call her "a puss," a term that has connotations not only of slyness but also more literally suggests, as the *OED* would have it, "one who scratches like a cat; a spiteful or backbiting woman," then we are left with the overwhelming sense that Mrs Quilp is right and that all these women have already, albeit unconsciously, begun their maneuvers to become the second Mrs Quilp. Finally, and perhaps most relevant here, is the fact that "puss" also has a sexual connotation; it is, as Eric Partridge so delicately puts it in his *Dictionary of Slang and Unconventional English*, slang for "the female pudend" (671). Taken in this register, then, the conversation among the women points unmistakably to the very physical relation they would all like to enjoy with Quilp.[8]

My point is not so much that sex plays an unnaturally important part in the Quilps' marriage, but rather that Dickens has created a figure who is unnaturally sexual. Quilp is both an unlikely sex object because he is so physically repulsive (Paul Schlicke calls him a "freak-show creature let loose"), and he is overly (and overtly) sexed in that every woman in this scene (and every woman in the world, according to his besotted Betsy) finds him attractive (101). I hope I am not being normative when I say that this is monstrous. The *OED* defines a freak of nature as "an abnormally developed individual of any species," and this scene suggests that it is not only Quilp's head that is oversized. Indeed, when we first see Quilp, the narrator takes pains to inform us that while he is "so low in stature as to be quite a dwarf," "his head and face were large enough for the body of a giant" (65). Again, we see the proliferation of absolutes that characterizes the miniatures and that suggests that these characters and their marriages are on display; here, Quilp is presented as both the world's sexiest man and, given that he is "quite a dwarf," the world's smallest dwarf. Further, his head is not just big, but gigantic. And while I am not aware of any theories as to the sexual significance of a big head, I am reminded of the connotations of a big nose. Quilp insists that his nose is "aquiline"; that is, that it is long and bony, a detail Cattermole's illustrations bear out. In fact, it is hooked and long, and it looks a great deal like Punch's nose in terms of both shape and proportion. Punch is also a violent husband—perhaps even the archetype of an abusive husband—and he is also a figure that has everything to do with the monstrosity of marriage and with *Curiosity Shop*'s continuing fascination with putting the institution of marriage on display.[9] We might argue that just as Betsy Quilp responds to her friends' criticism of her marriage by parading her enviable sex life in front of them, just as she displays the intimacies of her marriage in a deliberate fashion, and just as the narrator exhibits the charms of the little marriages of the miniature characters in such loving detail, so too does the Punch and Judy show perform a marriage in public and broadcast the private details of the institution for the most public of audiences.

There are many reasons to move from Quilp to a consideration of the Punch and Judy show: to consider the novel in the context of the show, and to consider the puppet show as it appears in the context of the novel. Paul Schlicke reminds us that both Quilp and Punch are comic characters most interested in satisfying their own appetites, that both are "little, ugly, violent and frenetically mirthful," and that Quilp, like Punch, "delights in surprises, pops up unexpectedly, feigns death, torments his wife, fights with a dog, and hurls verbal and physical abuse at everyone in sight" (125). Sue Zemka reads the novel as a sentimental, middle-class version of the puppet show's spectacular, carnivalesque lowbrow appeal, while Rachel Bennett argues that the novel is divided between the two opposing motifs of *The Pilgrim's Progress*, which she links to the novel's "lament for the inevitability of death," and Punch, which she associates with the novel's "celebration of life" (423). But the parallels between the novel and the puppet show do not end there. I want to elaborate on these comparisons, to consider Quilp and Punch as abusive, yet sexually attractive, husbands, and to explore the ramifications of the Punch and Judy show for the novel's pervasive concern with the unnatural institution of marriage. Punch and Judy are, indeed, of the greatest significance to *Curiosity Shop* because they shed a bright light on its obsessions, on the things with which it is perversely concerned but which it cannot announce as matters of primary importance in terms of plot and theme. Like Jasper Packlemerton, the novel's emblematic monster, the Punch and Judy show provides us with a metaphor for interrogating the novel and for uncovering its deepest anxieties.

There are many variations of the Punch and Judy show, but the version Dickens's audience would have known best begins with Punch singing, appealing to the audience with his wit and charm. He then calls to Judy, pats her affectionately (to which she responds with a slap), and they kiss. Judy brings out their baby, who cries, so Punch throws it out the window. This leads to a rough-and-tumble fight between Punch and Judy that culminates when Judy leaves the stage to fetch the beadle. At this point, a succession of characters (the beadle, the clown, a Jim Crow character or a foreign gentleman) come on stage, and Punch fights with them all— fights that are a combination of verbal raillery, slapstick, feints and dodges, and some violent punching and kicking. Then Judy's ghost appears behind Punch (we are led to believe that while Punch gave her a fatal wound, she lived long enough to go for the beadle), which causes him to tremble and quake, and finally to fall down in a fit, calling for the doctor. The doctor arrives, which leads to more verbal and physical antics, culminating in the entrance of several other characters we have seen before (the beadle and usually the Jim Crow character) who drag Punch off to jail. In jail, we have the famous scene between Punch and the hangman, where Punch manages to convince the hangman to hang himself by imploring him to demonstrate the workings of his noose. The clown comes back, and he and Punch perform the usual hi-jinks, culminating in a scene rich in slapstick and hide-and-seek that ends with Punch's routing of the clown. Left alone on stage, Punch begins to sing before the devil appears for one last fight—one that Punch wins in most versions. But in every version, Punch murders his wife, his baby, and the hangman.

This, then, is the show that runs throughout the novel, both literally and figuratively. Literally, the puppet show is continually playing in the background. We see a show soon after Nell and her grandfather meet the Punchmen, Codlin and Short, and we learn that on the road to the races Codlin and Short stop and put on a show whenever they come to a little town or even to "a detached house of good appearance" (191). "Sometimes they played out the toll across a bridge or ferry, and once exhibited by particular desire at a turnpike," practices which make it seem as if the puppet show is an ongoing performance, a sideshow endlessly enacted in the margins of the novel as we watch Nell try to beg for money at the races or keep watch over her grandfather. After Nell and her grandfather escape from Codlin and Short, we (and they) are always looking over our shoulders for the Punchmen, always listening nervously for the sound of the trumpet that advertises their show. In this sense, Nell is hunted and haunted by the monstrosity of marriage. She is continually pursued by Quilp and by Punch, by men who routinely beat their wives as a form of entertainment, just as she is in the midst of a nightmare journey because of her father's abuse of her mother.

The novel's obsession with the puppets continues in London with the single gentleman's "most extraordinary and remarkable interest in the exhibition of Punch" (353). The single gentleman has discovered that Nell and her grandfather have been seen in the company of a Punch and Judy show, and so "if the sound of a Punch's voice, at ever so remote a distance, reached Bevis Marks, the single gentleman, though in bed and asleep, would start up, and hurrying on his clothes, make for the spot with all speed" (353). Because the single gentleman brings all the Punch and Judy shows he finds back to Bevis Marks, the show is as much a presence in Dick Swiveller's and Sampson's and Sally Brass's daily existence as it is in Nell's. Just as we are aware of the puppets in the background as we watch Nell and her grandfather, we are made mindful of Punch and Judy as an accompaniment to the routines of Bevis Marks: to the quarrels of Sampson and Sally, the verbal raillery between Quilp and Sally, and the mutual rescue-cum-courtship of Dick and the Marchioness. And just as it seems as if Nell is forced to watch an endless Punch show on her travels with Codlin and Short, it is amazing to see how many Punchmen the single gentleman unearths. In a passage from the manuscript of the novel, the narrator ponders this incredible proliferation of Punches:

> what an enormous family of Punches there must be in the land, since no Punch appeared twice—or if he did, was never encouraged by the single gentleman— and yet these performances were constantly taking place by special desire and gave no signs of exhaustion. It must be left to political economists to deduce a new theory of supply and demand from these facts, or to cite them in support of an old one; but certain it is that as every day the single gentleman was ready for a new Punch, so a new Punch was every day ready for the single gentleman. (701, n.2)

The concept of a Punch and Judy show every day is, as Dick might say, "a wunner," and as such deserves to be examined at length and in context, for, as the narrator hints, it is crucial to the sexual, marital, and visual economies of the novel.

The daily Punch and Judy show at Bevis Marks mirrors the Punch and Judy shows going on inside the office between Sampson and Sally Brass and between Sally and Quilp, while it provides a counterpoint to Dick's curious courtship of the Marchioness. These stories of monstrous marriages and curious courtships alternate with each other; they come forward and recede almost at the same time. This doubling and reversal makes Punch and Judy serve as figures for the novel's implicit, covert, almost furtive interest in the monstrosity and curiosity of marriage. On the one hand, the quarrelsome relationship between Sampson and Sally Brass is an intriguing variation of Punch and Judy in that it reverses their gender roles. In this version, it is Sally who plays Punch and "delight[s] in nothing so much as irritating her brother," while Sampson is the Judy in that he "was at heart in great fear of his sister" (322, 323). The daily puppet show thus mocks Sampson's fear of a female, while it apes the aggression they exhibit towards each other. We can thus understand Sampson's irritation with the show ("nobody was rendered more indignant by these proceedings than Mr Sampson Brass," the narrator tells us), even as we recognize that his anger causes him to behave even more like the frenzied and violent puppets (354). Because he does not dare to offend his paying lodger, he resorts "to annoy[ing] the audiences who clustered round his door by such imperfect means of retaliation as ... trickling down foul water on their heads from unseen watering-pots, pelting them with fragments of tile and mortar from the roof of the house, and bribing the drivers of hackney cabriolets to come suddenly round the corner and dash in among them precipitately"—pranks which have much in common with the way in which Punch baits the doctor, plays hide-and-seek with the landlord, and throws his baby out the window (354). In this respect, Sampson looks more like Punch than Judy, and perhaps even more like Quilp, for here he resorts to what become routine acts of violence and trickery upon everyone in his vicinity.

While Sally behaves more like Punch with respect to her brother, she is a Judy when it comes to Quilp. Quilp's and Sally's constant sparrings are, in fact, notably accurate versions of Punch and Judy. The first scene we see between them consists of Quilp "ogling the fair Miss Brass" and exclaiming "There she is, there is the woman I ought to have married—there is the beautiful Sarah—there is the female who has all the charms of her sex and none of their weaknesses." Sally offers him a "grim smile" and a "hold your nonsense" in response (325). This scene repeats almost exactly the first scene between Punch and Judy as Mayhew records it. In Mayhew's version, Punch calls to his wife "Judy, Judy! my pratty creetur! come up stairs, my darling! I want to speak to you ... Here she comes, bless her little heart!" And Judy responds with a slap and a "Keep quiet, do!" (55) The accuracy of the parallel between Quilp and Sally and Punch and Judy not only suggests the very conscious way in which Dickens is using the puppet show as a counterpoint to the plots it plays alongside, but also makes us wonder where Betsy Quilp fits into the picture. That is, if Sally is such an accurate Judy, then how do we account for Betsy?

In an earlier version of Punch and Judy, Punch has a mistress, Pretty Polly. After throwing his baby out the window and killing Judy, Punch dances with Pretty Polly, kisses her, and holds her in his arms singing "I love you so, I love you so, I never will leave you; no, no, no: If I had all the wives of wise King Sol, I would kill them all for my pretty Poll" (Landes 16).[10] If we try to align *Curiosity Shop* with this version of Punch and Judy, we would no doubt begin by identifying Quilp with Punch, Mrs Quilp with Judy, and Nell with Pretty Polly. This version of Punch and Judy would suggest a jealous Mrs Quilp (not unlikely if we take her attachment to Quilp seriously) and a Nell that satisfies Quilp's fantasies in that she occupies the position of his mistress (again, an irresistible possibility given the similarity between Punch's "pretty Poll" and Quilp's "pretty little Nell"). This version is, in fact, the one Quilp would be most happy with, for it is the dream he masturbates to in Nell's bed come true. It is a useful version for my argument, too, for it emphasizes Quilp's sexual attractiveness, and it suggests both how cruel he can be to his wife and how dangerous he is to Nell and all the other little people in the novel. It suggests the threat he poses to the model behavior of the happy miniatures and diminutive figures of benevolence. But we could just as easily assign Sally Brass the role of Judy and make Betsy the pretty mistress, for if we take seriously the novel's implication that Quilp and Sally are the Marchioness's parents, then Betsy is, like Pretty Polly, a kind of replacement wife.

The similarities between Punch and Quilp in both versions are overwhelming and overwhelmingly suggestive. The one notable difference between Punch and Quilp is that Quilp does not murder his wife. While it is true that Dickens originally had him consider murdering Betsy, this is both a passage that does not find its way into the novel and a murder that is, even in manuscript form, only a fantasy.[11] The only husband who literally murders his wife (Nell's father, of course, could be said to have figuratively murdered Nell's mother) is the waxwork Jasper Packlemerton, who murders all fourteen of his wives by tickling them to death. But the way in which Packlemerton kills his wives suggests that he and Quilp do, in fact, have much in common. Jasper Packlemerton serves to illustrate the perversity of marriage in a way that illuminates, even as it violently exaggerates, the marriage of Betsy and her dwarf. For tickling is, as Adam Phillips has brilliantly pointed out, always erotic and potentially humiliating. Like Betsy's desire for Quilp, it is sexually exciting and potentially degrading. In his essay "On Tickling," Phillips reminds us that "the tickling narrative, unlike the sexual narrative, has no climax. It has to stop, or the real humiliation begins" (10). But tickling is like sex, Phillips makes clear, in that it is a "form of sensuous excitement," and it is better when someone else does it to you. Being tickled, Phillips explains, is a way of being "initiated in a distinctive way into the helplessness and disarray of a certain primitive kind of pleasure." Referring to the *OED*, Phillips reminds us that "the word speaks of the precarious, and so of the erotic. To tickle is, above all, to seduce" (10). As its potentially humiliating nature, the fact that it makes you helpless, and its association with the "precarious" all suggest, tickling renders the tickled powerless.

Dickens exaggerates, then, the powerlessness of the tickled in his creation of Jasper Packlemerton. Packlemerton is a tickler who does not stop before "the real humiliation begins," but rather goes on to exploit his power to its extreme. We would think that this extreme would be incontinence or perhaps, as Phillips suggests, hysteria. But it is in fact death. This is no figure of speech, as in "you scared me to death" or "I died laughing." Nor is it a figure for sexual satisfaction, as in "the little death" that connotes orgasm. This is, as Mrs Jarley makes clear when she tells Packlemerton's story, murder.

The waxwork figure of Packlemerton is, then, both the literalization of these figurative expressions and the embodiment of a figure of speech. Jasper Packlemerton is also a more literal version of a figure commemorated in Madame Tussaud's waxworks. In the category of "Remarkable Characters," Madame Tussaud includes "An old Coquette, who teased her Husband's Life out."[12] The coquette is a strange figure to find in Madame Tussaud's, not only because she is a type, rather than an actual character, but also because, judging from posters for the exhibition in 1812 and 1814, she is placed alongside historical figures, most of whom would be considered heroes of the French Revolution. The company the coquette keeps emphasizes the fact that she is not, like most waxworks figures, the re-creation of an actual person. She is not even given a name, only a descriptive label. She is a generic figure, not an actual one. Thus she is, like Packlemerton, the figure of a figure of speech, the embodiment of a familiar phrase. The similarity between a husband who tickles his wives to death and a wife who teases the life out of her husband is remarkable, but even more striking is the fact that both Tussaud and Dickens have commemorated and embodied these figures of speech for conflict in marriage. These images bring to the fore the violence implicit in these colloquial expressions for relationships between the sexes; in making figures out of figures of speech, Dickens and Tussaud have made the figure of speech literal. Dickens's figure is in fact doubly literal: not only has he turned the figure of speech into a figure, but his created figure is itself one who turns a metaphorical expression into a literal action. By the same token, in placing her coquette among historical figures like Marat, Robespierre and Charlotte Corday, Madame Tussaud suggests that the stereotype of a dominating spouse is to be taken literally. That both Packlemerton and the coquette are waxworks figures underscores this move of literalization and embodiment, for not only do these figures embody the colloquial, but they are also grisly manifestations of proverbial language. Unnaturally realistic figures of wax and grotesque manifestations of proverbial language, they are mimetic as well as linguistic exaggerations. They are also figures in an exhibition.

My point here has to do with both the peculiar properties of waxworks and the nature of an exhibition. On the one hand, I want to survey other instances of waxworks in Dickens, together with theories about their effect on the viewer. On the other hand, I want to gesture towards the way in which the novel itself is a gallery of waxwork figures (just as it is a freak show, a curio cabinet, and a Punch and Judy show). In other words, I want to talk about the nature and effect of waxworks, and then I want to make a larger point about the nature of a display, about what it means to direct an audience's attention towards a collection of objects. This latter point will take us back to my original question, to my concern with what the novel refuses to let us look at, to what it is so invested in hiding, and to what it wants to show us instead: to the marriages the novel so proudly and noisily parades before us and to the way in which that series of collections manages to keep us from seeing that the marriage of Nell's parents should be front and center in any and all of them.

There are scattered references to waxworks throughout Dickens. When Ralph Nickleby introduces Kate to Lord Verisopht, he replies "Well, then my ears did not deceive me, and it's not wa-a-x work," a remark that suggests both how hard he's been staring at her and how paralyzed with fear and shame she is at being put on display by her uncle (306). When Peggotty comes to London, David takes her sightseeing: they visit the Tower of London; they go to the top of

St Paul's; they visit Miss Linwood's Exhibition; and they go to see "some perspiring Wax-work, in Fleet Street," an exhibit the older David cannot help parenthetically disparaging: "melted, I should hope, these twenty years" (388).[13] As this litany of tourist attractions suggests, a trip to the waxworks is a customary part of seeing the sights, something to gaze and gawk at, a curiosity worth a special trip and a prolonged look. These associations come to the fore in a macabre manner in *Great Expectations*. But, in this instance, the allusion is purely figurative. While David and Peggotty go to see an actual waxworks exhibition, and while Lord Verisopht pretends to be surprised that Kate is real and not a model figure, the young Pip's response to Miss Havisham suggests that while he knows full well that she is alive and no effigy, he can only describe the effect her appearance has on him by comparing it to his visit to "some ghastly waxwork at the Fair" (87). While Lord Verisopht's response to Kate is the kind of reaction that Madame Tussaud must have fantasized about, and while David's description is no doubt the kind she most dreaded,[14] it is Pip's that captures most precisely the uncanny nature of a waxwork figure and that helps pinpoint the significance of the waxwork figure Jasper Packlemerton for *The Old Curiosity Shop*.

Here is Pip's response:

> Once, I had been taken to see some ghastly waxwork at the Fair, representing I know not what impossible personage lying in state. Once, I had been taken to one of our old marsh churches to see a skeleton in the ashes of a rich dress, that had been dug out of a vault under the church pavement. Now, waxwork and skeleton seemed to have dark eyes that moved and looked at me. I should have cried out, if I could. (87)

Pip is afraid that he is about to see the dead (or something that never even was alive) come (back) to life. He is afraid, not because Miss Havisham looks dead or artificial, but because, looking as she does, she moves. And she looks at him. What he is experiencing is what Freud would describe, 70 years later, as the uncanny. What he is focusing on is the aspect of waxworks that the art historian David Freedberg in *The Power of Images* identifies as the most important element in their composition and the element that has the most power to unnerve the viewer, regardless of the quality of the figure or the degree to which it achieves a kind of imitation or verisimilitude: the eyes.

Freud defines the uncanny as "that class of the frightening which leads back to what is known of old and long familiar" (220). Naomi Schor describes it as a "shock effect," as "the thrilling terror, the frisson universally produced by" an ultra-realistic figure (134).[15] For Pip, the uncanny effect of Miss Havisham does not have as much to do with her ultra-realism—she is, after all, an actual woman—but rather with her resemblance to a corpse. We might say that she is a kind of waxwork figure in reverse—not an inert artificial figure that looks alive, but a living, organic figure who appears to be artificial or dead. This confusion between what is real and what is not, what is alive and what might come to life, which is at issue for Freud in his investigation of the uncanny, is also what terrifies Nell when she works for Mrs Jarley.[16] Sleeping in the waxworks (a strange thing to do, but something of a *topos* in the annals of wax museums[17]), Nell becomes possessed by the fear that Quilp is lurking among the figures:

> she never retired to this place at night but she tortured herself—she could not help it—with imagining a resemblance, in some one or other of their death-like faces, to the dwarf, and this fancy would sometimes so gain upon her that she would almost believe he had removed the figure and stood within the clothes. (288–9)

That Nell cannot help entertaining this "fancy" is perverse enough, and the fact that she thinks the eerie effigies look like Quilp suggests yet another way in which the novel continually obtrudes him before our eyes and yet another collection of curiosities to which he might be said to belong. But most interesting here is the contagious effect of Nell's disturbed "fancy," her nightmare imaginings of Quilp in the clothes of a waxwork which give rise to a more pervasive fear of the figures themselves:

> Then there were so many of them with their great glassy eyes—and, as they stood one behind the other all about her bed, they looked so like living creatures, and yet so unlike in their grim stillness and silence, that she had a kind of terror of them for their own sakes. (289)

The eyes of the waxworks are again implicated, as is the indeterminate nature of the figures ("so like living creatures, and yet so unlike"), but what is most important to explore here is the fact that Nell's fear of Quilp—the defining and overpowering fear that shadows her throughout the novel, spurring her on the journey that leads to her death—here gives way to another kind of fear, to a "terror of them for their own sakes."

At this point I want to explain why, following David Freedberg, I have been focusing on the eyes of the waxworks (or, perhaps more accurately, why Pip and Nell have been drawn to these figures' eyes) and why it is the eyes that suggest, more than any other element in their make-up, that the waxworks occupy a sort of liminal state between the living and the dead, and thus have the power to terrify viewers who know full well that these are only objects put on display for their enjoyment.[18] Freedberg reasons that "we suspect the inertia of the material of which the image is made, but we cannot discard the impression of liveliness that it makes," a liveliness, he argues, that has much to do with the ways in which the eyes are represented in a statue—whether they are painted or represented by metal or crystal, or even left as blanks or holes. There is something about "the tension implicit" in our perception of the eyes in the context of the artificial that "may, at the very least, cause anxiety; at the most it may cause a terror that is not assuaged by the consciousness of the manmade status of the image or object ... fear of the lifelike haunts the warring perceptions of the image as reflection and the image as reality" (220–21). In other words, the eyes make the image hover uncannily between "reflection" and "reality," just as the contrast between the materials that make up the statue and the materials that represent the eyes makes the eyes the particular site of fear, creating what Freedberg so accurately terms the "fear of the lifelike." While we know that the figure is made of inorganic material, that it is constructed—made not begotten, we might say—the eyes create a sense of doubt in our minds because they look back at us. They reflect our vision and so suggest that they, too, can see. This suspicion leads to our strongest fear, which is that these images "might just come alive, just open their mouths, just begin to move. We fear the lifelike because the dead substance of which the object is made may yet come alive" (231). This is precisely Nell's fear and precisely why she is afraid of them "for their own sakes."

It is also important to remember that this is Nell's night-time fantasy, that it is "their dusky figures" that arouses this fear (and that Pip first sees Miss Havisham in a room dimly lit with candles). The passage from the German psychologist Ernst Jentsch's 1906 essay on the uncanny that Freud alludes to also focuses on the effect of lighting on our perception of waxworks figures:

> The disagreeable impression easily aroused in many people upon visiting wax-museums, wax-works, and panoramas is well-known. It is often difficult, especially in the half-darkness, to distinguish a life-size wax figure or similar figure from a person. (Naomi Schor 138)[19]

The emphasis on dusk and half-darkness not only helps explain the preponderance of nightmares about sleeping among the waxworks and accounts for Madame Tussaud's preoccupation with the lighting in her exhibition rooms (wax museums were illuminated by gas or candlelight well into the nineteenth century), but also helps us understand another way in which waxworks occupy a liminal status. Just as they are both lifelike and not alive (what Marie-Hélène Huet calls "not life itself, but a lifelikeness"), and just as it is hard to determine in the dusk or the half-darkness of candlelight whether they are actual figures or figures of wax, the arrangement of most wax museums (like the placement of Duane Hanson figures in art museums) is designed to confuse us (Huet 128).[20] Madame Tussaud herself was an especially confusing figure during her lifetime: visitors to her Baker Street museum would pay the actual Madame Tussaud at the entrance, only to be confronted by her wax image further down the hall; similarly, the carefully positioned figure of a bobby or a guard made of wax is a staple in such museums. Because, as Freedberg reminds us, the wax figure is designed to "arouse [our] wonder at the skill of the artist in approximating life so closely," the wax museum needs to be designed to exploit that wonder. Therefore, although we always know we are in a wax museum, we sometimes do not (immediately) know which figures are wax and which are real.

Mrs Jarley exploits this confusion when she sends Nell out to advertise her show. As a part of what the narrator approvingly calls her "inventive genius," she arranges for Nell and a waxwork figure to be driven throughout the town in a little cart "gaily dressed with flags and streamers" advertising the show (286). Much of this tactic's success arises from the fact that Nell becomes even more of an object of curiosity and delight than the wax figure she sits beside. This is, of course, a technique we see throughout *Curiosity Shop* and one that Dickens consciously set out to emphasize and exploit: "I had it always in my fancy to surround the lonely figure of the child with grotesque and wild, but not impossible companions, and to gather about her innocent face and pure intentions, associates as strange and uncongenial as the grim objects that are about her bed when her history is first foreshadowed," he tells his readers in his preface to the 1848 edition of the novel (42). The technique of arrangement by contrast also provides us with a way of better understanding the figure of Jasper Packlemerton, both as a figure of wax and as a figure for the monstrosity of marriage.

Jasper is, like those dusky figures that frighten Nell, a figure of some indeterminacy. It is hard to know what to make of him, both because he is the only figure Mrs Jarley describes in detail and because he is taken up at length, only to be absolutely forgotten—by Mrs Jarley, by Nell, by the narrator, and by the novel. Most readers forget him, too, reading right over his story's emblematic significance just as they fail to respond to the story of Nell's parents' marriage. Jasper Packlemerton occupies a very small moment in the novel (one paragraph in a novel of 73 chapters), but that moment is wholly characteristic of *Curiosity Shop* in its uncanniness. The way in which readers tend to read right over his story is an instance of the uncanny because the keynote figure is fully glimpsed and immediately forgotten. That is, just as Freud defines the uncanny as "that class of the frightening which leads back to what is known of old and long familiar," in attending to Jasper Packlemerton we are returning to a moment in the novel the significance of which we initially ignored, or perhaps even repressed. In honing in on the waxwork figure of Jasper Packlemerton, I mean to make explicit the link between the way in which he—or any other waxwork figure or uncanny object—is seen and the way in which we read his story, a story that is tucked into the plot much like a waxwork guard is tucked into a corner of Madame Tussaud's. In a more general sense, I am connecting a way of seeing to a way of reading as I look at the way in which these various displays of marriage structure our readerly attention. Specifically, I mean to suggest that the kind of response a visitor to Mrs Jarley's exhibition would have to the waxwork Packlemerton has much in common with the kind of response a reader of *Curiosity Shop* would have to his placement in the text. In both cases, Packlemerton is an uncanny figure.

The secret of Nell's parents' failed marriage is also tucked into the plot; as I argued at the outset of this chapter, like the failed marriages that generate the plots of *Twist* and *Nickleby*, it is buried so deeply and revealed so circumspectly that it barely causes a ripple on the surface of the novel's plot, though it has everything to do with the shape and the nature of that plot. I suggested that in taking a closer look at what the novel encourages us to consider in lieu of this marriage we might come to understand how the novel manages to keep its secret so well. One way in which the novel keeps its secret has simply to do with the understated fashion in which it is revealed and the fact that it is presented to the reader as an old, old story: one "known of old and long familiar" to the single gentleman, and one that is of interest only to him. That is, while we are given the details of Nell's mother's marriage and thus provided with the context we need for understanding the novel's plot and thematic concerns, this story is not presented to us as important information, but rather as something very familiar, something we have always known and thus paid little heed to.

This is uncanny in the way that the very familiar is at the root of that phenomenon. In this sense, it has much in common with the other marriages in *Curiosity Shop* we are encouraged to gaze upon, marvel at, and take a lesson from. That is, one reason we are so fascinated with these marriages is that they follow the contours of old, familiar stories. Implicit in the narrator's comparison of the young Garlands to Cinderella and her Prince and in my comparison of Kit and the elder Garlands to Goldilocks and the Three Bears and of the Quilps to Beauty and the Beast is the fact that they are all fictions come to life, fairy-tales come true. When, in a long, complex novel with some claims to realism, events start to accord quite markedly with the dictates of the fairy-tale, we have a textbook example of the Freudian uncanny. Freud holds that "an uncanny effect is often and easily produced when the distinction between imagination and reality is effaced, as when something that we have hitherto regarded as imaginary appears before us in reality" and precisely this effect is produced when a plot from the realm of the imagination, from the world of fairy-tale, appears before us in a realistic novel (244). Because these miniature marriages are uncanny, because they are figures of fiction come to life, marital bliss comes to seem like a familiar story that is very much a story—a fairy-tale that is not quite true.

These marriages, like the Punch and Judy show that runs throughout the novel and Mrs Jarley's waxworks exhibition, function as the novel's cultural unconscious. That undercurrent of deep skepticism over the institution of marriage is manifested in the embodied colloquialisms of the waxworks, the proliferation of bachelors, and the depiction of husbands that are either perfect or perfectly cruel. These elements are what Fredric Jameson would call the novel's "indispensable preconditions" (17). The reiteration of these very familiar images clues us in to the novel's ideological position vis-à-vis marriage, even as it presents them as context rather than as event. Thus these old familiar plots are displayed for the reader even as they are made so familiar and so frequent as to be of little moment. Because they are put on display, we are supposed to look at them. But because they are so prominently displayed we also do not bother to take a closer look, to analyze them. We think we know what we are seeing because these are plots we immediately recognize. Because these stories are literally uncanny, then, we fail to grasp their import or the import of the story they screen even as they anticipate and repeat its plot and its characters. Similarly, the etiology of the novel's plot is hidden from us even as it is reproduced all around us in a multiplication of uncanny images that suggest that marriage is either fictitious or monstrous, that it is either a story we do not quite believe in or a relationship of such exaggerated cruelty we cannot take it literally. Marriage in *The Old Curiosity Shop* is, then, an old, familiar story, and thus one to which we assign little significance. Were we to give it heed, to take that second look, we would find it frighteningly uncanny—even monstrous—or simply unbelievable.

It is not, in fact, until the middle of the century and in the midst of his career that Dickens will present the failure of marriage explicitly and overtly, not as a secret, but as a sensation. Accordingly, when Dickens does put the failure of marriage in the limelight, he presents us with such an exaggerated and overblown picture of marital failure that we tend to dismiss it as melodramatic and pre-plotted. I am referring of course to *Dombey and Son*, the novel in which Dickens dissects the failure of the mercenary marriage of Edith Dombey and sheds a glaring light on the institution to which Edith sacrifices herself, her self-respect, and, ultimately, her reputation. That marriage and the melodramatic mode in which Dickens plots its downfall will be the subject of Chapter 3.

Notes

1   I am referring, of course, to the time Dickens spent working at Warren's Blacking Warehouse and to the shame he felt at being reduced to a "poor little drudge" (Forster 1:25). This episode and its attendant shame stayed with Dickens and is not only a critical aspect of his biography, but also something of a *topos* in his fiction. Two of the most perceptive accounts of Warren's and its aftermath are Robert Newsom's essay, "The Hero's Shame," and Alexander Welsh's, *From Copyright to Copperfield: The Identity of Dickens*.

2   Yeazell makes this point in the context of Rousseau's *Emile* (1762). The quotation is from Sophie's father, as he explains to her why she should choose her own husband.

3   Critics have not entirely overlooked Nell's mother's marriage. In *Dear Reader*, Garrett Stewart points to the importance of this marriage for the novel's plot, though his larger argument has to do with the novel as elegy for Mary Hogarth. Accordingly, he is more interested in the single gentleman's renunciation of Nell's grandmother, which he compares to Dickens's renunciation of his own sister-in-law, than in the failed marriage of Nell's mother. But in making this comparison, Stewart does implicitly point to the importance of the failed marriage in making sense of the novel's plot. As he puts it, "the long-withheld (and autobiographically occulted) family structure behind the story—providing its very mainspring both as quest (via the single gentleman's searches) and as postmortem evocation (via Dickens' elegiac motives)—has in fact been thrown into unique relief by our longtime (though unacknowledged) narrator's one explicit 'narrative'" (194). Dianne Sadoff also acknowledges the importance of the single gentleman's story in *Monsters of Affection*, though she is interested in this story because of the way in which it simultaneously "discloses and disguises the facts

of genealogy" (20). She does mention that Nell's mother "married unwisely" and that her husband "beggared both herself and her father," but her emphasis is on this story as the tale of Nell's origins (20).

4   We learn of Oliver's father's failed marriage to Monks's mother in Chapter 49, and we hear the story of Oliver's mother in Chapter 51 of *Oliver Twist*, two chapters from the end. We learn of Ralph Nickleby's brief and unhappy marriage in Chapter 60 of *Nickleby*, five chapters from the end. And we learn about Nell's mother's miserable marriage in Chapter 69 of *The Old Curiosity Shop*, a novel that ends with Chapter 73.

5   The senior Garlands are described as "a little fat placid-faced old gentleman" and "a little old lady, plump and placid like himself," while their son bears a "wonderful resemblance" to his father "in face and figure" (164, 168). Kit thinks of them as "the little old lady, and the little old gentleman, and the little young gentleman" (220). Barbara is first introduced to us as their "little servant-girl," and she lives in a little kitchen that looks like it came out of a "toy-shop window." She has her own "little work-box" and a "little looking-glass" (233, 234). And we imagine that Kit is small, too, given that his "little" room over the stable is "just [his] size." Finally, the Marchioness, routinely described as "the small servant," is so small that Quilp, a dwarf, has to look down ("it was something quite new to him") in order to see her (473).

6   For another approach, see the compelling reading Hilary Schor develops of *The Old Curiosity Shop* by means of Stewart's notion of the souvenir in her *Dickens and the Daughter of the House*.

7   For a more detailed analysis of these wives and the implications of their failed marriages, see Chapter 4.

8   For a different reading of this scene, one that emphasizes the monstrous nature of "female combativeness" and contrasts it to Nell's more admirable feminine passivity, see Lisa Surridge's chapter "Private Violence in the Public Eye" in *Bleak Houses*, especially 29–30.

9   Punch and Judy shows pop up all over Dickens, but I am especially mindful of the fact that the puppets are at work demonstrating the routines of marriage when Edith and Dombey return from their wedding: "the carriages arrive at the Bride's residence, and the players on the bells begin to jingle, and the band strikes up, and Mr Punch, that model of connubial bliss, salutes his wife" (526). For a reading of this failed marriage and the spectacular way in which Dickens dissects it, see Chapter 3.

10 It is, of course, highly suggestive that this Punch offers to do exactly what Jasper Packlemerton has done: that is, kill all his wives. The parallels between the characters in the Punch and Judy show and the characters in *Curiosity Shop* thus come to seem, like the proliferation of Punches that so irritates Sampson Brass, infinite and infinitely flexible. The following juxtaposition will do nothing to diminish that impression, but will rather, I hope, serve to underscore the way in which Dickens uses Punch and Judy as figures for the master plot of this novel.

11 The manuscript for Chapter 61 includes this passage:

> "Humph!" said the dwarf, looking round. "Gloomy and dark! If I took it in my head to be a widower, now, I need only invite Mrs Quilp to take tea here one

foggy night—the water's very near the door to be sure. If she took the wrong turning and her foot slipped—Ah!"

He stood musing for a minute or two on the very brink of the wharf, holding the lantern so that its light was reflected downward on the water, and resting one foot upon the great iron ring, sunk into the coping.

"Yes," said Quilp, knocking this ring with his heels, "it's a tempting spot. If anybody I hate had fallen over, and was hanging by one hand to this, and screaming to me while I sat and smoked in Bachelor's Hall there, how very deaf I should be! I should hear the splash that followed though, for all that. Ha, ha, ha! I think I should hear the splash." (713–14, n.4)

That Dickens decides to assign this very death to Quilp instead and a happy remarriage to Betsy (financed by Quilp's ill-gotten gains, no less) is yet another way in which he tries to cover up his interest in the perversity of marriage. By erasing the perversity of the Quilps' marriage and substituting a more seemly version of matrimony at the end of the novel, Dickens warns us away from the monstrosity he has so delighted in depicting, gesturing instead toward the happy couples in the curio cabinet of the *Curiosity Shop*.

12 Posters for Madame Tussaud's 1810 exhibition in Edinburgh, her 1812 show in Hull, and her 1814 visit to Bristol make mention of this figure, listing it in a group that also includes Charlotte Corday, Marat, and the head of Robespierre after he had been guillotined. The coquette is thus associated with the bloody violence of the French Revolution, an association that suggests Tussaud's embodiment of a familiar phrase may be as literal and as chilling a figure as Dickens's Packlemerton. These posters are reproduced in Pauline Chapman, *Madame Tussaud in England* and in Pauline Chapman and Anita Leslie, *Madame Tussaud: Waxworker Extraordinary*.

13 Miss Linwood's exhibition is a gallery of needlework paintings, "one of the standard sights of early nineteenth-century London" according to Richard Altick (400). The waxworks in Fleet Street is probably Mrs Salmon's exhibition, a collection she inherited from her husband and which went through several changes of management after her death; this display enjoyed great popularity from the end of the seventeenth century through the beginning of the nineteenth century. Dickens probably had Mrs Salmon as much as Madame Tussaud in mind when he created Mrs Jarley, not only because we see him gesture towards her show ten years later in *Copperfield*, but also because her exhibit contained a figure much like Packlemerton. Altick cites a visitor to Mrs Salmon's in 1793 who makes special mention of the figure of "Renwick Williams, called the Monster, cutting the Miss Porters" (53). Renwick Williams was a famous eighteenth-century predator who was indicted for attacking a woman in the street. According to the transcript of his trial, he "wilfully, maliciously, and feloniously did tear, spoil, cut, and deface" several layers of Ann Porter's clothes (Hodgson 5). We might call Williams "the cutter," and his crime is like Packlemerton's in that it seems petty, but is (as evidenced by the fact that he cuts through Porter's cloak, her stays, three petticoats, and her shift) rather extreme, not to mention sexual and intrusive. That he is popularly called "the monster," both in the waxworks exhibition and in the transcript of

his trial, suggests not only a linguistic affinity with the husbands of *Curiosity Shop*, but also that he is put on display as a figure of warning.

14 In an 1860 *All the Year Round* piece entitled "Our Eye-Witness in Great Company," Dudley Costello describes Madame Tussaud's as "a large room, handsomely decorated, with the oddest-looking people in the oddest-looking dresses, and in the strangest attitudes, standing round about it" (249). This article disparages Madame Tussaud's for its emphasis on costume, the anachronism of the groupings, and the curious poses of the figures. In this respect it has much in common with the *Household Words* essay Costello wrote about Madame Tussaud's six years earlier, "History in Wax." But whereas in "History in Wax" Costello is more interested in critiquing the style in which the catalogue of Madame Tussaud's is written, in "Our Eye-Witness" he delights in reporting that the figures are all leaning precariously, that the King of Hanover "looks as if he had been drinking," and that the figures who are "supposed to be in motion" look like they are "skating" (251, 252).

15 Schor's subject is the sculpture of Duane Hanson, but I would argue that Hanson is our Madame Tussaud. Constructed out of fiberglass and polyester, dressed realistically and completely, and outfitted with accessories like beer cans, newspapers, grocery carts, and hair curlers, his life-size and highly detailed sculptures look so much like real people that they frequently fool the unsuspecting viewer into thinking that they are alive. The fear that Schor talks about in seeing a Hanson has to do not so much with being afraid that the sculpture will come alive or is watching you, but rather with the shock of realizing that something you thought was alive is not. In either case, the effect of the uncanny has to do with the confusion between the natural and the constructed, with the blurring of the boundary between real and artificial.

16 Freud begins the second section of his essay, where he takes up instances of the uncanny, with this very uncertainty:

> When we proceed to review the things, persons, impressions, events and situations which are able to arouse in us a feeling of the uncanny in a particularly forcible and definite form, the first requirement is obviously to select a suitable example to start on. Jentsch has taken as a very good instance "doubts whether an apparently inanimate being is really alive; or conversely, whether a lifeless object might not be in fact animate"; and he refers in this connection to the impression made by waxwork figures, ingeniously constructed dolls and automata. (226)

17 Nell sleeps with the waxworks "for their better security," but it's harder to understand the other instances of this phenomenon (288). Pauline Chapman notes that when Madame Tussaud's exhibition was being moved from one location to another, a "stupendous task" that took a week, "exhausted workers stretched out to sleep between the sheeted wax figures laid out on the floor awaiting transportation to their palatial new home" (*Madame Tussaud in England* 91). This strange practice is also depicted in Cruikshank's 1847 cartoon, "I dreamt I slept at Madame Tussaud's," which ran in the 1847 *Comic Almanac* and was accompanied by a verse that has much in common with my argument here. It runs in part:

> I dreamt that I slept at Madame Tussaud's
> With cut-throats and Kings side by side;
> And that all the wax figures in those abodes
> At midnight became revivified.
> (Qtd in Chapman, *Madame Tussaud in England* 79)

Finally, and more understandably, Thackeray, in his *Sights of London*, insists that "rather than be left alone in *that* Gallery at night with those statues, I would consent to be locked up with one of the horrid lions in the Zoological Gardens" (qtd in Chapman, *Madame Tussaud in England* 84).

18 That I bring in the idea of pleasure at this point may seem strange, and it is worth thinking about the fact that waxworks are a form of entertainment. That this is a form of entertainment that does not give pleasure is astutely pointed out by Costello when he refers to "the profound and awful misery of the place which provides the Englishman with an entertainment that does not make him happy" ("Our Eye-Witness in Great Company" 250).

19 I am indebted to Schor's chapter both for her translation of this passage from Jentsch and for her recuperation of his essay for a consideration of the uncanny. Freud alludes to this piece, but, as Schor makes clear, he does not play fair with it. He paraphrases it and quotes from it selectively, and he gives his readers neither an accurate nor a comprehensive sense of Jentsch's essay. See the "Freud/Jentsch/Cixous" section of Schor's chapter (134–39).

20 Like the figures of museum guards, bobbies, and Madame Tussaud in the nineteenth century, Duane Hanson's figures are carefully placed and chosen. So the figure of a derelict drug addict will be placed in the stairwell of a museum, while the figure of a woman collecting for a charity will be found in the hallway between galleries. Such figures and their placement are even more disturbing than the deliberately planted displays at Madame Tussaud's, for they make you wonder not only whether or not they are alive, but also how such people got in the museum, thus causing you to feel offended and slightly superior, and then, when you realize you have been fooled, embarrassed and perhaps a little anxious and irritated. In other words, they make the viewer very aware of the prejudices and preconceptions about art, about display, and about class and connoisseurship she brings with her to the museum.

Chapter 3
Making a Spectacle of Yourself, or, Marriage as Melodrama in *Dombey and Son*

This chapter on *Dombey and Son* interrogates the melodramatic way in which Edith Dombey leaves her husband and compares her actions to those of Caroline Norton—a Victorian woman who braved the publicity that surrounded her attempts to leave her husband and redress the wrongs the law allowed him to inflict upon her. Both of these women chose to make the intimate details of their domestic lives a public matter, and in so doing they shed a bright light on the private instantiation of the public institution of marriage.

This chapter, then, is about the failure of marriage as depicted in Victorian novels and enacted in Victorian lives. Consequently, it is about what Elaine Hadley calls "the melodramatic mode"—a technique she reads as both a "reactionary rejoinder to social change" and a "behavioral and expressive model"—and about the way in which Dickens and Caroline Norton deployed that technique (3). Functioning as a script for social protest, the features of melodrama provided Dickens and Norton with a way to demonstrate (and to demonstrate against) the inherent inequity of marriage as it was constructed in the nineteenth century. The goal of this chapter is to show how Dickens uses melodrama to dissect the failure of marriage, and then to explore why the failure of that institution is so often—and so effectively—figured in the mid-nineteenth century as a one-dimensional plot of spectacle and distress. More specifically, this chapter analyzes the similarity between Dickens's deployment of the melodramatic mode on behalf of the rights of a Victorian wife and the way in which Caroline Norton publicized her own failed marriage in order to defend herself against her husband's tyranny and effect reforms in nineteenth-century marriage law. Reading Edith Dombey's spectacular defiance of and flight from her husband as a melodrama makes available a feminist Dickens, or, at the very least, a Dickensian heroine who looks more like a New Woman than an Angel in the House.[1]

As Hadley astutely recognizes, the kind of protest couched in the melodramatic mode is often "a form of resistance especially difficult to see as resistance" because it "looks much like that [position] held by members of the dominant caste" (137, 138). Accordingly, this chapter reads Dickens's apparently conservative domestic plot for what it reveals about Victorian marriage and considers what putting the failure of a marriage in the limelight in this manner says about a culture. By implicating Edith, rather than her husband, in adultery, Dickens paradoxically works within the mainstream cultural climate and thus creates a form of protofeminism that looks a great deal like misogyny. But by reading Edith's actions as melodramatic and thus as highly symbolic and pre-plotted, we can begin to see the extent to which *Dombey* reveals that the guilty party is not Edith in particular. The fault lies not with her, but with the status and situation of a Victorian wife in general. Edith does betray her husband, but a melodramatic reading of this novel helps us see that she is not so much leaving her husband as she is abandoning the institution of marriage. By the same token, Dombey is not the object of the novel's blame or the villain, but rather the representative type of a domineering husband. He is, in accordance with the conventions of melodrama, a stock figure, just as Edith is. They "personify absolutes," to use Hadley's terms, and thus should be read as generic, rather than realistic, characters (3). Similarly, the novel points out the need for reform; it is not a narrative that imagines that reform. Like the stock plot of melodrama, it exposes an evil; it does not suggest a remedy.

Dickens deliberately presents his readers with an oversize picture of a failed marriage in order that we might read it paradigmatically, that we might take the Dombeys' marriage as a model of what's wrong with Victorian marriage. This is precisely how Norton intends her marriage to be read, as well. And the fact that her story is so often told (not only in the newspapers and periodicals of the day, but also in the several novels based on her life) suggests the efficacy of such a strategy. The goal of all these melodramatic stories of failed marriage is to make public the failure of individual marriages in order to illustrate the inherent inequities and cruelties of the institution.

Caroline Norton turned her life into the stuff of fiction, just as she read the versions of her life that other novelists wrote. Not only did she tell a version of her story in her novel *Stuart of Dunleath* (1851), but George Meredith also turned her life into fiction in his novel *Diana of the Crossways*, while Dickens turned Norton's adultery trial into fiction in the form of the breach of promise suit, *Bardell* v. *Pickwick*, portrayed in *The Pickwick Papers*.[2] These stories about Norton, along with the many journalistic accounts of her trials and travails, were circulated so widely and enjoyed such popularity that the figure of Caroline Norton came to seem more like a fictional character than an actual woman. Taking advantage of and further entrenching her status as a character, Norton utilized the features and patterns of melodrama to tell her own story. Specifically, she employed a genre that organizes the world into a reassuringly conventional plot of moral absolutes, yet also exposes the cruelty at the heart of social conventions. The fact that she came to be treated as a character can be read as both cause and effect of her decision to behave in such a scripted and performative manner.

Dickens also can be said to have acted out what he perceived to be his domestic persecution; in forcing his wife to leave him, he behaved in a calculated way and was always aware of his audience's attention. A figure who lived his life according to the dictates of the genre in which he worked, Dickens's life is a reflection on novelistic conventions. As Nina Auerbach puts it, the "self-dramatizing" Dickens "lived a myth that gives shaping energy to [his] fiction" (*Woman and the Demon* 184). This quixotic approach is suggested by the names he gave his children (Henry Fielding, Dora Annie, Edward Bulwer Lytton, Walter Savage Landor), and it is made especially clear in the way he plots the failure of his own marriage. The plot he writes for himself has much in common with—just as it comments upon and complicates—those plots of failed marriage he writes in his novels. A brief summary will suggest just a few of those correspondences. He forces Catherine to leave him so that he can present the failure of his marriage as the story of a wife's desertion. He complains about their incompatibility in terms that bring David Copperfield's dissatisfaction with Dora irresistibly to mind and in metaphors that revisit the monstrous marriages of his early novels. He makes public the failure of his marriage in detailed announcements to his reading public in both *The Times* and *Household Words*. Finally, most of his biographers agree that he wanted out of his marriage more because of his infatuation with the actress Ellen Ternan than because there was anything actually wrong with his marriage.

Dickens met Ellen Ternan when they played opposite each other in, appropriately enough, a melodrama. This melodrama was *The Frozen Deep*, written by Wilkie Collins and first performed in the Dickens's home in 1857—the year divorce was made legal and the year before Dickens turned Catherine out of their house. The coincidence of melodrama and failed marriage in Dickens's own life is suggestive, to say the least, connecting as it does the performative with the private and the exaggerated with the intimate. Given Dickens's own repeated assertions that he found his marital unhappiness impossible to bear after *The Frozen Deep*, we could say that a melodrama finally propelled Dickens to put an end to his marriage, just as that mode enabled him to plot the end of Edith Dombey's marriage 12 years earlier and, in so doing, finally to bring to the forefront the plot that appears so persistently in the margins of his preceding novels.

The Melodramatic Mode

I am certainly not the first to notice the melodramatic gestures and speeches of Edith Dombey. Nor am I the only reader to remark upon the melodrama of her failed-marriage/*faux* adultery plot. But whereas critics tend to remark upon the melodrama of Edith and her plot only to criticize Dickens for overwriting, I want to move beyond that kind of easy sophistication and think more analytically about why Edith is cast as a melodramatic, histrionic heroine and why the breakdown of her marriage to Dombey is plotted in such a predictable and theatrical fashion. I want to take her overacting seriously, to interrogate it rather than simply to dismiss it as an instance of the embarrassing excess to which Dickens's prose is sometimes prone. In order to discover the ramifications of the melodramatic mode in *Dombey*, I want to begin by suggesting that it is not only Edith's strand of the novel's plot that is melodramatic, but that the dutiful daughter plot is also what Peter Brooks describes as "a heightened and hyperbolic drama, making reference to pure and polar concepts of darkness and light" (*The Melodramatic Imagination* xiii). The entire novel is in fact a melodrama; Florence's plot, along with Alice Marwood's, John and Harriet Carker's, and Mrs Skewton's, need to be included in an assessment of the spectacular and one-dimensional plotting of *Dombey and Son*. By exploring the melodramatic aspects of the plot as a whole, I hope to suggest the ways in which the failed-marriage plot belongs, generically and structurally, to the overall novel, and to make clear what we sacrifice when we dismiss the melodrama of Edith and her plot as a stylistic mistake. This chapter, in other words, takes the genre of melodrama seriously; it considers why so much of this novel is enacted in a fever of rolling eyes and inflated rhetoric. It draws attention to the fact that a novel subtitled *Dealings with the Firm of Dombey and Son, Wholesale, Retail and for Exportation* is made up of heaving bosoms and piercing stares.[3]

In the basic plot of a melodrama, according to Brooks,

> a villain, the troubler of innocence, will come to insinuate himself, either under the mask of friendship (or courtship) or simply as an intruder. The intruder may be driven out temporarily, but only to return triumphant. ... The villain's return produces the topos of the interrupted fête, the violated banquet which ... represents the triumph of villainy, the fall, eclipse, and even expulsion of virtue. (29)

This paradigm neatly describes *Dombey and Son*, Chapters 1–47. Carker is the villain who insinuates himself into Dombey's life, first under the mask of professional friendship, then as the artful seducer. Edith drives him out by avoiding Florence and thus ensuring that Dombey will have no further need to reprimand her, via Carker, for her inappropriate behavior. But, of course, he returns triumphant to witness Edith's ultimate humiliation as she refuses to attend the "fête" that Dombey has arranged to celebrate their second anniversary. This "violated banquet" is so disrespected that it is pre-empted; Edith elopes with Carker on her anniversary day rather than participate in the empty celebration. When Dombey discovers her desertion (a desertion that represents not only Carker's temporary victory, but also Edith's "fall" and the apparent "eclipse of [her] virtue"), he responds by striking Florence and banishing her from the house, a particularly wrenching instance of what Brooks calls "the expulsion of virtue." "For the greater part of the play," Brooks continues,

> evil appears to reign triumphant, controlling the structure of events. ... Virtue, expulsed, eclipsed, apparently fallen, cannot effectively articulate the cause of the right. Its tongue is in fact often tied by the structure of familial relationships: virtue cannot call into question the judgments and the actions of a father or an uncle or a guardian, for to do so would be to violate its nature as innocence. ... Virtue fallen and eclipsed will, then, not so much struggle as simply resist. (*The Melodramatic Imagination* 31)

Again, Brooks's template accords with Florence's plot, accurately capturing the way in which Carker's machinations have rendered her powerless and the fact that her status as dutiful daughter renders her passive in the face of her father's extravagant cruelty. The virtuous heroine's supporters in this time of trouble are, according to Brooks, "a handmaiden, a fiancé, a faithful (often comic) peasant"; Florence has Susan Nipper, Walter, and Captain Cuttle (*The Melodramatic Imagination* 33). Order is finally restored in the melodrama's moral universe when virtue triumphs by being recognized as such, when that which has been misrepresented as fallen (Florence denounced by her father and thrown into the street) is reestablished as innocent and virtuous. Thus the extended family celebrated at the end of the novel—Walter and Florence and their two children, with Dombey rehabilitated as the doting grandfather—represents the happy ending of the melodrama that stars Carker as the villain and Florence as the heroine. Enshrined at the end of the novel is a tableau that represents "a reforming of the old society of innocence, which has now driven out the threat to its existence and reaffirmed its values" (Brooks, *The Melodramatic Imagination* 32). That this family is representative of "the old society" is made clear by the fact that the children are again named Florence and Paul. That they represent a reformulation of that society is suggested by their emblematic patronym, Gay.

The relationship between Edith's plot and Florence's, then, not only has to do with the bond between them, but is also a matter of genre. Both Edith and Florence find themselves in the midst of a melodramatic plot, both play the role of innocent heroine—an identification suggested most strongly when Edith's fall leads to Florence's expulsion from her father's house—and both are victimized by Carker who plays the villain to them both, insinuating himself into the most intimate details and controlling much of their day-to-day lives. These similarities are important, for they suggest that it is not only in plotting the failure of marriage that Dickens has recourse to a mode based on the absolutes of good and evil and the exaggeration of hero and villain into stock roles. Once we recognize that the novel as a whole relies on "providential plotting" and "universalizing tendencies," that all its plots depend upon "the anger-filled, inflated, black and white worldview of melodrama," then we can begin to see the way in which the dissection of marriage—like the plots that save Dombey, rehabilitate Alice Marwood, clear John Carker's name, reward his sister Harriet with a happy marriage, spectacularly kill their brother, and enshrine Florence—bespeaks a solid belief in what George Worth calls "a set of firm moral verities" and the conviction that virtue will triumph in the end (Hadley 230, n.3, Eigner, *The Dickens Pantomime* 34, Worth 1). That is, connecting Edith's plot to the rest of the novel enables us to see exactly what we mean when we call a plot melodramatic—that we are not only gesturing towards a genre characterized by "unbridled, if highly stylized, emotionalism," but also to a pre-plotted drama of good and evil in which good is seriously and repeatedly threatened, but always wins in the end (Worth 1). Such a reading reveals that Dickens is staging marriage as an institution which threatens the innocent, works by means of an intimate betrayal, and exploits the inherent structure of a family, thus working its most insidious evil by turning "the most basic loyalties and relationships" into "a source of torture" (Brooks, *The Melodramatic Imagination* 35). This reading also suggests that Dickens plots the resolution of Edith's story as a triumph of good over evil, that, like the morally satisfying endings he writes for the extended family of the Dombey-Gays and the Carker-Morfins, the appropriately grisly ends he scripts for Mrs Skewton and Carker, and the redemption he bestows upon Alice Marwood, Edith's plot has an appropriate and reassuring ending.

The question of Edith's fate is, perhaps, the sticking-point for an argument that positions her as the heroine in a melodrama of right versus wrong, and this is the time to consider the revised ending of the novel. As he would do 15 years later in *Great Expectations*, Dickens drastically altered the fate of his passionate heroine, and in both cases he wrote what we might call a happier ending for her. The initial role devised for Edith was that of "unwilling adulteress." Dickens's original intention suggests that he assumed his readers would accept her adultery and subsequent death, possibly by suicide, just as he expected his audience to accept the fact that Pip would not be rewarded with Estella (Butt and Tillotson 106). But like Bulwer Lytton's response to the last chapters of *Great Expectations*, Lord Jeffrey's response to Chapter 47 compelled Dickens to rewrite it. After reading "The Thunderbolt" (in which Dombey's and Edith's final clash of pride leads to Edith's elopement with Carker), Dickens's friend wrote that he refused to believe that Edith was Carker's mistress. Upon receipt of this letter, Dickens seems immediately to have decided to change Edith's fate, for the same day, December 21, 1847, he wrote to Forster proposing "a tremendous scene of her undeceiving Carker, and giving him to know that she never meant that." In his notes for the following number, he writes "Edith not his mistress" (*Letters of Charles Dickens* 5: 211 and n.6). In revising her plot, Dickens thus creates a character who is able to escape both her confining marriage and the trap of adultery. Doubtless, it is important to take into account the fact that she is banished from England not only because that is what so often happens to fallen women in Dickens (Monks's mother in *Twist* and Little Em'ly in *Copperfield*, for example), but also because, as Amanda Anderson points out, this move in Dickens always "has the appearance of a commuted sentence or a radical solution" (*Tainted Souls* 70). However, I want to suggest the possibility of reading that removal as a positive, if radical, solution to Edith's melodramatic plight.

It is important, first of all, to note that Dickens, not Dombey, sends Edith to the south of Italy with her cousin Feenix. The difference between being put away by your author and being put away by your husband is not only considerable, but also suggests two very different plots: one that has to do with preserving the sanctity of the world of the novel; the other with madhouses and lunatic asylums, the stuff of sensation novels rather than melodrama or the realistic novel. In emphasizing the fact that Dickens sends Edith to Italy, rather than having Dombey treat her as Rochester does his first wife or as Robert Audley does his, I mean to suggest that Dickens treats this wife more generously and more ambiguously than do those unhappy husbands who commit their wives to lives of imprisonment and insanity—both because Edith is not sent to a place of incarceration (she is not even sent to Australia, for that matter) and because she chooses to leave England.

I also want to underline the fact that she is accompanied to Italy by a relative named Feenix. That he is a relative is significant in terms of the way in which a melodrama is resolved. As Hadley argues, "the melodramatic mode plots the return of a society organized around a patriarchal family," and while she stipulates that this ending "idealizes and thus revises to some extent that culture by purifying its lineages" and that "estranged families reunite instead along primarily ethical lines," she hastens to add that those lines are still "dependent on the ideological coherence of the principle of blood lineage" (127). Her assessment of the end of a melodrama has much in common with Brooks's description of the kind of closure effected by the genre: "at the end, there is ... a reforming of the old society of innocence, which has now driven out the threat to its existence and reaffirmed its values" (*The Melodramatic Imagination* 32). Both Brooks's and Hadley's accounts help us read the end reserved for Feenix and Edith as a family reunion, as the purification of their family tree and a privileging of their blood relation that corrects "the scene of familial estrangement"—in this case, the "skewed" relations between Edith and her mother—that Hadley identifies as the traditional beginning of a melodrama's plot (124). The end of Edith's story is marked by the celebration of a domestic scene with Edith at its center.[4]

I also want to suggest, not entirely whimsically, that Edith's future looks promising because she is going to Italy with a relative named Feenix, someone at least phonetically related to the bird that rises from his ashes, is capable of a miraculous rebirth, and is rewarded with another long life after he burns himself on a pyre. While Edith is a Skewton by birth, not a Feenix, her association with ashes and fires and pyres suggest that she is closely related to her Feenix forebears.[5] And she does have some Feenix blood in her, for her mother is Mrs Skewton *née* Feenix. Edith, then, seems to have inherited the ability to rise from the ashes of her failed marriage and go on to live another life; she is rewarded with another life even after—in fact because—she burns herself on the pyre of her first.

To read her future in the terms of melodrama, Edith's fate accords with the dictates of the genre in that her virtue is finally recognized, both by her cousin and by Florence (whose exoneration is all she needs). Indeed, Edith's position at the end of the novel is much like Florence's in that her reputation has been salvaged and she is surrounded by familial love. While she is not awarded the traditional happy ending of a domestic novel and while she is transported, so to speak, to another country, it is hard to believe, given the contours of her marriage plot, that either marriage or a life in the England of *Dombey and Son* would constitute anything like a happy ending for her. What is more, all that threatened her happiness and her virtue (namely, her mother and Carker) has been wiped from the earth, while her double—Alice Marwood—has been redeemed. Thus, everything associated with Edith has been made right. While Edith's story is the stuff of melodrama, then, her part in that play is not what we have been given to expect. Her part, like Florence's, has a virtue-rewarded ending, not, like that of a fallen woman, a transportation-to-Australia ending.

The end Dickens rewards Edith explicitly denies that marriage is the stuff of happy endings or is necessary for establishing closure. While it is true that Florence's plot (and Susan Nipper's and Harriet Carker's) do end traditionally and conservatively, it is important to read these endings in the context of each other. As I argue in Chapter 2 with respect to early Dickens, there is a kind of counterpoint established between those plots that are resolved in marriage and those that find their resolution in the dissolution of that bond. In *Dombey*, this counterpoint can be read as a function of melodrama in that what Frank Kermode calls "the sense of an ending" has to do with the triumph of good over evil rather than with the conjugal. Sometimes this triumph is signaled by, or takes the form of, marriage, but, as Brooks reminds us in his comparison of melodrama to comedy, marriage in that case "is no more than another indication of virtue's right to reward" (*The Melodramatic Imagination* 32). By writing in the melodramatic mode, Dickens thus subordinates the role of marriage as narrative end, a move enabled by the fact that melodrama's overriding concern has to do with the realignment of the moral universe, with eradicating the villain and rewarding the heroine. Accordingly, I want to read the melodrama of Edith's and Dombey's marriage plot in these terms, to return to my earlier assertion that Dickens plots the resolution of Edith's story as a triumph of good over evil and that he stages marriage not as the institution that establishes closure or provides the novel's happily-ever-after ending, but rather as an institution that just as often threatens the innocent, that works by means of an intimate betrayal, and that exploits the inherent structure of a family and works its most insidious evil by turning Edith against her mother, forcing Florence to choose between her father and her stepmother, and making Dombey jealous of the affectionate bond between Florence and her stepmother.

Hadley argues that the melodramatic mode is characterized by "its always public and theatrical response to the classification of English society," and the mercenary marriage of Edith and Dombey exposes one of the worst inequities of that classificatory world, the common law doctrine of coverture (11).[6] Under the doctrine of coverture, when a woman marries she not only loses her identity under the law in that her legal existence is covered by her husband's, but she also becomes her husband's property. As Jeff Nunokawa points out, "undoing the boundary between the woman a man loves and the property he owns, the mercenary marriage dissolves the distinction between a species of property that is normally, or at least normatively, secure and one that is bound to be lost" (7). It reveals that a wife is a piece of property, like land or money or household goods, that she is a commodity and an object which circulates (or, more precisely, since she is denied agency under the law, is circulated). Proponents of the doctrine of coverture argue that her status as her husband's property suggests the care he will take of her, the protection he will give to something that belongs to him. But a mercenary marriage uncovers the economic nature of what we prefer to think of as an affectionate relationship.[7] Because it reveals the inequity of coverture upon which marriage is based, then, not only is it an effective vehicle for demonstrating the fundamental problems with the institution of marriage, but it also lends itself to a melodramatic performance, to a story of right and wrong that would be entirely legible to its audience. Under the doctrine of coverture, "the legal rules" of marriage "gave any husband who cared to invoke them virtually despotic powers over his wife" (Shanley, *Feminism* 8). Coverture gives any husband the opportunity to behave villainously, even as it stipulates that every wife must behave as passively as the helpless heroine of a melodrama. The institution seems tailor-made for the genre.

Dombey is well aware of the opportunities that the doctrine of coverture affords him. In fact, he is at his most villainous (not to mention his most melodramatic and one-dimensional) when he takes advantage of them and treats Edith as a piece of property. Consider the first altercation between Edith and Dombey, the scolding Dombey gives Edith after their first dinner party. In this scene it is clear that he feels entitled to correct Edith. His sense of their relationship is strictly vertical, and he talks down to her, rebuking her because her behavior does not accord with his wishes, which are the only wishes that count. He treats her as if she were an employee or, more precisely, as if she were in fact the "refractory slave" she later calls herself, anticipating the Queen's critique of marriage (748). As he explains to Carker and Mrs Skewton, both of whom, it is important to note, are present when Dombey reprimands his wife, "I have pointed out to Mrs Dombey that in her conduct thus early in our married life, to which I object, and which, I request, may be corrected" (604). His words bring to mind Browning's Duke and the pernickety and peremptory manner in which he would reprimand his wife: "Just this/Or that in you disgusts me; here you miss, /Or there exceed the mark" ("My Last Duchess" ll. 37–9). But remember that the Duke *would* reprimand his wife in this way were it not for the fact that to do so would be to "stoop to blame/This sort of trifling" (ll. 34–5). The Duke "chuse[s]/Never to stoop," but rather to give commands (ll. 42–3, 45). Dombey will come to resemble the Duke in this respect, too, for he decides soon after to relegate the stooping to Carker.

Dombey also shares with the Duke a delight in displaying his wife as a most satisfactory acquisition (even when he is less than satisfied with her behavior or, in the Duke's case, when such a display brings him very close to revealing the crime that her insufficiently grateful conduct caused him to commit). The Duke has no shame in displaying the portrait and telling the story of his "last duchess," nor does he mind revealing the way in which their marriage came to an end; by the same token, Dombey feels it perfectly appropriate to correct his wife in front of her mother and his employee. In fact, as we learn early on in their courtship, part of the reason he is attracted to Edith has to do with the kinds of display she will enable him to make—both of her and of her enslavement to him. When Edith makes a point of removing herself from all arrangements connected with the wedding in a show of exaggerated rudeness to her mother, Dombey is pleased to think that her "haughtiness and coldness" "deferred to him" and "seemed to have no will apart from his. It flattered him to picture to himself, this proud and stately woman doing the honors of his house, and chilling his guests after his own manner. The dignity of Dombey and Son would be heightened and maintained, indeed, in such hands" (509). "That's my Duchess," he might well exclaim, with an emphasis on the "my."

And while he is wrong in assuming that Edith "deferred to him" and had "no will apart from his," he is wrong about Edith, not about the role of a Victorian wife. When Browning's Duchess does not defer to her husband, "all smiles stopped together" and she becomes his last wife, his late (and latest) wife (l. 46). For husbands like Dombey and the Duke, it is not enough that their wives literally belong to them: they must also put their ownership and mastery of their wives on display. It is this display that lends an air of melodrama to Dombey's otherwise wooden manner, and it is also, as we will see below, Dombey's obsession with display that finally compels Edith to leave him.

Critics disagree as to how to describe Dombey. Kathleen Tillotson argues that he has a rich, albeit impenetrable, inner life; Edwin Eigner categorizes him with Ralph Nickleby as villains who are also "ironically the unwilling victims of a commercial system they seek to exploit" (*Dickens Pantomime* 34); Amanda Anderson argues that Dickens protects him and allows him to maintain his privacy, while he exposes Edith. But when it comes to his relationship with Edith, when he feels compelled to assert his mastery over and his ownership of his wife, Dombey is both unfailingly melodramatic in his speech and gestures and overwhelmingly villainous in his treatment of Edith. The appropriately, if somewhat ironically, titled Chapter 40, "Domestic Relations," begins with the narrator's description of Dombey as the first Mrs Dombey's lord and master: "He had asserted his greatness during their whole married life, and she had meekly recognised it. He had kept his distant seat of state on the top of his throne, and she her humble station on its lowest step" (647–8). Dombey not only behaves like a sovereign, but the first Mrs Dombey also encourages him in his assertion of command by her passive acquiescence to his authority. As he will do in the first scene of strife with his second wife, Dombey imagines himself to be positioned far above his wife; he is "distant," while she is "meek" and "humble."

Dombey's second wife, however, is quite another matter, and the contrast between his two wives reveals how important the doctrine of coverture is to his sense of self:

> He had imagined that the proud character of his second wife would have been added to his own—would have merged into it, and exalted his greatness. He had pictured himself haughtier than ever, with Edith's haughtiness subservient to his. He had never entertained the possibility of its arraying itself against him. (648)

Dombey thinks it goes without saying that Edith will, like his first wife, treat him as if he were the king of the domestic castle. He assumes she will display the proper wifely obedience to him, and that she will, in accordance with the principle of coverture, "merge" her character into his. While it may be tempting to think of the term "merger" in its business connotations and to assume that this is the language that Dombey of Dombey and Son would unconsciously apply to his personal life, it is more accurate to think of the way in which the merger he imagines describes the law that dictates a wife's identity be covered by her husband's, that she will, like Bella in *Our Mutual Friend*, disappear into her husband's coat.[8] Clearly, this is the sort of metamorphosis Dombey expects Edith to undergo. While Edith is, like Bella, a spirited and aggressive heroine, Dombey imagines that marriage will tame her. Given the state of marriage law in the mid-nineteenth century, such an assumption is not as unreasonable as the next ten chapters of *Dombey* reveal it to be. Because marriage completely deprives a woman of any agency or rights under the law, it stands to reason that she would relinquish her sense of self along with her legal identity. After all, she has no rights as a wife, so why not occupy what is her appropriate and "humble station on [the] lowest step" of her husband's throne? The image is accurate enough, so what is to be gained from resisting the arrangement?

But Edith does resist. While Dombey was lucky enough to find a first wife who both understood and accepted the reality of Victorian marriage, he is unfortunate in that his second wife understands it so well that she is compelled to submit to it even as she defiantly resists it. This paradox is, of course, beyond Dombey's comprehension: "He little knew through what a storm and struggle she had been driven onward to the crowning honour of his hand. He little knew how much she thought she had conceded, when she suffered him to call her wife" (649). This paradox, the contradictory impulses that drive her, is also what marks Edith's mindset as feminist, albeit *avant la lettre*. The deliberate inconsistency of the narrator's diction here suggests an ambivalence toward the institution of marriage characteristic of advocates of quite liberal gender politics. Marriage is both a "crowning honour" (a phrase that reminds us of Dombey's throne) and something that Edith is "driven" to; marrying Dombey is a concession that Edith makes to a mother who has devoted the last ten years to "secure" a "good establishment" for her and to a world that insists that marriage is security, that it serves to establish a woman for life (473). The narrator also reveals that Edith "suffered [Dombey] to call her wife," that the secure establishment her mother worked so long and hard for is something Edith must painfully endure. He assumes he is bestowing largesse, while she wears her bridal wreath as if it were "a garland of steel spikes put on to force concession from her which she would die sooner than yield" (594). While she concedes insofar as she marries Dombey, she will not concede so far as to act like a wife, or, more specifically, to be put on display like the acquisition she is.

Her attitude is, on the one hand, understandable. The way in which Dombey wants to exhibit her is precisely the kind of treatment she married to escape; "knowing that my marriage would at least prevent their hawking of me up and down; I suffered myself to be sold, as infamously as any woman with a halter round her neck is sold in any market-place," she confesses to Carker (857).[9] But, once purchased, she encounters another kind of "hawking," and she refuses to submit to this humiliation. Dombey insists upon "a positive show and confession of deference before the world"; he demands that she advertise herself as his wife (652). And while we might think that Edith would understand that the system that compels her to sell herself would also require that she allow her purchaser to display her as his latest acquisition, Edith has determined that the only way she can maintain her self-respect is to refuse the role of subservient wife or grateful servant. The deference Dombey demands would, in her mind, obliterate the last traces of her "better self":

> the broad high mirrors, showed her, at full length, a woman with a noble quality yet dwelling in her nature, who was too false to her better self, and too debased and lost, to save herself. She believed that all this was so plain, more or less, to all eyes, that she had no resource or power of self-assertion but in pride: and with this pride, which tortured her own heart night and day, she fought her fate out, braved it, and defied it. (503–504)

She assumes that everyone sees the emotions she feels with all the clarity the melodramatic mode brings with it. She thus acts out her pride as a kind of defense against what she perceives as the revelation of her fallenness. Cast in a melodrama of failed marriage, her actions both highlight and resist the doctrine of coverture.

Edith knows that her marriage is an economic matter, but she reads the bargain as one that entitles her, rather than—as Dombey and the common law doctrine of coverture would have it—one that makes her beholden and powerless. Just as she maintains the "power of self-assertion" with which her pride arms her, she believes that she still has the agency to fight "her fate out," to "brave it and defy it." Although she has legally given up her identity by marrying, Edith is still scripted as a character with a powerful sense of self, a character with more than enough agency to reason that she has earned the power her husband's money and position give her. Accordingly, she refuses to accept the notion that his purchase entitles him to any of the privileges or kindnesses associated with marriage:

> nothing that his wealth could do, though it were increased ten thousand fold, could win him for its own sake, one look of softened recognition from the defiant woman, linked to him, but arrayed with her whole soul against him. ...even for its sordid and mercenary influence upon herself, she spurned it, while she claimed its utmost power as her right, her bargain—as the base and worthless recompense for which she had become his wife. (584)

She lays bare the logic of their marriage when she reveals that it is the power of Dombey's money that compensates her ("base and worthless" though that compensation may be) for her share in the bargain. And she implies that what Dombey gets from the bargain is her, that, in return for his money, "she had become his wife." What that means, however, is confusing. She will not defer to him, but rather is "arrayed with her whole soul against him"; she will not be civil to his guests, act as hostess in his house, or obey his commands. Further, he seems to be a stranger to her rooms, while she seems to live a life that is completely separate from his. What has Dombey purchased, we wonder? Edith's answer would be "me." But the only way in which she acknowledges that ownership is by going through the marriage ceremony and living in Dombey's house (and wearing the jewels he buys her, spending his money, and allowing him to support her and her mother).

When we think about the bargain of their marriage in this fashion, we may find ourselves grudgingly in sympathy with Mr Dombey, who is not only frustrated with Edith's absolute refusal to behave like a wife in any way, but is also unaware of the shame and abasement she feels. Dombey's frustrated rage comes to a head in Chapter 40, a chapter that, as we have seen, begins by contrasting the first and second Mrs Dombey, and a chapter that reveals most explicitly both Dombey's literal reliance on the doctrine of coverture and Edith's refusal to admit the power of that doctrine—both in general and as it applies to her own marriage. This chapter also reveals the ways in which Dickens is staging a melodrama about the institution of marriage, with Dombey playing the role of Patriarchal Villain, and Edith the Victimized Wife. That is, Dombey embodies the patriarchy, just as Edith represents the victimized status of wives in the 1840s. To use Hadley's terms once again, they "personify absolutes" and thus act out a drama of moral absolutes.

The pivotal Chapter 40 begins by comparing Edith to Dombey's first wife, and it ends by comparing her to Alice Marwood. That the chapter begins with a kind of angel in the house and ends with a fallen woman has much to do with its melodramatic indictment of Victorian gender politics in that it suggests, in the black-and-white fashion of melodrama, that these are Edith's two choices. The fact that she cannot embrace the first and only acts as if she has chosen the second points both to her limited options and to the fact that a melodrama is the perfect vehicle for illustrating those limited options. There are only a certain number of roles in a melodrama, and they are all rigidly prescribed. By the same token, there are only a certain number of roles available to a Victorian woman, and they are also quite limiting. When Dickens tries to increase the options open to one of his characters, he has to straddle and combine roles, to make Edith an innocent fallen woman or a loving mother who would rather not be a wife. To make clear the paucity of her choices and the complexity of her desires, Dickens packs this chapter full of revelations and explanations. Dickens plots the end of "Domestic Relations" as a melodrama, then, and a close reading of those pages yields a very specific answer to the more general cultural inquiry about the coincidence of melodrama and failed marriage in the nineteenth century with which I began this chapter. Melodrama, I would argue, is an excessively energetic presentation of the conventional—one that yields an overabundance of creative power, and a force that can lead to a rescripting of the conventional roles that melodrama would seem to enforce. In what follows, I want to attend to the energy and the spectacle of the scene at the end of the chapter and also suggest the ways in which this enactment of the evils of coverture makes available a very different story of marriage.

I begin my interrogation of this scene after Dombey has made it clear to Edith that she is his "dependent," and after he has given her to understand, "in a tone of sovereign command," that he is "to be deferred to and obeyed" (652). Assuming an attitude of dictatorial magnificence, Dombey fully inhabits the role of villain, while his reminder to Edith of all she owes him and of her absolute powerlessness as his wife is designed to reduce her to the role of passive victim. In an attempt to underscore her powerlessness, Dombey appends a threat to the string of demands with which he has presented her: he reminds her that he can and will use Carker as an intermediary again, for "it would be derogatory to my position and reputation to be frequently holding trivial disputes with a lady upon whom I have conferred the highest distinction that it is in my power to bestow" (653). This part of the scene is marked by Dombey's sense of majesty, by his insistence upon the respect due him, and by his announcement that it is beneath him to argue with his wife, whom he views as the most privileged, yet still one, of his subjects. This portion of the scene ends with Dombey "rising in his moral magnificence" and assuming that he has made his point (653). In other words, it closes with an exaggerated picture of a Victorian husband, and the highly charged scene in which Dombey and Edith enact the stereotypical roles of husband and wife underscores the conventions of marriage in a patriarchal society.

Edith's response initially suggests that she is following the same script and playing the obedient wife to Dombey's domineering husband, for she responds by pleading with him to stay and listen. But her subsequent questions are defensive and accusatory, and they begin to reveal the way in which melodrama's excess energy can lead to a rescripting of the roles it would seem to impose upon its players. Specifically, Edith's questions suggest that she is trying to communicate her own peculiar understanding of marriage to Dombey:

> Did I ever tempt you to seek my hand? Did I ever use any art to win you? Was I ever more conciliating to you when you pursued me, than I have been since our marriage? Was I ever other to you than I am? Did you think I loved you? Did you know I did not? Did you ever care, Man! for my heart, or propose to yourself to win the worthless thing? Was there any poor pretence of any in our bargain? Upon your side, or on mine? (654)

Edith thus reminds Dombey that she never played the role of passive wife, and that she never acknowledged his right to play the role of exacting husband. She makes it clear that the kind of behavior he is now demanding of her is precisely the role she has been careful never to play. By the same token, she suggests that he only wanted to acquire her, that he never gave her to understand that the marriage would involve any pretense of affection.

By framing her understanding of their arrangement in these terms, Edith reveals her assumption that they were acting out quite another kind of drama. And, indeed, the one-sided and economic nature of Victorian marriage, governed as it is by the doctrine of coverture, does make available another story. Just as it sets up the benign fiction of a happily passive wife married to a husband whose absolute power is justified and redeemed by his love for her, it also sets the stage for a scenario in which both husband and wife accept the economic basis of marriage and act accordingly. The possibility for melodrama inherent in the doctrine of coverture, then, makes available both a conventional story and one that breaks out of those conventional bounds. Edith knows that marriage is, above all, an economic arrangement. Because she is "regularly bought," as Cousin Feenix so precisely puts it, she sees no need to pretend otherwise (598). As she makes clear to Dombey, "I feel no tenderness towards you; that you know. You would care nothing for it, if I did or could. I know as well that you feel none towards me" (655). Further, she explains her cold and haughty attitude toward him as a reflection of his bearing to her: "since our marriage, you have been arrogant to me; and I have repaid you in kind. You have shown to me and everyone around us, every day and hour, that you think I am graced and distinguished by your alliance. I do not think so, and have shown that too" (655). Edith thus assumes a sort of parity between them: she assumes that her reasons for marrying must be like his; that her reluctance to assume the role of a wife must be akin to his unwillingness to act as a husband; and that her disdain for him is as acceptable as his arrogance towards her. In this moment it becomes clear that we are being presented with something doubly remarkable: a woman in a Victorian novel thinking very clearly about the inequity of marriage and articulating that understanding most precisely, even as the plot of the (melo)drama in which she finds herself underscores the fact that in the economy of a Victorian marriage, and in the economy that governs Dombey's sense of family, she is disastrously wrong in assuming that she can act out and upon her sense of the institution in which she finds herself trapped.

But while we, as readers of Victorian novels, know that she is wrong to think that she can alter her role in accordance with her clear-eyed understanding of what it really means to be a wife, Edith has not yet come to a full understanding of the double bind of coverture. She follows up her lucid explanation of the state of her marriage with the suggestion that she and Dombey agree to "forbear," a word she repeats three times. The word's financial connotation, that of forbearance, refers to a refraining from the enforcement of something (as a debt) that is due. Thus Edith reveals with her carefully chosen diction that it will take a great deal of effort, on both their parts, for them to continue to play the role of husband and wife, even as she suggests that to do so would be to give up the right she thinks they both have to demand a very different kind of behavior from each other. Even as she humbles herself to suggest a more accommodating form of behavior, she assumes an equivalence between them. She does not say, "I will forbear," but rather makes her forbearance contingent on his: "If you will promise to forbear on your part, I will promise to forbear on mine" (656). Even her grammar reveals her conviction that they are equal; the parallel construction places them in positions of equal rhetorical weight.

Accordingly, disaster ensues when Dombey makes it clear to Edith that she has misread her script. Her response to his absolute refusal to consider her suggestion is the highly melodramatic "Go, Sir!"—a command accompanied by the appropriate gesture: "pointing with an imperious hand towards the door" that demonstrates her assumption that she has as much right to issue ultimatums as he does. This response discloses, perhaps more clearly than anything else she does, the extent to which Edith misunderstands the role of wife. While she is aware of her reified status, and while she knows that she belongs to Dombey, she does not seem to understand that she is thus completely disenfranchised. She does not behave like the passive heroine of a melodrama or a legally nonexistent *femme covert*. The protofeminism of the novel becomes clear as she contemplates, accepts, and endures her mercenary marriage. Instead of making her passive and powerless, instead of reflecting her lack of agency in her lack of personality, Dickens scripts an Edith that rebels and ignores her husband as if he were "an unseen spider on the wall" (657). Edith refuses to behave like the piece of property she is, and, in so strenuously resisting that role, she finds a way to refashion it. That is, while Dombey makes it clear that she has misread her script, Edith persists in her misreading. In refusing his conventional understanding of the roles of husband and wife, she creates a new part for herself, and she is able to do so precisely because of the energetic way in which Dombey melodramatically plays the conventional role of husband and because of the creative energy she expends in resisting the conventional role of wife. The excess of conventionality inherent in melodrama thus leads to a series of unconventional readings and roles; it makes available a transgressive, even subversive, script for the story of a marriage.

My argument that the conventional makes available such liberating strategies relies on an awareness of the contours and the power of those conventions. While Edith refuses to behave like the chattel she in fact is, she has always been well aware of her status as commodity. And that awareness carries with it the seeds of the rebellion she stages in Chapter 40. The histrionic scene in Chapter 27, wherein Edith insists that her mother acknowledge that Dombey "has bought me, or that he will, to-morrow," reveals Edith's cognizance of her disenfranchisement in an articulation that is itself an act (suggestive) of rebellion (472). "He has considered of his bargain; he has shown it to his friend; he is even sufficiently proud of it; he thinks that it will suit him, and may be had sufficiently cheap; and he will buy to-morrow," she continues (472). Edith knows that she has been displaying herself in the hopes that he would bid for her, and she is aware that, by putting herself on display in this manner, she has reduced herself to the status of an object. (It is not unimportant that she refers to herself here as the "it" that Dombey has shown to his friend, the "it" that Dombey is proud of, and the "it" that comes quite cheaply.) But in this scene she also reveals her "conscious self-abasement" and her "burning indignation" at being treated like an object. She admits the humiliation she has been subjected to and the paradoxical fact that she has been the agent of that humiliation, that she has consented to being treated like an object. "There is no slave in a market: there is no horse in a fair: so shown and offered and examined and paraded, Mother, as I have been," Edith declaims in one of her most melodramatic moments (473).

But neither slaves nor horses have a choice in the matter, while Edith, as long as she remains unmarried, does have control over her actions and her destiny. That she feels she does not, that she feels as powerless as a slave or a horse, leads her to make a spectacle of herself—both as she exhibits herself for Dombey and as she rails against her mother for having forced her to do so. I thus want to connect her theatrical behavior on the night before Dombey makes his purchase with the kind of performance and display that Edith has been subject to for most of her life. That is, Edith is making a scene here, and I want to draw attention to the fact that this bit of scenery-chewing is, like *Dombey*'s most melodramatic moments, related to the victimizing law of marriage in the nineteenth century that allows a man to buy a woman and call it matrimony. Just as melodrama is the perfect genre for exposing the villainous nature of the law of marriage in the nineteenth century, this kind of spectacle "dismantle[s] the boundary with which several centuries of discursive formation have sought to separate woman's estate from the anxieties of the marketplace" (Nunokawa 6). In other words, Edith's overwrought but accurate accusations melodramatically reveal the lie upon which the doctrine of separate spheres is based. As Nunokawa so incisively points out, this doctrine calls upon us to accept that "a man's home is his castle, a shelter from the mean streets of the cash nexus" and that his wife, "essence and ornament of a domestic sphere defined by its distance from the marketplace," represents "a kind of value that transcends the commodity form" (6). But Edith's fit of truth-telling compels us to acknowledge that a man's home is in fact formed by means of the cash nexus and that the angel he buys to adorn it is, as the word "ornament" so precisely suggests, simply another object and one whose worth is actually quite easy to calculate.

Her status as object, and her awareness of that status, is made most clear when she refers to herself as a slave. She does so in this scene, and she does so again the night she leaves her husband, when she declares that she "will be exhibited to no one, as the refractory slave you purchased" (748). But in between calling herself a "refractory slave" and revealing the truth of that nomination by leaving Dombey, she asks him for a separation. This request marks a crucial moment in the history of the novel as it begins to develop strategies for plotting the soon-to-be-legalized institution of divorce. This moment is also important for it brings up, if only momentarily, the possibility of a separation by mutual agreement rather than by means of the law. What was called a separation agreement or a private separation was, strictly speaking, extralegal, but it allowed many husbands and wives—who either did not have the money to go through the expensive three-court process or who did not have the necessary grounds for divorce or who wanted to avoid the shame and the acrimony involved in pursuing a legal divorce or separation—to escape the bonds of matrimony. Even after divorce was legalized and streamlined into a one-court process in 1857, many couples still arranged the ends of their marriages in this way. This is precisely the arrangement that Dickens had recourse to when he no longer wanted to be married to his wife, and it is also the way in which Caroline Norton managed, at least for a time, to obtain financial support from the abusive husband she abandoned. A legal separation also figures in the way Norton plots the end of her heroine's marriage in her most autobiographical novel, *Stuart of Dunleath*. The heroine's stepbrother asks his sister's adulterous husband "to arrange terms of separation, and make his wife an allowance," but, like Dombey, Sir Stephen "flatly refused" (123). Although the separation that Edith asks Dombey for is quite different from the virtual banishment that Dickens inflicts on Catherine, and although the separate existence that Caroline Norton managed to lead for the last 41 years of her life provides us with yet another kind of story about the end of a marriage (just as Eleanor Raymond's flight from her tyrannous husband in *Stuart of Dunleath* reflects one more way in which the failed-marriage plot may be resolved), all of these instances suggest an arrangement in which the wife exercises (or tries to exercise) as much, if not more, control over the way her marriage will end as her husband does. Further, Edith, Caroline Norton, and Eleanor Raymond all take matters into their own hands and make sure that they do manage to put an end to their unhappy marriages. Even when the husband refuses to come to terms, as in the case of Dombey and Sir Stephen, even when he tries to dictate the terms of the separation, as in the case of Dickens and George Norton, the process of drawing up a separation deed ensured that some kind of agreement, if only a putative one, would be reached between the parties.

That Edith asks Dombey for a separation is telling, and it is also an important parallel between her story and that of Caroline Norton, another woman forced into a mercenary marriage and falsely and most publicly accused of adultery, who begs her husband to "release me, then, from the chain by which I am bound," and who is tyrannized by her husband yet refuses to accept the inequity that the law of coverture inflicts upon her (*Dombey* 749). In the second half of this chapter, I want to read *Dombey*'s melodrama of failed marriage alongside the story of Caroline Norton's life as she tells it—in her self-exculpatory pamphlet *English Laws for Women in the Nineteenth Century* (1854) and in *Stuart of Dunleath*— and alongside the story that Dickens tells of his growing unhappiness with his wife and their eventual separation in 1858. These may seem like strange stories to read together. Caroline Norton is regarded today as an early champion of women's rights, viewed as largely responsible for the first law that gave separated wives custody of their children and for having significantly affected the final form of the 1857 Divorce Act.[10] Conversely, Dickens is at his most autocratic and demanding when he decides to end his marriage. He insists that Catherine agree to a separation on his terms, and he publicizes the news of their separation in *Household Words* and *The Times*, thus turning what should have been a very private matter into a public scandal and turning his wife of 22 years into an embarrassing object of pity. Even the most loyal of his friends—Mark Lemon, Edmund Yates—and his most sympathetic biographers—John Forster, Edgar Johnson—condemned his actions. What makes things even more complicated, but also suggests the need for a more nuanced reading of the way these Victorians plotted the ends of their marriages, is the fact that Norton's novel has a very conservative ending and is decidedly anti-divorce, while *Dombey and Son* is, as I have been arguing, a novel with a remarkably strong-minded heroine and a text that not only makes a compelling case against the law of coverture, but also compels feminist critics usually unsympathetic to Dickens's contribution to the Woman Question to acknowledge and applaud the critique of the doctrine of separate spheres he writes into *Dombey*.[11] Finally, as I assert at the beginning of this chapter, these stories all rely on the genre of melodrama to portray the failure of marriage.

In this first section, I have demonstrated the several ways in which *Dombey and Son* is a melodrama, and I have analyzed the appropriateness of casting the story of a Victorian marriage in that mode. I want now to turn to the multiple and varied instances of melodrama and failed marriage in Victorian culture.

Melodrama and Marital Discontent

Caroline Sheridan first encountered George Norton on a school excursion through the grounds of his estate. She apparently caught his eye, for he sent a message to her teacher that he wanted to marry her. Caroline's biographers suggest that she was as thrilled by the romance of a sudden proposal as she was unexcited by the proposer. Not only was he a fierce Tory, while all the Sheridans were solid Whigs, but he was also "rather dull and slow and lazy," whereas Caroline was lively and intelligent (Perkins 10). Caroline's mother refused the proposal on the grounds that Caroline was only sixteen, but George was willing to wait until she came of age. In the intervening years, George was elected to Parliament, and Caroline was presented at court. At the end of the three years, Norton again proposed. While it may seem incredible, given the obvious differences in their personalities, their political differences (because, as we will see, politics were very important to all the Sheridans and no less so to Caroline), and the fact that George and Caroline hardly knew each other, Caroline accepted him. Her first biographer, the sympathetic, if not overly analytical, Miss Jane Gray Perkins, writing in 1909, accounts for her decision in this way:

> So at the end of her second season, with another sister coming on after her, having learned by this time that the world was not entirely made for girls like herself—girls who had neither great family nor great position to make up for their lack of dower—in a mood of momentary disgust at what the world had hitherto given her, or submission to her obvious duty to her family, touched and misled no doubt by the permanence of the passion she seemed to have excited in this one lover, she married George Norton, July 30, 1827, he being at that time twenty-six, and she nineteen. (13)[12]

To fill in the blanks of this account, let me add that it took her older sister two seasons to find a husband, that the younger sister now coming out was the most beautiful of the Sheridan girls and it was beginning to seem, given that Caroline had not found a husband during her first season, that she might stand in her sister's way. Further, the expense of the social season was not inconsiderable, and

Caroline was raised, much like Edith, with a clear understanding of the necessity of marrying, and of marrying for money.

In telling the story of her marriage and its failure, Caroline is silent about her reasons for accepting George, but in turning her life into fiction, she suggests, as Perkins implies, that she married for money and because she felt that she had no other choice. The heroine of *Stuart of Dunleath*, Eleanor Raymond, is convinced to accept Sir Stephen's proposal after she discovers that her guardian, with whom she is in love, speculated with and lost her fortune, and then committed suicide. Left with no means of subsistence for herself or her invalid mother, convinced the man she loves has ruined her and drowned himself, Eleanor agrees to marry a man she met in her first season. Eleanor's decision is even more heart-wrenching than the one we can imagine Caroline Norton making; while Caroline knew little about George, what Eleanor remembers most about her brief acquaintance with Sir Stephen is that he beat her dog for attacking his. Eleanor's first reaction to the man that will become her husband is to exclaim, with "her eyes filled with tears," "the man will kill my dog!" (32). She cannot think of him without remembering the violence of their initial encounter, a violence that will prove prophetic, for Sir Stephen is an abusive husband both physically and mentally (34). When Sir Stephen writes to press his case, insisting that Eleanor's poverty makes no difference to him, her reaction to the generous renewal of his offer is unequivocal: "never—I can never be his wife" (44). Only when her villainous half-brother Godfrey reminds her of her responsibilities toward her mother, and her chaperon encourages her to consider Sir Stephen's proposal seriously (confessing that she too loved another, but married the man her family wished her to because of his "great expectations of inheritance" and learned to love him and to enjoy "a married life of unbroken sunshine") does Eleanor relent (45). The narrative of courtship in *Stuart of Dunleath* thus heightens and exaggerates a social status and a set of feelings that usually impose a more mundane kind of oppression into a lurid story; in telling the story of her life in this fashion, Norton melodramatizes both her situation as an impoverished aristocrat and the emotional predicament, not uncommon in Victorian novels, of being compelled to marry without love. She thus turns not only her life, but also a fairly typical Victorian plot, into a story of victimization and oppression.

Perhaps most revealing of Caroline's feelings about marrying George is Eleanor's reaction to the letter of acceptance her half-brother writes for her, a reaction worthy of an actress in a melodrama: "she tossed her clasped hands above her head with a despairing wail; and dropping down again in her chair, she sobbed as though her heart would break" (45). Eleanor's reaction is a wordless tableau worthy of the stage and one that, to borrow Peter Brooks's description, "gives the spectator the opportunity to see meanings represented, emotions and moral states rendered in clear visible signs" (*The Melodramatic Imagination* 62). Brooks finds that melodrama has "recourse to tableau at moments of climax and crisis, where speech is silenced and narrative arrested in order to offer a fixed and visual representation of reactions to peripety," and this scene of sorrow and supplication captures and exaggerates Eleanor's sobs of despair (61).

Yet Norton demands that we take this picture seriously, that we view it not as a moment of theatrics or a calculated performance, but rather as the manifestation of deep and sincere feeling. Godfrey disapproves of Eleanor's emotional tendencies, and he reacts to her outburst by exclaiming, "Don't be so like an actress, for Heaven's sake!"—a response that corrects the reader who would dismiss Eleanor's reaction as exaggerated or unnecessarily extreme by showing that this judgment is characteristic of the highly unsympathetic Godfrey (45). Further, Norton turns to her reader (another standard move in melodrama) and explains:

> This was a favorite phrase with Godfrey; as it is with many persons of impassive manners. It never seems to strike them that the actress copies nature—nature, it may be, in her exaggerated moments, but nature still. The stride of the savage, the gesticulation of the Frenchman, are foreign to us, but natural to them. I have heard and smiled at the observation, "What a beautiful moonlight! it is like a scene on the stage!" Was the moonlight less real for the comparison?
> But these were reflections Godfrey never made. (45)

Eleanor's reaction, then, is "natural" and "real," and it is only "persons of impassive manners" who think otherwise. This scene thus suggests not only how Caroline might have felt upon determining that she must marry George Norton, but also a way in which we might read Dombey's reactions to Edith's more impassioned performances. If we follow Caroline Norton's logic, we can attribute Dombey's refusal to take Edith's pleas seriously as evidence of "reflections never made," of a general pattern of unthinkingness and "impassiveness" that accounts for our lack of sympathy toward his not inconsiderable marital woes.

More specifically, reading Eleanor's and Edith's reactions as performances that are consonant with their feelings, rather than as scenes they are staging or fits they are throwing, suggests the importance of distinguishing between the dramatic and the theatrical, between a way of manifesting or dramatizing one's emotions and the overt and flamboyant mode of self-presentation we associate with a highly stylized and self-conscious performance. Joseph Litvak points out that "the trope of 'theatricality' enables us both to unpack subjectivity as performance and to denaturalize—to read as a *scene*—the whole encompassing space in which that subjectivity gets constituted" (xii). On the other hand, as Mary Jean Corbett argues, the dramatic "is a mode of expression that reveals the innermost thoughts and emotions of the actor as private utterances spoken only for the relief of the speaker" (112). The context of Corbett's remarks is the actress Fanny Kemble's autobiographical writings, and specifically a passage where the actress reveals that while she finds the public aspect of her profession distasteful and improper, she considers the acting itself not only proper and pleasurable, but also supremely natural because it allows her to reveal her own sincere emotions. If we view Eleanor's and Edith's moments of explicit despair as dramatic revelations of their most intimate feelings, as unwitting performances rather than calculated scenes, then, we see that Dickens and Norton are making palpable their heroines' "innermost thoughts and emotions," representing a subjectivity that is natural as opposed to the kind of theatrical performance that Litvak would have us denaturalize.[13] That is, while Eleanor and Edith are making spectacles of themselves, they are not doing so for the benefit of an audience but rather as a means of giving shape and substance to their emotions. Their behavior may be stagy, but it is not staged.

That the dramatic, and even the melodramatic, can be understood as genuine is also made clear in the double melodrama of a failed marriage we find in the Laure subplot of *Middlemarch*. This chapter on the spectacle that the nineteenth century so often makes of a failed marriage would be incomplete without a consideration of Laure and Lydgate, for not only does their story involve a fatally failed marriage, but the ultimate failure of that marriage also takes place within the performance of a melodrama. Eliot's subplot thus makes literal the connections I have been drawing between the melodramatic mode and the plot of a failed marriage, while it demonstrates most vividly the fact that the actress often does, as Norton's tableau of Eleanor in despair reminds us, express genuine emotion—that melodramatic scenes and tableaus of despair may be enactments of genuine feeling rather than acts or performances. Acting out, making manifest, and figuring forth are all efforts to get at the ineffable by making an emotion tangible, concrete, palpable. Norton suggests that only an unsympathetic villain like Godfrey would fail to understand that Eleanor's actions represent how she really feels; in much the same fashion, Dickens alternates explanations of Edith's state of mind with vivid and graphic demonstrations of those emotions. Similarly, but more directly, Eliot succinctly and terribly demonstrates to her reader that Laure's actions, although they are performed on stage, are genuine evidence of how she feels. She thus demonstrates the way in which the excess and energy of a melodrama can suggest the possibility of new roles to its players and that its heightened portrayal of a conflict makes available a revisionary, sometimes even revolutionary, script.

Laure is a second-rate actress who performs in melodramas and has thus captured Lydgate's heart. In the play that Lydgate routinely goes to see, her part is to stab her lover, whom she mistakes for the play's villain. In a bit of casting that begins to suggest the blurring of the actual and the performative that Laure's story figures forth, the actor who plays her lover is actually her husband. One night when the time comes for the heroine to pretend to stab her lover, "the wife veritably stabbed her husband" (180). After an official investigation, it is determined that her husband's death was an accident; Laure's foot slipped. But soon after, the reader—and Lydgate—learn that this bit of stage business was not, in fact, performance gone awry, but rather exactly what it looked like: a woman stabbing her lover. For as Laure reveals to Lydgate, "I meant to do it." What is more, she explains that while she did not plan to kill her husband (who had begun to annoy her with his overfondness), she did *mean* to kill him. And she got the idea for his murder from performing a facsimile of it night after night. "It came to me in the play," she says (182). Andrew Miller calls this scene "a lesson on the correct viewing of effective theatrical representation." That is, while "the initial horror of the scene comes from our discovery that what has appeared theatrical has become 'real,'" "the final shock of the scene" comes when we realize "not that the theatrical became real, but that it was real all along" (201). Furthermore, because Laure got the idea from the play, her behavior is an example of the way in which "drama produces the real" (Andrew Miller 202).

Eliot's subplot is especially important for my purposes because Laure learns how to dissolve her marriage from a melodrama: by performing in an exaggerated form of drama, she learns how to make reality accord with her desires. The outsized nature of the genre in which she performs helps her determine what she wants and what she really feels. By performing the stagiest of scenes, she finds a way to act out and upon her own emotions. Miller refers to the "theatrical" in this scene, and he is certainly right to use that term about the plot of the melodrama in which Laure performs. But Laure's acting is more dramatic than it is theatrical in that she is acting out and upon her own genuine emotions. As Corbett argues, "the dramatic, unlike the theatrical, allows the actress to make a role her own, or, as it is more typically represented, to be 'possessed' by it" (112). The melodrama is an especially productive site of the dramatic because its oversized roles and exaggerated characters provide its players with a great deal of room. Its plots are so clearly artificial constructs that they suggest the ways in which other patterns (lives, marriages) might be similarly recreated and refashioned. In this sense, Laure's re-creation of her role, from unhappy wife to relieved and vindicated widow, has much in common with another Victorian actor who discovered that his marriage was unendurable through his performance in a melodrama, for Dickens and his biographers would have us believe that he realized while playing the role of the noble hero Richard Wardour in *The Frozen Deep* the extent of his unhappiness with his wife of 22 years.

Just a few days after the last performance of *The Frozen Deep*, in August of 1857, Dickens wrote to his close friend John Forster and insisted that

> Poor Catherine and I are not made for each other, and there is no help for it. It is not only that she makes me uneasy and unhappy, but that I make her so too—and much more so. She is exactly what you know, in the way of being amiable and complying; but we are strangely ill-assorted for the bond there is between us. God knows that she would have been a thousand times happier if she had married another kind of man, and that her avoidance of this destiny would have been at least equally good for us both. ... Nothing on earth could make her understand me, or suit us to each other. Her temperament will not go with mine.
> (*Letters of Charles Dickens* 8: 430)

Dickens also suggested in this letter that his marital problems were not new, that "what is now befalling me I have seen steadily coming, ever since the days you remember when Mary was born," but the editors of the Pilgrim letters insist that "there is no sign whatever of their incompatibility" around the time their daughter Mary was born, and that in fact Dickens's letters from that period "give new evidence of their happy relationship" (*Letters of Charles Dickens* 8: 430, 430 n.1). Whatever the case may be, it was only after *The Frozen Deep* that he began to articulate his distress. And when we consider that the last performance of the melodrama occurred at the end of August of 1857, and that by the beginning of the following June, all the arrangements for Dickens's and Catherine's separation were in place and they were living apart, it does seem that the play was in some way involved in, if not responsible for, the break-up of their marriage.

That Dickens began to take seriously his marital discontent, to publicize it, and to consider how it might be alleviated because of his role in *The Frozen Deep* is suggested most explicitly by his complaint in a letter to Wilkie Collins of an "unhappiness" "so strong" that "I can't write, and (waking) can't rest, one minute. I have never known a moment's peace or content, since the last night of The Frozen Deep" (*Letters of Charles Dickens* 536). Jean Ferguson Carr suggests that

> Dickens's participation in the play overlapped with two major changes in his life—his decisions to leave his wife Catherine and to begin public reading tours. Both threatened to damage his reputation as a moral institution, and his letters of 1857 are full of defences against potential criticism. The letters move back and forth between exuberant descriptions of his successes as Wardour, grim concern over his domestic crises, and threats that he will do something destructive unless he distracts himself with something like the public reading tours. (36)

Edgar Johnson finds that "the tone of Dickens's unhappy letters to Collins and Forster during all the time between the last night of *The Frozen Deep* and the time of the separation discloses an entirely new intensity of personal misery far exceeding the restlessness of years before" (2: 991), while Michael Slater believes that "once the excitement of acting *The Frozen Deep* was over Dickens found it impossible to resume normal domestic life" (140). And all of his biographers (with the exception of his loyal friend Forster) note that it was only a few months after the last performance that he wrote to Catherine's maid and asked her to have a door put up between his dressing room and Catherine's bedroom and to put a bed in his dressing room—renovations which allowed him to move out of Catherine's bed just seven months before he would move her out of his house (*Letters of Charles Dickens* 465).

In the introduction to his edition of the play, Robert Louis Brannan suggests that "in his appearances as Wardour, [Dickens] found relief from the marital unhappiness and well-known unrest that agitated him during 1856 and 1857. Months after the last performance, he continued to refer to this relief" (3). Many Dickens scholars would bring up Ellen Ternan at this point, for it is now generally agreed that Ellen was Dickens's mistress for the last 12 years of his life, and it is true that he first met her when she played in *The Frozen Deep*. However, because the evidence strongly suggests that Dickens was initially interested in her older sister Maria, rather than in Ellen,[14] and because of the way in which Dickens's acting in the melodrama was described, I want to tease out the connection between Dickens's experiences on stage and his new resolve to end his marriage. I want, that is, to look more closely at the role that provided him with such relief and ultimately suggested that he might create another role that would provide him with similar relief, and I want to analyze the way in which he played that role, the way in which the energy and exaggeration of melodrama enabled him to think so very flexibly about the drama of his own life and to turn his marriage to the self-effacing Catherine into a melodrama of desertion.

The Frozen Deep is a story of renunciation and heroic self-sacrifice. It is also a story of unrequited love, broken engagements, and a kind of ferocious self-discipline. The hero of *The Frozen Deep* is Richard Wardour, a "terribly headstrong and passionate" young man, in love with Clara Burnham, whom he has grown up alongside and to whom he thinks he is engaged (Collins, *The Frozen Deep* 112). As Clara explains to her best friend, "I did all I could to show that I was willing to be like a sister to him, and that I could be nothing else. He did not understand me, or he would not—I can't say which. ... He never spoke out—he seemed to treat me as if our future lives had been provided for while we were children" (112). Operating under this assumption, he leaves on an African voyage with this goodbye for Clara: "If I live, I shall come back promoted, and we both know what will happen then!" (112). He kisses her, and then disappears. Clara reproaches herself for not objecting, and although she writes to him to clarify her feelings, he never receives the letter. While Richard is in Africa, Clara meets Frank Aldersley; they fall in love and become engaged. Months later, Wardour returns to claim his wife, only to learn that she has promised herself to another. He responds with an "awful, awful look of fury and despair," and his parting words to Clara, "The time may come when I shall forgive *you*, but the man who has robbed me of you shall rue the day when you and he first met," set up the plot which the melodrama will play out (113). For it turns out that Frank is about to sail for the Arctic, an expedition that Richard joins at the last minute, after Clara has refused him: "They have sailed away together—away to the eternal ice and snow—the man who is to marry me and the man whose heart I have broken!" Thus, the conflict *The Frozen Deep* enacts is established, and the first act ends.

It is, of course, a conflict that will prove Richard's heroism, even as it tests his love for Clara. *The Frozen Deep* was inspired by the story of the Franklin Expedition (1845–59); accordingly, the ships on which Richard and Frank sail are lost, and the survivors have been stranded in the Arctic for three years. When the second act begins, the remaining sailors have determined to make one last attempt to reach the nearest settlement. Frank is seriously ill, and though he determines to go with the search party, he cannot keep up with the other men, and Richard stays behind, ostensibly to take care of him. Left alone with his enemy in the Arctic, he has the perfect opportunity to make good on his threat; all he would have to do is leave Frank in the snow, and his death would be assured. But instead he saves him, at the expense of his own life. As he says to Clara with his last breath, in the last act of the play, "Saved, saved for *you*! He's footsore and weary, Clara. But I have saved him—I have saved him for *you*! I may rest now—I may sleep at last—the task is done, the struggle is over" (158). *The Frozen Deep* is thus a story of heroic love and self-sacrifice—a story of devotion and selflessness writ large.

Peter Ackroyd calls the devoted and selfless Wardour "a part into which [Dickens] could pour himself, and even at rehearsals his identification with it was seen to be something quite extraordinary" (773). Fred Kaplan notes that "reviewers commented with almost awestruck praise on Dickens's innovative naturalistic performance, in which he acted with an emotive restraint that made the character's feelings especially expressive" and suggests that "audiences sensed the identification between Dickens and his role" (358). Like Laure's actions, Eleanor's despair, and Edith's diatribes, Dickens's performance seemed to be more genuine than it was theatrical. Jean Ferguson Carr concludes that "to the reviewers of the play, Dickens's performance seemed 'true', 'natural', not because he made them forget the illusion of theatre and think they were seeing Wardour, but because they felt they were seeing Dickens himself, through the disguised and assumed role" (39). Similarly, Edgar Johnson posits that "the emotional power of the play was derived from the intensity he gave to the character of Wardour, into which he poured all his own concealed desperation" and that he "felt a kind of agitated relief in projecting and symbolizing an emotion not unlike his own" (2: 868, 904). And the play's author, Wilkie Collins, testified that Dickens played the role of Wardour "with a truth, vigour, and pathos never to be forgotten by those who were fortunate enough to witness the performance" (Collins, "Introductory Lines" 3).

Perhaps most helpful in terms of figuring out exactly why Dickens's audiences thought they were seeing something so natural is the prologue to the play, 34 lines of heroic couplets that Dickens himself wrote—lines that, as Carr notes,

> invite the audience to attempt a vicarious exploration of the geographical and psychological extremes of a polar expedition, to journey into a secret and covered realm and observe the hidden depths, not only of the main character, but of "us".... The audience is invited to compare the physical events experienced by the explorers with the more private and psychological events facing those at home. Dickens thus appears to offer his theatrical audience a key to self-revelation, a way of reading him through his theatrical role. Dickens, as Wardour, will stand before them, revealed, intimate, with protective surfaces melted, normally-frozen depths exposed. (34–5)

With its announcement that "the secrets of the vast Profound/Within us, an exploring hand may sound," the prologue suggests that this play will be as much about "the frozen deep" of an "ice-bound soul" as it will be about an expedition to the polar regions, and that its goal will be to "test the region" of that frozen soul, to "seek [its] passage," to "soft'n the horrors of its wintry sleep," and ultimately to "melt the surface of that 'Frozen Deep'" (Dickens, *Miscellaneous Papers* II: 487). In other words, the prologue makes it clear that we are to take the play both as a psychological drama and as the story of a dangerous and adventurous expedition. Further, we are to think of the fictional story of the Arctic voyage and the love triangle of Wardour, Frank, and Clara in terms of "the secrets" that dwell "within us"; the spectacle of distress and relief the melodrama enacts will also reveal truths about our own most private selves.

Dickens recurs to the way in which melodrama makes available new roles and new plots for his own life in his preface to *A Tale of Two Cities*. There he explains that he first came up with the idea for this novel while acting in *The Frozen Deep* (another example of "it came to me in the play"), and that

> a strong desire was upon me then, to embody it in my own person; and I traced out in my fancy, the state of mind of which it would necessitate the presentation to an observant spectator, with particular care and interest. As the idea became familiar to me, it gradually shaped itself into its present form. Throughout its execution, it has had complete possession of me; I have so far verified what is done and suffered in these pages, as that I have certainly done and suffered it all myself. (29)

While this preface is somewhat difficult to decipher, it is clear that Dickens is trying to suggest the intimate connection between this story and his own experiences. Alexander Welsh interprets the "strong desire ... to embody it in my own person" as evidence that Dickens "meant either to write such a story of his own or to act out the role in real life" (*The City of Dickens* 110). He did, in fact, write a version of this story as the triangular relationship of Lucie, Carton, and Darnay, but instead of playing the part "in real life," Dickens played it on stage. That is, he says that "a strong desire was upon me *then*, to embody it in my own person," meaning that while he was performing in Collins's melodrama he determined to play this part as naturally and as realistically as possible. By taking on this role, letting it take "complete possession of me," he can, as Carr would have it, "posit himself as another person" and thus "explore dangerous emotions and desires in front of large audiences. He can display himself on stage in his most devastating posture, but in the disguise of someone else" (36-7).

When Dickens says that the role of Wardour "had complete possession of me," he is suggesting that his performance is more dramatic than it is theatrical, that it is more genuine than it is staged. To be possessed by a role means, on the one hand, that you have made it your own, that you have taken it over for yourself. Or, to put this phenomenon in precisely the opposite way, it means that you have lost yourself in the role. Either way, there is a strong and unstable resemblance between actor and role. Mary Jean Corbett brings together these formulations when she reminds us that the "loss of self" in a role is

> at the same time, an affirmation of self. Although the boundaries between who [Kemble] is and the role she is playing temporarily blur ... by momentarily losing her sense of difference from that role in being "seized" by it, she recognizes her

> ontological difference from it as well as her capacity for being selves other than
> her own ordinary one. (112)

This capacity to be someone else, to play other roles, is precisely what the melodramatic mode makes available and exactly why and how the failure of marriage is so often depicted melodramatically in nineteenth-century British culture. Because melodrama suggests the fluidity of a role, a script (a marriage, a life), it provides a template for taking on other roles, for rescripting your life, for ending your marriage. It is, in fact, a genre that suggests possibilities and that often produces radical plots. And, perhaps most importantly, it is a genre that privileges the revelation of feelings, one that valorizes the exposure of one's most subjective and interior self.

Taken together, Dickens's prologue to *The Frozen Deep* and his preface to *A Tale of Two Cities* suggest that he sees melodrama in just this way—as a means of revealing a complex interior life and a way of expressing genuine emotions—while his actions after performing in *The Frozen Deep* suggest that he took seriously the idea that he might play other roles as naturally as he had played the role of Catherine's husband. It would thus seem that crafting your own role in a melodrama makes the role you play in your actual life seem as much a construct open to re-creation and revision as the role you play on stage. As I've been suggesting throughout this chapter, the fact that Norton and Dickens (and Eliot's Laure) find a way to end their marriages by acting in (or, in Norton's case, by writing herself into) a melodrama has much to do with the nature of the genre. Melodrama is highly conventionalized, but it also has a kind of fluidity and exaggerated energy to it. Players assume roles, the script can be rewritten, the distinction between the real self and the performed self wavers. It thus presents itself as the perfect strategy not only for dramatizing a conflict between good and evil, but also for discarding one role for another—for abandoning the pose of contented spouse, for stepping out of a domestic role and into a more public part. It is no accident that Dickens and his biographers talk about the end of his marriage and his decision to begin a program of public readings in the same breath. An important part of his abandoning the role of husband is his simultaneous undertaking of the role of public performer, and his letters make it clear that he is taking up the more active and public role as a means of coping with his unhappiness in the role of husband.

Extrapolating from his writings and actions from 1857 to 1859, then, we can read his earlier creation of the melodramatic Edith Dombey as the sympathetic portrait of a woman who was not afraid to substitute one role (fallen woman) for another (Victorian wife). Rather than creating a one-dimensional tragedy queen or giving us an exaggerated picture of a recalcitrant wife, Dickens is working in a mode he considers highly realistic and revealing in the extreme, as is Caroline Norton when she tells the story of her life in the form of a melodrama. As Elaine Hadley maintains, Norton "found it necessary to adopt what seems like a pronounced melodramatic narrative and to depict herself as a beleaguered heroine precisely because she wanted to employ the style of theatricality that privileged visibility, disclosure, and public authenticity" (158). I began this section by looking at the way Norton turned her life into fiction, at the way in which she revealed her feelings about marrying George Norton through the creation of the melodramatic Eleanor Raymond. I now want to consider another version of her melodramatic autobiography, her political pamphlet *English Laws for Women in the Nineteenth Century*.

Both *Laws for Women* and *Stuart of Dunleath* are autobiographies, the first disguised as a protest against the gender bias of the 1854 divorce bill, the second a domestic melodrama.[15] In both, the Caroline Norton figure is cast as the victim, the innocent heroine forced to abandon the passivity appropriate to her role and her gender because the law does not exist that would protect her from her husband. Whereas in melodrama all is almost magically made right and the heroine's innocence is proven as a matter of course, *Laws for Women* argues that the law guarantees that Norton's situation will not be made right, that it will obliterate her rights and her identity, rather than reveal her innocence and publicly exonerate her as a wrongly maligned victim. Norton argues that the law interferes with the role she has been taught to play as a Victorian wife, forcing her to abandon the part of angel in the house and take on, instead, a public and controversial role—to leave her husband, to advertise her sufferings, and to expose the inequity of marriage law in the nineteenth century.

Before I look at the way Norton, like Dickens, abandons her private role for a very public one (and in so doing, like Dickens, advertises the details of her failed marriage), let me outline the story of her failed marriage. In 1830, when George lost his seat in Parliament upon its dissolution on the death of George IV, Caroline used her family's connections to find him a new job, ultimately convincing Lord Melbourne (who was later to become Victoria's Prime Minister) to appoint him as a magistrate. Caroline and Melbourne were just beginning a friendship that had its genesis in his fond memories of her grandfather; after he gave her husband a job, they became very close friends. In 1836 Caroline and George quarreled over their children's visit to Caroline's brother (a trip which George was explicitly not invited on because Caroline's brother had witnessed his brutal behavior to Caroline), and Caroline went to her brother's alone. She returned to find her children gone; upon tracking them down she was denied access to them, at which point she vowed to leave her husband. He responded by initiating divorce proceedings, naming Lord Melbourne, then Prime Minister, as her lover. The trial attracted a great deal of publicity (Dickens reported it for the *Morning Chronicle*), but the evidence was obviously manufactured and bought; the witnesses clearly perjured themselves. Without even hearing the defendant's case or leaving the box, the jury found Melbourne innocent.[16] It is generally agreed that the whole affair was more political than personal in nature, due to Lord Melbourne's position as Prime Minister of a Whig government.[17] Lord Melbourne emerged from the affair unscathed, but Caroline's reputation was seriously damaged by the trial. Furthermore, since the case had failed, George could not divorce her and Caroline could not divorce George (despite his having committed the requisite crime of adultery aggravated by cruelty) because, having returned to him after a short separation two years earlier, she had, according to what she called "the negative and neutralizing law for married women in England," forgiven him and thus forfeited her right to sue for divorce (Norton, *English Laws for Women* 161). Caroline and George continued their rocky, quarrelsome relationship for the next 11 years, living apart, sometimes on more amicable and sometimes on the bitterest of terms.

In 1848, however, George tried to persuade Caroline to allow him to raise money on her marriage settlement. This settlement, legally and exclusively hers unless signed over to him in the presence of witnesses, was created by her father upon her marriage. She agreed to sign the settlement over to him in return for an increase in her allowance and the formalization of their separation agreement (precisely the kind of separation Edith asks Dombey for). These terms were agreed upon in a legal deed, signed by both George and Caroline, but three years later she discovered that, in her husband's words, "by law, Man and Wife were one, and could not contract with each other; and the deed was therefore good for nothing" (Norton, *English Laws for Women* 78). In fact, not only did George claim, correctly, that the law did not compel him to keep his word to his wife, but he also withdrew the small allowance he had originally agreed to pay her. At this point Caroline decided to retaliate, and she used the doctrine of coverture—the law George cited in his defense—for her own ends. She refused to pay her debts, arguing that as a wife whose identity was subsumed under her husband's, she actually had no debts; all her debts were really his. George was eventually sued for nonpayment of her debts, at which point he claimed in a court of law that because Melbourne left her a legacy upon his death, she could in fact pay those bills. Whether or not Caroline had the money to pay her debts was not the subject of the trial, but presenting this piece of evidence allowed George informally to retry Caroline for adultery and to suggest that the original verdict was in error because Melbourne's legacy put their relationship in a suspicious light. As it turned out, the jury found for George on a technicality, a further legal injustice that compelled Caroline to make public all the wrongs she had endured. She first wrote to *The Times* with an account of all she had suffered,[18] and then she published *English Laws for Women*, a document that advertises itself as political pamphlet in response to the Divorce Bill that was introduced in June of 1854, but is in fact a detailed account of her failed marriage and the ways in which the law underwrote its failure.[19]

In telling this story, Norton insists that she cannot remain passive as the heroine of a melodrama should because her story has no hero to vindicate her reputation and rescue her from the clutches of the evil villain. As Mary Poovey puts it, "if George is the villain here, and Caroline is the lady-in-distress, who … is to be the lady's defender? In the current, lamentable state of society, there is no one else to play the role but Caroline Norton herself" (*Uneven Developments* 67). Norton thus seeks to avenge herself not only against her husband, but also against the law that allows him to mistreat her with impunity. The way in which Norton tries to straddle and combine roles, to cast herself as both the wronged innocent heroine and as the hero who will unmask the villain and save the heroine should remind us of the way in which Edith tries to find a role that fits her, of the way in which she tries to move between the alternatives of angel in the house and fallen woman that are her only options. Like Norton, Edith is also unable to restrict her behavior to the silent, trusting, inactive pose of a heroine. While the innocent heroine "cannot call into question the judgments and the actions of a father or an uncle or a guardian" without forfeiting her status as virtue personified, Edith is virtually defined by her criticism and defiance of the evil practiced upon her—by both Carker and, in adherence to the roles of melodrama, by her mother (Brooks, *The Melodramatic Imagination* 31). While Brooks points to "the structure of familial relationships" that renders the heroine mute, the fact that Edith is twice the victim of her mother's mercenary marriage plots in no way inhibits her or stops her from speaking out against her mother's actions (31).

By the same token, the fact that the intimate details of Caroline Norton's marriage had twice been made public in a court of law in no way deterred her from making even more of a spectacle of herself and her marriage by speaking out against the treatment she received at the hands of her husband and the law. Indeed, her response to her husband's very public attempt to dredge up her relationship with Lord Melbourne was to make her private life even more public by writing a series of letters to *The Times* and then reprinting portions of these letters in *English Laws for Women*. These letters are Norton's attempt to expose the lies that her husband told in court, to insist all over again that she never had an affair with Melbourne, and to reveal the various ways in which her husband abused her over the years. Her letters, not surprisingly, elicited replies from her husband, which in turn provoked replies from several of the lawyers who had been involved with the case, all of which George Norton felt compelled to reply to. Caroline, in turn, could not resist replying to her husband's replies, and when *The Times* became reluctant to print any more of the Nortons' correspondence, she began to write *English Laws for Women*. Her response to the public plots her husband hatched against her was to make even more details about her private life public, to persist in publicizing the details of her marriage, both by replying to her husband's letters and by reprinting selections from their exchange in her political pamphlet.

One of the most curious moments in this exchange occurs in the last paragraph of the last letter she wrote to *The Times*, where she explains why she behaved in a way that seems to violate the doctrine of separate spheres. Given her mania for advertising the story of her marriage, the fact that she would even admit the existence of an ethos that underwrites the public silencing of women is curious. But her account of the consonance of her behavior with traditional gender politics is important to unpack, for it is a move that reminds us that Norton, like Dickens and Eliot's Laure, is performing the end of her marriage, that she is playing a carefully constructed role in the very public drama she writes for readers of *The Times*. She concludes her last letter by reminding "those women who have the true woman's lot, of being unknown out of the circle of their homes" to "thank God for that blessing" for "it *is* a blessing" (Norton, *English Laws for Women* 122). That is, she both insists that a woman's place is in the home and that it is "a blessing" to be so confined, even as she laments the fact that she does not enjoy the blessing of that confinement: "Publicity is no longer a matter of choice. Defence is possible to me—not silence." In what follows, Norton addresses those who need to be reminded of the domestic protection they enjoy, those to whom she must explain her actions, "those who think that the right of a husband so indefeasible, that a wife ought rather to submit to the martyrdom of her reputation, than be justified at his expense." In what is perhaps her most agile move, she insists that she sides with those who believe that a woman should keep silent about her sufferings. Thus Norton, a woman clearly hell-bent on making her sufferings known and advertising her husband's slander and perjury, manages to occupy the role of passive, silent, and long-suffering victim. "I *have* refrained," she insists. "All I state now, I might have stated at any time during the past unhappy years; and I never did publicly state it till now." In other words, Norton claims that she does subscribe to the conventional view of marriage, and she takes care to articulate deferential sentiments and to show that she has occupied a conservative role. It has been my argument throughout this chapter that melodrama displays the conventional with an excessive energy that can lead to the rescripting of stock sentiments, scenes, and characters, and that rescripting is made explicit here when Norton insists that she tried to play the passive heroine, that she still believes in the doctrine of separate spheres, but that the circumstances of her marriage (circumstances inherent in the doctrine of coverture) made it impossible for her to go on with the show, so to speak. It is precisely Norton's argument, counterintuitive though it may be, that it was her determined adherence to the confines and conventions of Victorian marriage that ultimately made it impossible for her to submit to those strictures. Only when she realizes that the law that denies her a legal identity is also the law that allows her husband to swindle her does she break her womanly silence and speak out against him and the institution that gives him unlimited power over her.

The fact that Caroline Norton and Edith Dombey speak out—that they accuse those who have wronged them and reveal the fundamental inequity of marriage as it is institutionalized and enacted in the mid-nineteenth century—brings to mind what is perhaps the most famous passage in *Dombey*, the "oh for a good spirit who would take the house-tops off" passage at the beginning of the chapter in which Edith elopes with Carker (738). Here the Dickensian narrator fantasizes about the immeasurable good such a spirit could do by exposing the social evils that beset "a Christian people" and revealing the "stumbling-block of their own making." The vision he pines for is an amazingly powerful one, "for only one night's view" of these "scenes of our too-long neglect" would "make the world a better place." And the entity that could show us this vision is, appropriately enough, "a good spirit." By using the word "spirit," Dickens conjures up the domestic angel, this time moving outside her customary sphere, no longer the angel in the house but now taking off the very top of that refuge, revealing what is inside the home she presides over. Dickens thus reaffirms his allegiance to the protecting domestic spirit and links her work of protecting the house to a flamboyant opening up and exposing of it, Edith-style. Like Caroline Norton's pained insistence that she cannot remain within the house, playing the role of passive heroine, the Dickensian narrator here insists that the domestic sphere must be violated in order, ultimately, to be protected.[20]

That Caroline Norton's and Edith's behavior violates the domestic sphere would seem to go without saying, but Caroline Norton purports to protect that sphere, like the good spirit Dickens imagines; she valorizes the doctrine of separate spheres she violates by speaking out and in public. In other words, while my argument about Norton's strategic employment of the melodramatic mode stresses the creative excess, the overabundance of energy, and the exaggerations of the mode that ultimately allow her to embrace a new role and a new script, at the end of *Laws for Women*, Norton abandons the role of angry avenger for the more passive role of "lady-in-distress in search of a champion." While playing that role she could, as Poovey points out, "ask only for protection," and that protection could only "be enforced by male legislators and magistrates" (*Uneven Developments* 84). Caroline Norton, then, while melodramatizing her plight, ultimately "remained within the terms of the ideology whose discursive rules she violated" (*Uneven Developments* 83). One reason Poovey characterizes Norton's politics in this way is that while Norton exposes the double standard inherent in Victorian marriage law, based as it is on the doctrine of coverture, while she calls attention to "the defective state of Laws for Women in England," to "the whole framework, in short, of those laws by which her existence is merged in the existence of another," she does so all the while insisting that she does not believe in "the wild and stupid theories advanced by a few women, of 'equal rights' and 'equal intelligence'" (*English Laws for Women* 14, 20, 165). "I, for one " she declares, "(I, with millions more), believe in the natural superiority of man, as I do in the existence of a God" (*English Laws for Women* 165). As the inferior sex, she argues, women need to be protected. If men neglect their God-given duty, then that duty must be performed by the state: "failing her natural protector, the law should have power to protect" (*English Laws for Women* 161–2). Thus, she advocates the reform of Victorian marriage law not because she believes that women have a right to leave their husbands, but rather so that women will be provided for and protected—by the state, if not by their husbands.

My interest in the popularity and efficacy of melodrama as a strategy for depicting the failure of marriage in the mid-nineteenth century necessarily means that I want to think more about Norton's strategies than about the sincerity of her politics, that I want to think more about the role she embraces than about the pronouncements she makes while playing that role. That Norton asks for a kind of paternal protection in her political pamphlet is, of course, a contradictory strategy. And while Norton insists that "petitioning does not imply assertion of equality" (*English Laws for Women* 165), Poovey is surely right when she points out that "Norton's usurpation of the defender's role ... and her entry into political discourse have already collapsed the very differences she seems to support" (*Uneven Developments* 69). But it is those very differences in which I am most interested.

While Poovey argues that "to the extent that she formulated her complaint in terms derived from the prevailing ideology, her challenge actually reinforced the idealized domesticity she seemed to undermine," a disjunct that distresses Poovey because she reads the contradiction between Norton's method and her goals as evidence that either one or the other must be false, I am most intrigued by Norton's writing when the fissure between her strategy and her announced purpose is most evident (*Uneven Developments* 81). To highlight that rhetorical chasm, I want to consider another Victorian heroine who seems to operate under a similar double bind: the ultra-capable Mrs Bagnet in *Bleak House*. I bring up "the old girl" not only because, like Caroline Norton, she "reinforces the idealized domesticity" that her firmness of mind and the fact that she is in charge of virtually every aspect of her family's life (from washing the greens to telling her husband what he thinks) would "seem to undermine," but also, and perhaps more importantly, because Caroline Norton brings her up at the outset of *Laws for Women*.

The epigraph to this pamphlet—"It won't do to have TRUTH AND JUSTICE on our side. We must have LAW AND LAWYERS"—comes from Mrs Bagnet. That is, Norton begins her diatribe against the law of coverture and the exposure of her husband's abusive behavior by quoting a wife who seems as unlikely to be subsumed under her husband's identity as she is to be taken advantage of by him—or by any other man, for that matter. Norton quotes Mrs Bagnet in her appeal to members of Parliament to create the law that would protect a defenseless woman. But Mrs Bagnet, certainly not a defenseless woman, uses them to impress upon Mrs Rouncewell the need to convince her son George to get a lawyer, not because the law provides the kind of protection that Norton here insists that it does, but because he needs "every sort of help to put himself in the right, and clear himself of a charge of which he is as innocent as you or me." "It won't do to have truth and justice on his side," she continues, "he must have law and lawyers" (803). Norton's transcription of these lines is almost exact; the only discrepancy is a matter of capitalization and of pronoun reference. However, she uses these lines for a very different purpose, for the narrator reveals that Mrs Bagnet is "apparently persuaded that [law and lawyers] form a separate establishment, and have dissolved partnership with truth and justice for ever and a day," while much of Norton's rhetoric relies on an entirely opposite understanding of the relationship between justice and the law (803). True, she admits that the reason she has been so mistreated by her husband for 27 years has to do with the fact that the law does not do justice to the rights of women. But her earnest entreaty to her audience to correct this mistake suggests a fundamental faith in the institution of "law and lawyers." Elaine Hadley maintains that "the main aim of Norton's documents" is "to advocate reform of the laws regarding marriage and divorce so that the law and not the husband would be the ultimate source of benevolence and obligation in the family" (160). This "conservative-minded reform" stands in stark contrast to Mrs Bagnet's more cynical attitude toward the law, but it would seem that Mrs Norton and Mrs Bagnet share a belief in the efficacy of appealing to the doctrine of separate spheres, in the strategic deployment of the kind of paternalistic ethos that underwrites Norton's appeal to the law. Both of these Victorian wives behave in ways that suggest they know the value of that Victorian ideal, whether or not they actually subscribe to such patriarchal logic. Both Mrs Norton and Mrs Bagnet gain access to power while putatively remaining within the status quo.

Reading Caroline Norton's behavior in terms of the fictional Mrs Bagnet highlights the fact that Norton embraces and strategically employs the tension that exists between the various roles and plots she can utilize—in her life and in her writings. Indeed, her political pamphlets and her melodramatic novel suggest a variety of strategies by which a woman can plot the course of her marriage even as they suggest that Norton is consciously and strategically deploying the tensions inherent in the role of Victorian wife. In *Laws for Women* Norton seems perfectly happy to appeal to the law for protection; she seems as comfortable with its paternalism as Mrs Bagnet is with her husband's fiction that she is only articulating his opinions for him, rather than telling him what to think and how to behave. We do not stop to wonder whether Mrs Bagnet really believes in the role her husband has created for her (or is it a role she has created for him?) any more than we wonder how she feels about the constant tribute to her abilities that he makes to everyone but her, everywhere but to her face. We do not wonder about these things because there is no such thing as how Mrs Bagnet really feels, because there is no such thing as Mrs Bagnet. She is words on a page, a fictional construct, just as the fiction that upholds their marriage is a rhetorical strategy that Dickens crafted. By the same token, the wife whose plight Norton chronicles in *English Laws for Women* is also a construct, and the exact nature of the politics she espouses in that text is also a strategy rather than a verifiable actuality.

If we resist the temptation to privilege the story Norton unfolds in *English Laws for Women* because it is what she calls a "Story of Real Life," if we read this melodrama in the same way we read a Dickens novel, we can see that her stance is no more to be questioned than Mrs Bagnet's real feelings are to be discovered (*English Laws for Women* 141). Rather, they are texts to be analyzed, and their writers employ strategies that we can interrogate, not beliefs we need to verify. This approach helps us see that Caroline Norton scripts for herself a daughterly reliance on a paternalistic law, just as she chooses to depict herself in the role of passive heroine. In contrast, we can see that Dickens scripts for Edith a much more rebellious role. While the melodramatic role Norton chooses ultimately leads her to valorize the protectionist ethos of the doctrine of coverture, Dickens, in casting Edith's actions in the melodramatic mode in much the same fashion, concentrates instead on the energy necessary to escape the paternalism of marriage in the nineteenth century. Both Mary Poovey and Elaine Hadley convincingly demonstrate that Norton performs a passivity that flies in the face of her otherwise active and rebellious behavior. Dickens, on the other hand, writes for his heroine a role that employs the melodramatic mode to demonstrate the glaring inequities built into the Victorian construction of marriage. Working within a genre that privileges the triumph of good over evil, he creates an Edith who follows through on her threats against the patriarchal confines of the house of Dombey. Instead of writing a plot that eventually turns Edith into a passive angel, he lets her out of the house in order to expose the evils within the domestic sphere. And he lets her stay out.

That we find a plot that more closely accords with our ideas of feminist behavior and more completely satisfies our demands for ideological upheaval in a Dickens novel rather than in what we might call a feminist tract suggests something of historical moment about Dickens's strategy of representation and his particular deployment of the melodramatic mode. This is something that will, I hope, mark the beginning of a new appreciation for the plots he fashions, a new awareness of the potential inherent in the excesses and exaggerations of melodrama for creating socially revisionary work, and the beginning of a new kind of inquiry into the many strands of the Woman Question and those who posed it.

Notes

1   Lisa Surridge describes Edith as "a threat that loomed on the Victorian horizon: the aggressive feminist claiming equality or independence" (65).

2   Micael M. Clarke argues that Thackeray also turned Norton's life into fiction. She suggests that Norton is the "original" of *Barry Lyndon*'s Lady Lyndon, *Vanity Fair*'s Becky Sharp, and *The Newcomes*'s Clara Pulleyn. She also suggests that Norton's life story "exemplified" for Thackeray "the injustices under which women lived" and thus contributed to his "remarkably liberal views regarding the nineteenth-century women's movement" (333).

3   Kathleen Tillotson argues that Carker's revenge plot is written as a melodrama and that Carker is a rather typical melodramatic villain. However, while this plot necessarily involves Edith, she insists that Edith does not belong in a melodramatic plot: "Melodrama is Carker's native air, but it is not Edith's. Perhaps the single flaw in this novel is that Dickens, having conceived a character so complex as hers—behaving so consistently with her nature and situation and yet producing such exciting turns of the action— allows her to be drawn into a sphere which distorts her effect" (177). In *The Dickens Pantomime*, Edwin Eigner argues that *Dombey*, like all the novels from *Nickleby* on, is structured so that it "chang[es] genres every five installments." Thus, the first quarter is pathetic (Paul Dombey's section), the second and third are melodramatic, during which "the melodrama grows, at first somewhat comically, and then, following the catastrophe of the 'keystone,' the precise center of a Dickens novel, it takes on greater and greater seriousness until the fifteenth number, when a melodramatic climax is reached" (30). While Tillotson and Eigner think quite carefully about the conventions of melodrama as they apply to *Dombey*, they both find that that generic label applies only to the Edith–Carker plot. Similarly, Amanda Anderson focuses on this strand of the plot in her argument about the way in which Dickens spectacularizes and exposes the plight of the fallen woman. Anderson's argument has much in common with mine, particularly her assertion that "Edith's 'melodramatic' moments constitute the most heightened display of her commodity status and, more important, establish a troubling inverse relation

between self-reflexivity and interiority, between reading the self and having a self." Ultimately, however, she is more interested in the way in which melodrama "gives expression not to a stable embodiment of vice or virtue but to a form of perpetually falling selfhood" (*Tainted Souls* 85). While Anderson's is a supple critique of the melodramatic mode in *Dombey* and while she naturally focuses on Edith's and Alice's plots in her study of fallen women, I am struck by the fact that she, too, reads Edith's plot as somehow separate from the rest of the novel, both generically and structurally.

Other critics who comment on the melodrama in *Dombey* include John Carey, who makes fun of "the preposterous melodrama" of the scenes between Edith and Carker and finds the picture of Edith "spurning her bosom" "ridiculous" (60–61); and F.R. Leavis, who complains that the novel serves as "license for endlessly overworked pathos, for lush unrealities of high moral insistence, for childish elaborations of sensational plot, and for all the disqualifying characteristics (a serious theme being proposed) of melodrama" and bewails the "unreal" characterization of Edith. "It is impossible to make moral sense of her attitude towards her marriage, and only in the world of melodramatic rhetoric could there be any illusion to the contrary," he declares (Carey 60–61, F.R. Leavis 2, 24). Similarly, William Axton finds that "Edith's speech, with its elaborate parallelisms, rhetorical questions, elevated diction, and heroic metaphors, carries with it as strong an odor of gaslight and painted canvas as her stylized gestures and the stagey blocking" of Edith and Carker (152). For a vigorous defense of such staginess, see George Worth's *Dickensian Melodrama*; Worth argues that in *Dombey* "melodramatic features are largely shifted from the speech of the characters to the language of the narrator," but offers little perspective on how the melodramatic mode reflects and shapes gender politics (25).

4   This account also explains why Dombey is rehabilitated, rather than exorcised, at the end of the novel.

5   Edith's connection to fire is suggested by the narrator's tendency to employ images of conflagrations barely under control when describing her. She is "a lady ... in whom some passion or struggle was raging" (458). "Concentrated into one handsome face" is "the burning indignation of a hundred women" (472). She declaims "with a burning brow" and "flashing eyes" (473). The beginning of Chapter 47, "The Thunderbolt," (a natural phenomenon that also produces fire) describes the "flinty opposition" between Edith and her husband that "struck out fire between them which might smoulder or might blaze, as circumstances were, but burned up everything within their mutual reach, and made their marriage way a road of ashes" (736). When Edith and Carker meet at Dijon, Carker is afraid of her "towering fury" and of the "intense abhorrence sparkling in her eyes and lighting up her brow." These portents of her anger "made him stop as if a fire had stopped him" (854). When she reminds him of "how often" he "fanned the fire on which for two years, I have writhed," we begin to suspect that the fire of her marriage has caught hold of her, that she is now being burned up by what "has most tortured me" (856). Accordingly, Edith is described throughout this chapter as if she were on fire, "with eyes that seemed to sparkle fire" and a resolve to "die and make no sign," as if she were prepared to immolate herself if it would guarantee her revenge against Dombey and Carker (860).

6   This is neither the first time Dickens has told the story of a mercenary marriage, nor are
     the specific contours of Edith's plot new to Dickens. Her situation has much in common
     with that of Oliver Twist's father in that she allows herself to be forced into a loveless,
     mercenary marriage by a plotting parent, only to leave that marriage when it becomes
     unbearable, and go on to commit shameful acts for which she is made to pay dearly.
     Similarly, if we read Edith as a victim of her mother's machinations, we can see the
     way in which her plot echoes and amplifies the plight of Madeline Bray in *Nicholas
     Nickleby*. By the same token, Dickens's plot for Edith follows through on the aborted
     plot that Ralph Nickleby tries to arrange, in concert with Sir Mulberry Hawk, for his
     niece Kate, and it is a more carefully planned and executed version of the marriage that
     Frederick Trent tries to plot between his sister Nell and Dick Swiveller.

7   Mary Lyndon Shanley argues that this is an inaccurate, even deluded, view of the
     institution of marriage, reminding us that

> when Victorian feminists began their crusade to change the laws regulating
> marriage, they explicitly and forcefully challenged what they regarded as
> society's sentimentalization of family life. They would have looked askance at
> the interpretation of many modern historians that "companionate marriage"—
> characterized by "affective individualism," "romantic love," and "a conscious
> ideological egalitarianism"—was the norm in both England and the United States
> by the mid-nineteenth century. (*Feminism, Marriage, and the Law* 7 and see
> n.12).

While historians like Lawrence Stone and Carl Degler insist that the nineteenth century
was marked by what we might calls the rise of the affectionate or companionate
marriage, Victorian marriage law flatly contradicts such a rosy view of the institution
(as does John Stuart Mill, as I argue in the Introduction).

8   Or, as Amy Dorrit insists, "if you loved any one, you would no more be yourself, but
     you would quite lose and forget yourself in your devotion to him" (*Little Dorrit* 648).

9   Edith seems to be referring to the practice of wife-sale, which was used in England
     from the sixteenth through the nineteenth centuries as a form of self-divorce. Lawrence
     Stone explains that

> the details of the ritual were designed to emphasize the final nature of the transfer
> of property, by imitating as closely as possible the sale of a cow or a sheep.
> A halter was used to lead the wife from her home to the market, and from the
> market to the house of the purchaser; money was paid in exchange for her; and
> the seller paid the clerk of the market a toll for his wife, just as he would have
> done if he had sold a cow. To make the parallel with a cattle sale closer still, some
> early sales even involved the nominal selling of the wife by her weight. (145)

E.P. Thompson, in his essay on the subject, finds that "the consensus of mid nineteenth-
century enlightened opinion was that the practice [of wife sale] existed only amongst
the lowest stratum of the labourers" and "that the wife sale was most strongly supported

in … plebeian or proto-industrial communities," suggesting that Edith is insulting Dombey's class status here, as well as her own status as commodity. Thompson also argues that "the halter was central to the ritual" and "that it was a shaming ritual for the wife is explicit in the ritual" (413, 446, 419, 448).

10 Karen Chase and Michael Levenson argue that "we can now look back on the struggle to pass the Infant Custody Bill as the first Victorian attempt to reform family law. The ultimate passage of the legislation would open the way for the reform of the divorce law and the law of married women's property later in the century," though they hasten to add that "in 1837 history had not yet revealed its intentions. For Norton the decision to publish her views on custody was an anxious new movement into the civic space" (40).

11 Feminist readings of *Dombey* that acknowledge its undermining of the doctrine of separate spheres include Jeff Nunokawa's chapter in *The Afterlife of Property*; Jonathan Loesberg's "Deconstruction, Historicism, and Overdetermination: Dislocations of the Marriage Plots in *Robert Elsmere* and *Dombey and Son*," Hilary Schor's chapter in *Dickens and the Daughter of the House*; Helene Moglen's "Theorizing Fiction/ Fictionalizing Theory: The Case of *Dombey and Son*," and Nina Auerbach's "Dickens and Dombey: A Daughter After All."

12 Perkins thanks Norton's grandchildren for their "kind hospitality" and for giving her access to letters, family pictures, and "a scrap-book," which, in addition to "personal recollections of Mrs. Norton" "have greatly aided me in my work" (v). As this indebtedness suggests, Perkins's biography is something of an appreciation, but it is also styled as an attempt to replace Norton in the canon as a poetess and novelist and to re-enshrine her as a reformer of the laws affecting "her own kind" (xiv). Perhaps most importantly, however, and certainly crucial to keep in mind for my purposes, Perkins begins *The Life of Mrs. Norton* by describing her subject as "a beautiful, unfortunate woman, the target of a great deal of cruel scandal, ill remembered, but never quite forgotten" (xiii). In contrast, Norton's most recent biographer, Alan Chedzoy, celebrates Norton's infamy, titling his biography *A Scandalous Woman*.

13 I do not mean to suggest that Litvak is wrong to draw our attention to moments of theatricality that need to be deconstructed in terms of sincerity and authenticity. In fact, I find his argument about theatricality in the Victorian novel highly suggestive. My point is that a distinction between theatricality and dramatization is extremely useful here. Although the two terms have been collapsed of late, it is important to register that Edith's and Eleanor's behavior is dramatic, not theatrical. Indeed, Norton's and Dickens's strategy is to present their heroines' melodramatic behavior as natural so that they can present their marriages as paradigms, so that we can read them for what they reveal about the institution of Victorian marriage.

14 See Storey's and Tillotson's preface to volume 8 of the Pilgrim *Letters of Charles Dickens*, especially xiii.

15 Hadley defines domestic melodrama as "a subgenre that focused on the trials and tribulations of women both good and bad" (133). Martha Vicinus describes it as "the working out in popular culture of the conflict between the family and its values and the economic and social assault of industrialization" (128).

16 The letters that formed the principal portion of the plaintiff's evidence were completely innocent of the slightest suggestion of any sort of liaison between Melbourne and Caroline Norton. Dickens used these letters as the basis for the comically non-incriminating letters written by Pickwick to his landlady and used as evidence in *Bardell* v. *Pickwick*.

17 If he had been found guilty, he would have been forced to resign, which would quite possibly have toppled the government. George and his Tory friends would have benefited greatly from such a turn of events.

18 Dickens also advertised his failed marriage in *The Times*. For the full text of his statement, see Dickens, *Letters* 8: 744.

19 Mary Poovey argues that Norton published *Laws for Women* (and also her 1855 pamphlet, *A Letter to the Queen on Lord Chancellor Cranworth's Marriage and Divorce Bill*) in order to get back at her husband, at Melbourne for being more concerned about his political reputation and the discomfort the trial would bring to the young queen, and at the government that buried the story of her innocence for political reasons. Such a strategy brings to mind Edith's elopement with Carker—a move that costs her her reputation but is designed to pay back her husband for his betrayal. See *Uneven Developments*, especially 65–6.

20 As Surridge argues, "far from buttressing middle-class status by portraying the lower classes or the gentry as violent, *Dombey and Son* worked to expose domestic violence in the middle-class home" (54).

Chapter 4
Estranging *David Copperfield*

Halfway through *David Copperfield*, in the chapter in which David becomes engaged to Dora (in fact, just a week before he proposes), David observes a divorce case at Doctors' Commons. One Thomas Benjamin appears before the court and sues, successfully, for a divorce under what David calls "an ingenious little statute" (391). This "statute" is actually the loophole created by the sloppy wording of the Marriage Act of 1753, wording that "made null and void any marriage in which there was the slightest mistake, however trivial or accidental, in the wording of the banns or license with respect to age" and thus "accidentally opened up a new avenue for self-divorce ... pushed up the number of nullities in the London Consistory Court and created scandal by giving the appearance of being the equivalent of divorces" (Stone 132).[1] Thomas Benjamin's divorce has nothing to do with age, but rather rests on the fact that his name on the marriage license appears simply as "Thomas." As David puts the matter, Thomas Benjamin conveniently leaves off his last name

> in case he should not find himself as comfortable as he expected. Not finding himself as comfortable as he expected, or being a little fatigued with his wife, poor fellow, he now came forward by a friend, after being married a year or two, and declared that his name was Thomas Benjamin, and therefore he was not married at all. Which the Court confirmed, to his great satisfaction. (391)

That Dickens addresses the legal loophole which David—in a moment of ironic foreshadowing, given that he will soon "not find himself as comfortable as he expected" in his own marriage—calls "an ingenious little statute" is more than a little interesting given my argument in this chapter, but even more significant is the fact that while this process is, strictly speaking, an annulment, David calls Benjamin's case a "divorce-suit," thus echoing that panic Lawrence Stone identifies on the part of Londoners who perceived—correctly—that men and women were being allowed legally to put an end to their marriages, despite the fact that divorce would not be written into law until 1857. That panic shapes and informs the many plots of *David Copperfield* and gives rise to the despairing depictions of marriage which permeate the novel—marriages fraught with anxiety and lacking in trust, marriages between people who apparently could not be more incompatible. From the foolishness of Dora and David and the improvidence of Wilkins and Emma Micawber to the suspicion which characterizes the marriage of Annie and Dr Strong and the heartache which marks both the union of Clara and Murdstone and the strange separation of Betsey Trotwood and her rake of a husband, Dickens's most autobiographical novel is concerned in a multiplicity of ways with the institution of marriage and the miseries it causes. Appearing in the year that saw the formation of a Royal Commission to study the state of marriage and divorce law—a commission formed in large part because, as I discuss in Chapter 1, so many people were managing to obtain divorces despite the fact that they were, strictly speaking, illegal—*David Copperfield* both participates in and reacts against the general unrest which resulted in the legalization of divorce seven years later.

Thus my claim: *David Copperfield* is a novel of adultery, of second marriages, and of what *Hard Times'* Stephen Blackpool will, four years later, call "th' supposed unpossibility o' ever getting unchained from one another" (57). *David Copperfield* is, in fact, a novel of divorce. This is a surprising claim, to be sure, but if it is true that no one can remember reading *David Copperfield* for the first time, if the novel is so very familiar, then perhaps it is our familiarity with it that makes this claim seem so surprising—that numbs us to the suggestions of desire and the stories of divorce that it inadvertently tells. Alexander Welsh maintains that "the main action of *David Copperfield* might be described as the replacement of one wife by another," and by estranging the novel, by fracturing our familiarity with it, perhaps we can arrive at a reading which recognizes the vast amounts of time and energy the novel puts into determining just how such a replacement might be effected (*From Copyright to Copperfield* 125). We can, in other words, begin to recognize just how emblematic Thomas Benjamin's "divorce-suit" is.

The usual claim is that *Copperfield* is a novel about marriage in a very traditional sense. According to Hillis Miller, "*David Copperfield* is the first of [Dickens's] novels to organize itself around the complexities of romantic love. For the first time, marriage, in a more than conventional way, is seen as offering a solution to the problem of solitude and dispossession" (*Charles Dickens* 150). It seems to me, however, that *Copperfield* presents us with a view of marriage as an institution that does not solve problems of identity and selfhood, but rather creates such problems, as the string of marriages with which we are presented in this novel serves to illustrate. What is it, then, about the novel that leads critics to assert the primacy and efficacy of marriage in its plotting? After all, this is a novel in which a woman—Emma Micawber—reads over her vows by the light of a candle to ascertain whether or not she can leave her husband. This is a novel in which Miss Betsey Trotwood leaves her husband and assumes her maiden name; a novel in which the hero is an apprentice at Doctors' Commons, the ecclesiastical court which deals with all legal aspects of marriage, including divorce; and in which Dora bequeaths her husband to his second wife, and David is rewarded with Agnes. This is a novel that endorses, encourages, even preaches the wisdom and rightness of second marriages. Miller is right in his assertion that marriage is presented as the solution in this novel, but it is not a final solution. The temporary nature of marriage in *Copperfield* suggests that the novel is more about desertion than unity, more about separation than marriage. David fantasizes about never having married Dora. Emma Micawber's frequent declaration, "I never will desert

Mr Micawber," leads us to suspect that she protests far too much for us not to attribute a barely repressed desire to her oft-repeated assertion, and further causes us to wonder if, to her, the wish is not almost as good as the deed. Furthermore, Aunt Betsey does leave her husband, while Little Em'ly deserts her fiancé, her home, and the only family she has ever known. Similarly, Clara Murdstone and Dora Copperfield desert their husbands through the benevolent agency of death.

That *Copperfield* immediately follows *Dombey and Son*—itself a novel that centers around the failed marriage of Edith and Paul Dombey and that takes as its focal point Edith's desertion of her husband—is not unimportant. One could argue that *Copperfield* distributes and disperses *Dombey*'s climactic point, taking the spectacle of a marriage's dissolution and making it part of the novel's very texture. Whereas marriage's failure is presented in *Dombey and Son* as a highly melodramatic and isolated occurrence (albeit one we are to read paradigmatically), *David Copperfield* portrays the end of marriage as something less than an event, certainly not at all spectacular, melodramatic, or theatrical. In *Copperfield*, the end of a marriage is common and commonplace, frequent and frequently unnoticed, an occurrence to be expected—almost a part of the usual order of things.

Furthermore, although there are no instances of adultery and, as we have seen, only one divorce in the novel, the very lack of such explicit occurrences serves to highlight the degree to which both adultery and divorce are presented as desired and, although obliquely, desirable. If, as Ruth Yeazell contends, the English novel refuses to deal explicitly with instances of sexual misconduct such as adultery, then this studious inattention must be recognized; the novel's silence on these subjects is one to which we must learn to listen. In "Podsnappery, Sexuality, and the English Novel," Yeazell observes that "English novels tell of awakening consciousness, not sexual acts" and, like Podsnap in *Our Mutual Friend*, they continually invoke the ever-present "cheek of the young person" in order to avoid the discussion of any subject that might suggest a consciousness of things sexual (346). Following Foucault, Yeazell points out that censorship of this sort is a titillating technique, since to subject everything to the test of female innocence is "implicitly to convert all knowledge into sexual knowledge, to translate every possible speech into the very language which no Young Person may hear" (340).[2] If things sexual cannot be mentioned, then they are to be found everywhere. Yeazell's conclusion, and my point of departure for this chapter—"the silences of the novel are part of its discourse"—points out just how telling it is that we are given no adulterous relationships and only one brief glimpse of what seems almost a sham divorce in Dickens's 1850 study of divorce (357). The Podsnappish silence that *David Copperfield* (and David Copperfield, for that matter) preserves on the subject of extramarital sexual desire is an indication of just how vitally concerned the novel is with such desires.

My aim in this chapter is to provide a way of listening to the novel's silences, a way that shows that, rather than preserving a prudish silence on subjects like adultery and divorce, *David Copperfield* actually never stops talking about such things. The structure of the novel encourages us to preserve the Podsnappish silence, distributing our attention in such a way that we are encouraged to read over its suggestions of desire. Estranging the novel will allow us to read it in a fashion which is alert to these suggestive, nervous silences—silences which bespeak a competing vision, silences which point to another novel buried beneath the surface of the fiction we are so accustomed to reading. Learning to listen for what is suggested rather than said, for the indications of desire Dickens liberally places throughout *Copperfield* is, in fact, the way to understand the extent to which this novel exposes the inequities of nineteenth-century marriage. Sexual desire, failed marriage, divorce—these are, to use Frank Kermode's terminology, the sorts of narrative secrets the novel encourages us to ignore.[3]

However, the novel does not preserve a total silence where sexuality is concerned; that silence is broken, significantly enough, in order to discuss another forbidden instance of sexuality—that occasioned by the fallen woman. The stories of Martha Endell and Little Em'ly provide an opportunity for moralizing about the evils of desire, while maintaining a marked distance from the carefully protected realms of hearth and home. These narratives serve as screen stories that deflect our attention from the real concern of the novel—the possibility of remarriage—by taking up the question of extramarital desire in a way that is decidedly removed from the environs of the established and revered institution of marriage. Fallen women are separate and separated from marriageable women. Dan Peggotty will not let his niece Emily associate with Martha, although they had been friends and co-workers. Even Ham describes Martha as someone that Little Em'ly "doen't ought to know no more" (273). Women of such ilk are kept at a distance from those who have entered, or may soon enter, into the sacred institution of marriage.[4] Thus they can safely be used as vehicles through which to explore that side of Victorian morals which Steven Marcus terms "other."[5] Similarly, Dickens made much of his involvement with fallen women at Urania Cottage, but shrank from the publicity his own separation received, even though, as we saw in the previous chapter, he invited the public's interest in his failed marriage by publicly announcing it in *The Times* and in *Household Words*. Even more striking is his refusal to divorce his wife and his fear of the publicity that Catherine's attempt to divorce him would surely create.[6]

Divorce is a taboo subject for the Victorian novel (which is not to say that it is a subject the novel does not admit, but rather that it represents it as something beyond the pale, scandalous, and proscribed) and a relative impossibility under Victorian law for reasons that are markedly Podsnappish. As Leo Bersani points out, "realistic fiction serves nineteenth-century society by providing it with strategies for containing (and repressing) its disorder within significantly structured stories about itself" (63). The marriage plot is traditionally seen as establishing closure, as insuring the social order. For this reason the divorce plot is rare in the Victorian novel and is almost always a subplot; it is also a reliably scandalous plot, in large part because divorce bespeaks the existence of extramarital desire within a marriage. Divorce is thus as sexual and as "not English" a subject as adultery or procreation precisely because the granting of a divorce would make available a relationship that was, in some sense, adulterous.[7] Furthermore (and quite ironically), well into the twentieth century adultery itself was the only grounds for divorce. In other words, the subject of divorce goes beyond the suggestion of extramarital desire, beyond the possibility of adulterous inclinations, and suggests a way of obtaining the satisfaction and validation of such desires. Fallen women are punished and shunned; they are clear indices of a society that will not tolerate such advertisements of sexuality. Divorce, on the other hand, asks society to condone a desire that ignores the enclosed institution of matrimony, a desire that flaunts its rejection of the tacitly agreed-upon code of behavior, a desire that threatens to overthrow the hegemony of sexuality that a Podsnap would preserve at all costs.

It thus seems that *David Copperfield* is implicitly obsessed with the dissolution of marriage, whether the severing of this tie takes place in fantasy, reality, or fiction. More particularly, it is almost obscenely interested in the phenomenon of wives who leave their husbands. That is, while Bersani points to the way in which the nineteenth-century novel provides strategies (plots, conventions) for "containing" and "repressing" the disorder of society, *Copperfield* can only barely contain the disorder signaled by the failure of marriage. This chapter is engaged in the process of estranging the novel, of making it unfamiliar so that we might read the plots of divorce and desertion buried beneath the novel's more familiar, conventional plots, so that we can see just how much effort it takes to keep those plots under control. In order to make strange *David Copperfield*, then, I turn my attention to the women who want to leave their husbands—Dora Copperfield, Emma Micawber, and Betsey Trotwood—and their repressed plots of marital unhappiness.

What Dora Knew

Like the little heroine of Henry James's *What Maisie Knew* (1897), Dora knows a great deal more than her elders give her credit for. She is aware of her shortcomings, both before and after she marries, aware of David's love for Agnes, aware of Agnes's greater and prior claim to her husband, aware that she is dying when all those around her try desperately to deny it, and aware that her husband is much too hard on her, that he is changing the rules of the game in mid-play. And most importantly, like Maisie, Dora knows something of the secrets of unhappy marriage, of divorce, and of remarriage. But one crucial difference between Maisie Farange and Dora Copperfield is that while the adults in Maisie's life—her parents and their lovers—intuit the extent of her knowledge and are curiously charmed by all she knows, the adults in Dora's life prefer to act as if she really were the child she asks to be called. It is not surprising that the one adult in James's *What Maisie Knew* who does not realize that Maisie is so prescient, her nurse, Mrs Wix, is the one character who is implicitly Dickensian and explicitly reminiscent of *Copperfield*. Indeed, Mrs Beale, Maisie's stepmother, says of Mrs Wix: "like Mrs Micawber—whom she must, I think, rather resemble—she will never, never, never desert Miss Farange" (113). That Mrs Wix is said to resemble Mrs Micawber is telling, for the comparison brings to mind unhappy marriages, powerless wives, and overblown sentiment, not to mention misplaced devotion. Above all, the fact that the James novel which explores the effects of divorce upon children should hearken back to Dickens's divorce novel leads us to question the connection between knowledge and childhood.[8] For if Maisie knows more than a child of her age perhaps should, if she knows more than anyone can quite believe, then might not the same be true of David's child-wife?

Dora's knowledge is most clearly revealed on her deathbed. Her dying words to her husband make it clear just how much she realized during her brief wedded life: "But, as years went on, my dear boy would have wearied of his child-wife. She would have been less and less a companion for him. He would have been more and more sensible of what was wanting in his home" (627). This prophecy encourages us to view her death as an escape from marriage, an escape for which she is eager, perhaps even more eager than David. For it is painfully clear that these words are an indictment of their marriage as it is and was, rather than as what it might become. The proper tense is actually the present, rather than the future, a fact which is made evident by David's response: "Oh, Dora, dearest, dearest, do not speak to me so. Every word seems a reproach!" (627). He takes her words not as a warning about what their marriage would have become, but as an indictment of their past and present married life. And every word of Dora's is an implicit reproach to him, for she thus indicates that he has made it clear that he wants to erase their marriage.

It is also important to note that Dora has been just as aware of their incompatibility as David, a fact she makes clear to him before she dies: "I loved you far too well, to say a reproachful word to you, in earnest—it was all the merit I had, except being pretty—or you thought me so" (627). This pathetic admission of her limited appeal is a stinging and not entirely implicit reproach, for Dora is really saying that she was made to feel that her only virtues were a pretty face and an ability to hold her tongue. These are virtues straight out of a Victorian conduct book; in *The Wives of England: Their Relative Duties, Domestic Influence, and Social Obligations*, Sarah Stickney Ellis preaches that it "is unquestionably the inalienable right of all men, whether ill or well, rich or poor, wise or foolish, to be treated with deference, and made much of in their own houses" (1:28). Dora has subscribed to this doctrine, or at least she has played along with the game. But in her deathbed confession it becomes clear that she is reproaching David for wanting both a child-wife and a companion. This is, of course, a paradox built into the cultural climate of the day. On the one hand, Mrs Ellis advises wives to be ciphers:

> It is unquestionably the best policy then for a bride to be in all things the opposite of eccentric. Her character, if she have any, will develop itself in time; and nothing can be gained, though much may be lost, by exhibiting its peculiarities before they are likely to be candidly judged or rightly understood. (1:19)

But wives should also be educated, intelligent companions for their husbands:

> If, then, a husband finds in his wife a degree of ignorance which renders her
> incapable of judging rightly in common things, if he finds that she has never
> made any proper use of her powers of observation, that she has not been in
> the habit of thinking to any rational purpose, of discriminating, comparing, or
> drawing right conclusions from what she has seen and heard, it would be hard
> indeed to require him to believe that she will act with prudence and propriety
> as the mistress of a house; and the natural consequence is, that she must be
> watched, suspected, and in some degree treated as a child … If, therefore … I
> have earnestly recommended to the Daughters of England an early, and diligent
> cultivation of their mental powers, it has not been that such embellishments of
> character … should merely give zest to conversation, or throw an intellectual
> charm over the society of the drawing-room; it is that the happy individual who
> possesses these advantages, may, on becoming a wife, become also a companion
> in which her husband can perfectly, and at all times, confide. (1:39)

Dora is not, at least in David's eyes, "a companion in which [he] can perfectly, and
at all times, confide" and thus, according to Mrs Ellis (and David), she "must be
watched, suspected, and in some degree treated as a child" or at least as a child-
wife. But Dora speaks in her own defense and in the defense of all wives who are
taught to fill such a paradoxical role when she asks at the end of this confession,
"Is it lonely down-stairs, Doady?… Is my chair there?" (627). She thus reminds her
husband that she has been his companion, that she will leave a void in his life, that
she has been a wife to him, rather than a mere plaything. Dora will not be easily
discarded, and despite the fact that she paves the way for her replacement, she
does not do so without first reminding her husband that she will be missed. Thus,
on her deathbed we see the extent of her knowledge, both of David's complaints
against her and of her true value to him.

Indeed, long before Dora miscarries, sickens, and dies, we can see that she
is not merely a "Little Blossom," not simply the pet that David and Aunt Betsey
make of her, but that she is, rather, a perceptive young woman. Dora is wise in that
she realizes long before David does that she probably cannot make him happy and
that this inability to be a proper companion is due to the quality of her education.
Dora's realization of her inadequacies comes after she first meets Agnes, and, as
Michael Slater has astutely noted, her growing sense of her deficiencies "implies
a dawning awareness that her own upbringing and social conditioning, though it
has been everything that is considered fitting for a young lady, has nevertheless
stunted her in some very damaging way" (248). Genuinely perplexed that David
should have fallen in love with her, rather than with Agnes, Dora tries to solve
this riddle, but David refuses to take her questions seriously and instead focuses
on her girlish sexual attractiveness. When she asks "Don't you think, if I had had
her for a friend a long time ago, Doady, I might have been more clever perhaps?"
David is concentrating on "her bright eyes shining very brightly, and her little right

hand idly busying itself with one of the buttons of my coat" rather than on the seriousness with which she asks such a revealing question (499). The fiancé who, just one chapter before, was afraid "that I had fallen into the general fault, and treated her like a plaything too" now refuses to take her legitimate fears seriously and responds to her questions with such patronizing answers as "What nonsense!" and "Suppose we had never been born!" (495, 499–500). Not surprisingly, the whole of this exchange is given to us by David with more stress laid on Dora's body than on her mind. While she wrestles with a sense of her own inadequacies and the clear discrepancy between herself and Agnes as potential wives for David, he is concentrating on her physical self. This split is clear throughout their dialogue, but it is most disturbingly clear when he professes to consider the nature of her thoughts for a moment: "I wondered what she was thinking about, as I glanced in admiring silence at the little soft hand travelling up the row of buttons on my coat, and at the clustering hair that lay against my breast, and at the lashes of her downcast eyes, slightly rising as they followed her idle fingers" (500). While Dora is wondering why David wants to marry her, she is providing him with the answer. As Alexander Welsh discerns, David "married only for sex" (*From Copyright to Copperfield* 136). David is so interested in Dora's body (and in what she is doing to his own body) that he misses the import of her questions. Similarly, Dora has been so acculturated that she cannot ask these questions of her fiancé without involving her body, which is the answer to her own questions.

The eroticism of the passage buries the dialogue and causes us—and David— to treat Dora's grammatical questions as if they were merely rhetorical. Dora's attempt to discover the nature of David's attraction to her is unsuccessful because he is more interested in what she is doing to his buttons. Literally and figuratively, Dora's education has taught her how to push the right buttons, but the lessons prove to be useless once the courtship is over. Dora knows well enough how to use her charms to entrance her fiancé, but she does not know how to deal with him in ways other than those that emphasize her sexuality. Yet she suspects that this is a knowledge worth having; the fact that she even attempts to discover the reason David prefers her to Agnes suggests that "dawning awareness."

This awareness seems to have further developed on their wedding day, for as they drive away after the ceremony Dora asks her new husband, "Are you happy now, you foolish boy? ... and sure you don't repent?" (517). The words "foolish" and "repent" have a resonance about them, not unlike Aunt Betsey's awful "blind, blind, blind." "Foolish" is what Dora has so often been called and so often asks to be called, but in this instance she wisely applies the epithet to her husband, who will soon come to suspect that he was indeed a "foolish boy" to marry Dora. "Repent" brings to mind Congreve's "Married in haste, we may repent at leisure," which is an accurate assessment of the situation they find themselves in after the wedding. And these wise predictions and accurate judgments belong to Dora. In fact, wisdom in the guise of foolishness seems to be Dora's chief characteristic throughout her married life. Aware of her inadequacies, both because she is perceptive and because David is transparent in his dissatisfaction with her, she seeks to compensate for them by asserting them all the more strenuously, as if she hopes to discount the gravity of her shortcomings by constant allusion to them. This endeavor is responsible for the "child-wife" mythology she creates as a form of self-defense:

> "When you are going to be angry with me, say to yourself, 'it's only my child-wife!' When I am very disappointing, say, 'I knew, a long time ago, that she would make but a child-wife!' When you miss what I should like to be, and I think can never be, say, 'still my foolish child-wife loves me!'" (526)

By indicating her insecurity about "what I should like to be, and I think can never be" she acknowledges her failings and transfers responsibility for them onto David. This approach also serves to remind David of his earlier fear ("that I had fallen into the general fault and treated her like a plaything too"), which he refused to act upon. Thus, poetic justice is served: because of his earlier refusal to take her seriously, she now refuses to be taken seriously. By admitting her failure as a wife, Dora tries to avoid being taxed with her failure.

Though she knows the extent of her failure all too well, what Dora does not know is how to turn herself into the wife David demands she become. So Dora compensates in the only way she knows: she relies on her love for David and on the beauty that occasioned his love. Her advice to him, "say, 'still my foolish child-wife loves me!'" is her last hope for establishing their marriage on a more solid footing. She reminds her husband four chapters later, after more attempts on his part to "form her mind," that it is hopeless to rely on her to be anything but a sexual companion. Yet again, as Dora tries to make clear to her husband the extent of her capabilities, he sees more than he hears:

> "It's not a bit of use," said Dora, shaking her head, until the earrings rang again. "You know what a little thing I am, and what I wanted you to call me from the first. If you can't do so, I am afraid you'll never like me. Are you sure you don't think, sometimes, it would have been better to have—"
> "Done what, my dear?" For she made no effort to proceed.
> "Nothing!" said Dora. (567)

David sees the "pretty enquiry of the raised eyebrows" and "the parted lips" and misses the import of the half-question Dora cannot bring herself to articulate completely (567). To have done nothing does not mean, as David thinks, "it would have been better to have done nothing than to have tried to form my little wife's mind" but rather it literally means to have done nothing, not to have married. But these thoughts cannot be admitted, for to admit the truth of Dora's half-uttered suggestion would be to admit the question of divorce into the newlyweds' cottage.

The fact remains, however, that Dora tries to raise the issue; she looks squarely at the nature of their troubles, as she has been trying to do from the moment she first met Agnes. Dora, like Maisie, knows when the threat of divorce has entered her house. And she is not made nervous by the thought of divorce and second marriage like the guilt-stricken David is. Rather, Dora effects her own divorce and paves the way for her husband's marriage to Agnes; she dies for David's convenience.[9] Embracing death allows her a way out of a marriage in which she is constantly made to feel like a failure, and allows her still-precious Doady to find happiness with Agnes. Dora graciously allows him to remarry by leaving him in such a way as to preserve his reputation and ensure his marriage to Agnes, while guaranteeing that she will be free of him in a way that nothing else but a legal divorce (which was unavailable to her) would make possible.[10] Her last words to Agnes make it clear that her death is a self-willed flight from the unbearable, a muted, self-sacrificing version of Edith's flight from Dombey. These last words are her request that, in Agnes's words, "only I would occupy this vacant place," and they make it clear that what Dora knew was that her husband was in love with their closest friend (708).

Emma Micawber's Fantasy of Desertion

Dora is not the only woman in *David Copperfield* unafraid to confront the possibility of dissolving her marriage. Emma Micawber considers the option on a regular basis, as we learn from the constant repetition of her decision "never [to] desert Mr Micawber." She repeats this conclusion so often that it comes to seem like a verbal tic, even as it suggests that she is continually weighing her options and pondering the possibility of leaving her husband. James Kincaid finds that Emma's verbal tic "is representative of the imaginary resolution with which the family meets imaginary crises" (68). But there is nothing imaginary about her resolution or about the crises in her marriage to the cheerfully improvident Mr Micawber. This is the woman who reads over her marriage vows by candlelight in an attempt to determine whether or not she can "desert Mr Micawber":

> "I am a wife and mother, and I never will desert Mr Micawber ... That," said Mrs Micawber, "that, at least, is my view, my dear Mr Copperfield and Mr Traddles, of the obligation which I took upon myself when I repeated the irrevocable words, 'I, Emma, take thee, Wilkins.' I read the service over with a flat-candle on the previous night, and the conclusion I derived from it was, that I never could desert Mr Micawber." (433)

In this manner, Emma Micawber repeatedly asserts the limitations and restrictions the sacrament of marriage imposes on her. And once we learn that she has studied her options and has discovered herself to be trapped with a husband who "has kept [her] in the dark as to his resources and his liabilities, both," we can see that her repeated assertion of fidelity is actually an admission of powerlessness (138–9). What Emma Micawber really means to say is that she never *can* desert

Mr Micawber, so, of course, she never will. Her tag is not indicative of loyalty, nor is it meant to provide reassurance. Rather, it is a pathetic, repetitive bleat of despair, and we hear it whenever she is especially overwhelmed by the state of her marriage, whenever she is struck anew by the fact that she is trapped.

What I find most striking about Emma Micawber's behavior is not so much the frequency with which she repeats her resolve, but rather the method to which she resorts to determine her options. Reading over one's marriage vows is a most interesting way of determining one's rights, but it is also, judging from her conclusion, a reliable one. And it seems it was not an uncommon thing for Victorian wives to do, or at least to be encouraged to do. Lawrence Stone tells us that "as late as 1808 a popular magazine catering to middle- and upper-class women was urging them to 'read frequently and with close attention the matrimonial service, and take care in doing it not to overlook the word OBEY'" (2). Similarly, we learn from the 1869 case of *Kelly* v. *Kelly* (which was influential in effecting changes in the laws punishing matrimonial cruelty) that such a practice was utilized as a means of taming a disobedient wife: Mr Kelly "repeatedly lectured her on the duties of a wife, read the marriage service to her, and even called in two fellow clergymen to explain the religious basis of a wife's obedience" (qtd in Hammerton, "Victorian Marriage and the Law of Matrimonial Cruelty" 290). What these two examples have in common is their reference to the importance of the word "obey" in the marriage service. It is clear why husbands and domestic magazines, both agents of discipline, were so eager to stress the concept of obedience, along with the Biblical source of the vows themselves, but Emma's recourse to her vows is puzzling, for it seems to partake of the same strategy which these patriarchal forces employed. But Emma reads over her vows not only in an attempt to impose discipline upon herself, but also in an effort to make sure that she really cannot "desert Mr Micawber." Instead of resorting to her vows as a means of strengthening her resolve, Emma seems to refer to the words she repeated on that fateful day in order to check and see if she can leave her husband. The fact that her actions mirror those advised by domestic magazines and tyrannical husbands sheds a rather bright light upon the ways in which the marriage service itself was being examined in the nineteenth century. Emma literally performs what many women were doing figuratively at mid-century: rereading the institution of marriage with an eye to the options and escapes it might possibly afford them. And, for many of these women, the conclusion they were forced to reach—that they could not leave their husbands without being viewed as deserters of their homes and their social positions, and without losing what little rights and property they enjoyed—was hard to accept.

Yet while Emma pays lip service to the "irrevocable" nature of the marriage bond, her behavior stands in stark contrast to that allegiance. If she is completely convinced that the words she spoke when she married Wilkins are irrevocable, then why does she so frequently feel compelled to assert that she will not break her word and dissolve the bond that joins them? And to whom is she making this assertion? When we first hear Emma declare her admirable intentions in

Chapter 12—"'But I never will desert Mr Micawber. No! … I never will do it! It's of no use asking me!'"—we are made to feel as confused and uncomfortable as David, "as if Mrs Micawber supposed I had asked her to do anything of the sort!" (138). And it is true, the question "Who asked you to, indeed?" comes to mind, as it will again and again in the course of the novel. Of course this declaration of loyalty is directed to no one but herself, and it is a response to no one's questionings but her own. The oath of allegiance she is constantly swearing—an oath that only serves to make us more acutely aware of her untenable situation—functions as a kind of mantra for her. To repeat it over and over is to remind herself that she has no choice, unless she would brave the application of the word "desertion" to her actions. Emma believes her marriage is an "obligation" and a peculiarly taxing one, in that it is an obligation she can never discharge.

Yet she still hopes, and the frequency with which she asserts her fidelity is also an indication of the frequency with which she fantasizes about leaving her husband. Each time we are confronted with Emma soliloquizing about her fierce loyalty we are actually seeing the results of her latest indulgence in fantasy. Her pledge of allegiance is the means she employs to bring herself back to reality. And it is no accident that each time we are shown Emma in this state we are also shown the Micawber family in yet another financial catastrophe. David remarks upon Emma Micawber's amazing ability to recover so rapidly from these recurring situations of impending doom—"I have known her to be thrown into fainting fits by the king's taxes at three o'clock, and to eat lamb-chops, breaded, and drink warm ale (paid for with two teaspoons that had gone to the pawnbroker's) at four"—but what he does not comment upon is the source of these mood swings and the fact that she really has no other choice than to enjoy her chops and ale (129). David is so impressed with this "elastic" quality of hers that he never stops to consider the incredible strain—both emotional and physical—that such constant flexibility must create. Similarly, readers of *Copperfield* are generally so captivated by the humor of the Micawbers that the nature of Emma's assertion is rarely considered. Even more ironic is the fact that it is the very frequency of her despairing cry of fidelity that numbs us to its meaning and import. Just as a word repeated over and over takes on the quality of nonsense, Emma's constant reiteration of her intent to stand by her man robs her declaration of its explicit and implicit meanings. And while I find her verbal tic evidence that she is, in fact, protesting too much—while, for me, the constant reiteration is a plea for help and a sign that all is not right with the Micawber marriage—it is also true that Dickens's creation of a woman who so constantly alerts us to the inequity of marriage serves to numb us to the true horror of the situation of the many Emma Micawbers who had no choice but to stay with their husbands. For the alternative was, in the eyes of the dominant culture, "desertion," and such an alternative was neither attractive nor acceptable, as the story of Betsey Trotwood makes clear.

The Married Miss Trotwood

Like Dora Copperfield and Emma Micawber, Betsey Trotwood does not hesitate to consider the prospect of leaving her husband. In fact, she goes a great deal further than Dora and Emma dare, for, rather than dying or implicitly threatening, she really does leave the man she married, despite her vows. Yet, as the story of the married Miss Trotwood makes clear, even she could not truly leave her husband. Miss Betsey always fears her husband's next appearance; she remains passive in the face of his frequent assaults, unable to divorce or renounce him. For as Dickens so insistently reminds us, Miss Betsey still loves her unnamed husband. Along these lines, Q.D. Leavis, one of the very few critics to write about this enigmatic character, argues that although Betsey Trotwood "follows the voice of Reason in separating herself from her husband and quite logically reverting to spinster status ... a rational solution to the problem of an unhappy marriage, a legal separation, can't make happiness" (68). Leavis rightly suggests that Miss Betsey's decision to leave her husband was a sensible one; it would be wise for a woman who has been thrown "out of a two pair of stairs' window" to leave the man who did the throwing (2). But what is not so clear about Leavis's argument is what she calls Miss Betsey's logical reversion to spinsterhood. First, Miss Betsey is not a spinster, for that would imply that she had never been married. If she had never been married, the Miss Betsey plot would make no sense. She would never have been moved to take in Mr Dick if she had not felt sympathy for his distress, occasioned by his sister's mistreatment at the hands of her husband,[11] nor would she be so averse to her servants marrying, even to Peggotty's marrying, so insistent upon the birth of Betsey Trotwood Copperfield, and so wise about the nature of David's "blind, blind, blind" infatuation with Dora. Far from reverting to spinsterhood, Miss Betsey rather advances to the state of bitter divorcée. Leavis seizes upon the fact that Miss Betsey takes her maiden name as proof of her spinsterhood, but such a view distorts the fact of the matter. Aunt Betsey is not a spinster, and in fact she isn't even a divorcée. Miss Betsey is married. But Leavis can no more imagine a married "Miss" than can we, and rather than examine that paradox to discover its significance within this novel of marital desertion, dissolution, and replacement, Leavis simply asserts that Miss Betsey is exactly what her name implies.

Similarly, Leavis suggests that she cannot accept a woman happy to be separated from her husband. Leavis insists upon Miss Betsey's unhappiness because of what she views as her "rigidly monotonous existence in which her tending of Mr. Dick is (till David enters her life) her substitute for husband and child and the natural instincts for intimate human relations." She goes even further and insists that Miss Betsey "has to vindicate her own judgment against society's" (68). I do not know where Leavis finds proof of the "rigidly monotonous existence" Aunt Betsey supposedly endures, nor can I imagine upon what she bases her claim that Miss Trotwood is even remotely interested in society's judgment, much less determined to "vindicate her own." Yet while I do not think there is evidence that

Miss Betsey is unhappy after her separation, Leavis's insistence that such is the case is understandable, given Dickens's own insistence that Miss Betsey still cares for her husband, and even (dangerously) still finds him attractive: "'he was a fine-looking man when I married him,' said my aunt, with an echo of her old pride and admiration in her tone" (562). Notice that, like David's affection for Dora, Miss Betsey's enduring loyalty to her husband has much to do with the physical nature of their relationship. Although Dickens thus presents us with a woman who does leave her husband, he nevertheless insists that that woman remains in love with the husband she leaves, even if that love might more accurately be described as a powerful combination of loyalty and sexual attraction. Thus, the significance of the Miss Betsey plot is buried beneath the narrative convention of the loyal wife, which leads Leavis to assert that "a legal separation ... can't make happiness." This convention is so powerful that it blinds more readers than Leavis to the numerous clues in the novel which point to the fact that a legal separation can indeed make a woman happy—clues that suggest that divorce is lurking everywhere and that Miss Betsey is just one of the many women who refuse to stay in marriages where they are abused.

Yet Miss Betsey never ceases to care about her abusive husband, and her behavior at the end of the novel, especially when she tells David the story of her marriage and when she buries her husband of 36 years, seems to give the lie to all the preceding sentiments which we might call feminist. For all her independence and strength, Miss Betsey looks quite traditional at the end of the novel. Instead of a virtual divorcée or a precursor of the New Woman, she appears more like a modest heroine than anything else. Despite the fact that she left her husband, Miss Betsey has always loved him. Despite the fact that she herself admits that her faithfulness is something to be ashamed of—"This is my grumpy, frumpy story, and we'll keep it to ourselves, Trot!"—and that it has more to do with the sexual than with the sanctity of marriage, we are encouraged to accept the most conventional and conservative view of this abused wife (562). We would prefer to believe that, like a modest heroine, she loves only once and she loves steadfastly.[12] The story of divorce that Dickens almost tells becomes a more conventional story, and Miss Betsey seems more like Esther Woodcourt than Edith Dombey, more like Richardson's Pamela than the willful heroine of a novel by Hardy or Gissing.

Yet Betsey remains married to her husband for reasons other than her physical or emotional love for him. One important reason she does not divorce her husband is simply because she cannot. Given that the novel is set in the 1820s, she has no legal grounds upon which to file for divorce.[13] She could, however, obtain a judicial separation, or a *divorce a mensa et thoro* (literally, a divorce from bed and board). The only grounds necessary for this kind of separation were adultery or cruelty. Miss Betsey is aware of her rights, for she tells David that her husband "had been so cruel to me, that I might have effected a separation on easy terms for myself; but I did not" (561). She could also, if her husband agreed, work out a private separation agreement with him. This kind of arrangement (effected by means of a separation deed drawn up by a lawyer between a husband and his wife's representative) established the monetary arrangements and the conditions of contact between the two parties. Such separations were actually quite common from the eighteenth century until well into the twentieth century; forms for such deeds can be found in legal handbooks from the eighteenth and nineteenth centuries. As I discuss in Chapter 3, this is the kind of arrangement that Caroline Norton works out with her husband, that Edith suggests to Dombey, and that Dickens employs when he and Catherine separate. This also seems to be the way Rawdon arranges the end of his marriage to Becky Sharp in *Vanity Fair*: "it was found that he could not spare to his wife more than three hundred pounds a year, which he proposed to pay to her on an undertaking that she would never trouble him" (740).

However, Miss Betsey does not seek such a remedy to her situation. For that matter, neither does Rawdon, and the reason he does not is remarkably similar to the one Miss Betsey gives in defending her actions. Thackeray's narrator reveals that Rawdon offers his wife the aforementioned arrangement not as a strictly legal proposition, but as something that should be agreed to in order to avoid "scandal, separation, Doctors' Commons" (740).[14] Similarly, Aunt Betsey refuses to separate herself legally from her husband because she wants to avoid the unpleasant consequences of such an action:

> Sooner than have him punished for his offences (as he would be if he prowled about in this country), I give him more money than I can afford, at intervals when he reappears, to go away. I was a fool when I married him; and I am so far an incurable fool on that subject, that, for the sake of what I once believed him to be, I wouldn't have even this shadow of my idle fancy hardly dealt with. (562)

Rather than sue for a judicial separation and bring in the law to punish him, she will endure his continued pleas for money; rather than admit publicly that she was the fool she recognizes herself to be, she will suffer the humiliation which his subsequent conduct inflicts upon her. In other words, to save him from punishment and to save herself from the shame such punishment would cause her, she allows him to make a pauper of her, to take another wife, and to remain a constant reminder of the mistake of her own "undisciplined heart." Finally, she takes up her old role as his wife and is with him at the end of his life, even as he is buried. Despite her insistence that "He is nothing to me now, Trot,—less than nothing," she is only too willing to believe that he had changed at the end of his life—"He was sorry then. Very sorry" (562, 639). Thus, the two reasons Miss Betsey cannot divorce her husband—her love for him and the law of divorce as it existed in the 1820s—converge into one reason which seems to have more to do with the convention of the modest heroine and her faithful love than it does with issues such as divorce law, married women's property, and the status of marriage as an institution—issues the novel nervously circles around.

Thus while Dickens presents us with women who want to leave their husbands, and even with women who manage to do so after a fashion, he does not portray wives who do not love their husbands. This is an omission peculiar to *Copperfield*. Women in Dickens novels pre- and post-*David Copperfield* leave their husbands and resent, even hate these men. Think of the scorn with which *Nicholas Nickleby*'s Madame Mantalini treats her ne'er-do-well husband from whom she insists "on being separated and left to myself ... If he dares to refuse me a separation, I'll have one in law—I can" and of the marriage of Smike's parents in the same novel—"Angry quarrels and recriminations took place, and when they had been married nearly seven years ... she eloped with a younger man and left him" (669, 888–9). Think also of the intense disgust Edith feels for Dombey, or of Monks's parents who happily put an end to their mercenary marriage and go their separate ways. Think, too, of the loveless marriage of Bounderby and Louisa and her flight from Stone Lodge in *Hard Times*. Clearly, the insistence with which Dickens presents loving wives in *Copperfield* is peculiar to this novel. In fact, one could argue that while we have failed marriages in this novel, we do not have loveless marriages: even the evil Mr Murdstone loves Clara, at least in the sexual way that also characterizes the unions of David and Dora and of Betsey and her husband. So we are left with the teasing contradiction that the novel that explores the nature of marriage, the possibility of escaping from marriage, and the chance for a second marriage simultaneously reveals the enduring love of wives for their husbands. Alexander Welsh, Hillis Miller, and Q.D. Leavis all find the fascination with marriage, with its capacity for social change, with its status as a social institution, to be at the heart of *David Copperfield*. Perhaps it is the fact that the novel examines marriage—as a sacrament and a commitment, as well as a legal institution—the fact that *Copperfield* confronts what Leavis calls "the problem represented by the marriages of the two David Copperfields" that accounts for its insistence on loving wives (56). The relatively ad hoc fashion in which the marital gap is filled with love might be read, like Emma Micawber's mechanical insistence that she will not leave her husband, as false reassurance, as a re-covering of the convention laid bare. *David Copperfield* is, finally, a novel of divorce in which no one gets a divorce but Thomas Benjamin (a character few readers even remember)—a novel in which almost every wife wants to leave the husband with whom she is permanently in love.

Thus it makes a kind of narrative sense that even Betsey Trotwood, the most independent, strong-minded woman in *Copperfield*, perhaps in all of Dickens, cannot take legal action against her "adventurer ... gambler ... cheat" of a husband (562). Here, as in the stories of Dora and Emma, the missing divorce, the gap in the story where a divorce might occur, calls for an explanation that comes only in the form of an evasion. Dickens does motion toward the subject of divorce as it relates to women; he goes so far as to suggest that Miss Betsey has taken refuge in the law and obtained a legal separation from her husband. The novel's first explanation of the Miss Betsey plot has her arranging "a separation by mutual consent" which is, with the help of the ecclesiastical courts, exactly what a *divorce a mensa et thoro* is. Further, in this initial version of the story we are given a husband who dies in India and so can no longer torment his wife. But Dickens cannot leave this story alone: he keeps adding things, even changing things. The elements with which he tampers are the kinds of details we tend to read right over, details which the overall plot contradicts, details which, if read carefully and even perhaps out of context, alert us to the nature of the question with which Dickens is absorbed as he writes this pseudo-autobiographical novel. These are elements that lead me to view *David Copperfield* as a novel of divorce. In submerging the first version of her story beneath the second, more conventional, version, he leaves us with a modest heroine tending her dying husband and declaring her steadfast love for him. He thus gives us a woman who, as Edwin Eigner points out, "has a richly ambivalent attitude toward men and toward sex" ("David Copperfield and the Benevolent Spirit" 4). But the most precise conclusion we can come to about her is that she is "ambivalent." We cannot even refer to her or her husband very easily: the contradictory phrases "Miss Betsey's husband" and "the married Miss Trotwood" underline her contradictory characterization. Because we never find out the name of "Miss Betsey's husband" we never learn her married name and are forced to use a phrase that linguistically repeats the oxymoronic status of "the married Miss Trotwood." We are thus forced to repeat within our own discussion the confusion with which Dickens plots her story. In other words, by withholding his name and forcing us to talk about "Miss Betsey's husband," Dickens literally makes the subject of this section very hard to talk about. While he gives us a novel of divorce with one hand, he takes it away with the other. While he presents us with a novel in which all wives seem to want to leave their husbands, he insists upon the existence of love in all these failed marriages.

Annie Strong and the Not-So-Pious Fraud

While Dickens gives us two versions of the Miss Betsey plot, he makes it clear that the story of the wrongly maligned Annie Strong can only be interpreted in one manner. The statements Annie makes when declaring her loyalty to her husband become the morals of the book and the means by which David's "blind, blind, blind" eyes are opened. Annie's three morals are all directly related to the question of fidelity in marriage, to the lessons that must be learned in order to avoid the threat of divorce and the temptation of a second marriage. These morals—"There can be no disparity in marriage like unsuitability of mind and purpose"; "The first mistaken impulse of an undisciplined heart"; and "My love was founded on a rock"—serve as correctives to the potentially subversive nature of the marriages of Dora and David, of Emma and Wilkins, of Betsey and her husband, and even as correctives to Emily's aborted engagement to Ham and her disastrous affair with Steerforth (540–42).

Thus it is not unimportant that these morals appear in what seems to be an explicit adultery plot, nor is it unimportant that Annie's story is actually one of intense loyalty, faith, and trust between husband and wife. The love-triangle of Jack Maldon, Annie, and Dr Strong is, of course, a fiction of Mr Wickfield's and

Uriah Heep's creating. But so much attention is paid to this apparent instance of marital infidelity and so much weight is placed on an affair that never took place (an affair which was never even contemplated by the wrongly maligned Annie) that we begin to wonder about the function of this plot. As the focus of our attention, it serves to screen the deterioration of David's and Dora's relationship from our view, to distract us from Dora's gradual death, and to encourage us to ignore the import of Emma Micawber's alienation from her husband. Because the weight of the narrative at this point in the novel is placed on the tension between Annie and Dr Strong, we overlook the potential divorce plots in the marriages of Dora and Emma. By directing our attention to what seems to be a failed-marriage plot, Dickens steers us away from the truly failed marriages of the Copperfields and the Micawbers. By telling a story of loyalty which looks like infidelity, he buries the stories of desertion that look like happy marriages.

The conventional view of the Annie Strong story and her morals seems to be that espoused by Gwendolyn Needham in "The Undisciplined Heart of *David Copperfield*." Like my argument, her reading of *Copperfield* places great importance on the function of Annie's morals within the novel, and she points to the ways in which they shape the novel as a whole. Yet my sense of the Annie Strong plot as a screen story is diametrically opposed to Needham's view. She asserts that

> the theme of the undisciplined heart ... emphasizes and illumines the character
> of David, showing that his function is far greater than that of narrator; it works
> within the novel's frame of retrospection to shape the structure; it gives deeper
> significance to and closer integration of minor episodes with the novel's larger
> unity; thus it contributes largely to the novel's total effect and pervading tone.
> (81)

The theme of the undisciplined heart is prescriptive, corrective, and positive in Needham's view. It sets everything right and guides David's progress toward the true heroine, Agnes. Yet the morals of Annie Strong, as well as the plot in which they are found, are actually a kind of red herring, directing the reader toward a happy ending that seeks to escape the consequences of the rebellious plots contained in the novel. Perhaps Needham is correct in her assertion that this theme "contributes largely to the novel's total effect and pervading tone," but, if so, it is as a kind of narcotic, lulling us passively and placidly to rest in the belief that all is well, that marriage does establish closure, that, in fact, the institution of marriage stabilizes and orders society. We can only maintain this conservative view if we ignore the desertion plots discussed above and if we read over the insidiousness and deception at the heart of the cover story Dickens writes in the Annie Strong plot.

At this point it seems important to consider who is involved in this deception, who casts suspicion on Annie's character and the Strongs' marriage. The cast of accomplices would have to include Mr Wickfield, Uriah Heep, David himself, and

Jack Maldon. But it would be difficult to discover the origin of this deceit, whether it began with Jack Maldon's attentions to Annie or with Mr Wickfield's suspicions of her. Mr Wickfield sets the plot in motion, but perhaps some of the blame should be placed on Dr Strong for the innocent trust he has in his young wife—a trust which places her in a very awkward position and which causes her to have to deal with both Jack Maldon's advances and Mr Wickfield's suspicions. And the "Old Soldier," Mrs Markleham, is greatly to be blamed because rather than protecting her daughter from such advances as a good mother should, she sees no harm in Jack's continued presence and, in fact, she constantly pesters the doctor to do favors for her nephew Jack.

But what is the point of asking questions about agency and blame? While the plot does not quite spontaneously generate itself—there are Jack's inappropriate actions and remarks and Mrs Markleham's insinuations, and there is that cherry-colored ribbon which disappears from Annie's dress—and while it is not hard to explain how the rumor achieves such wide currency—Wickfield, for one, believes it because he is always ready "to look for some one master motive in everybody, and to try all actions by one narrow test"—there is still something striking about the way in which the purported adultery plot spreads so quickly and gains so many believers (503). My point is that this plot is the most obvious and readily available way of thinking about a failed marriage. It translates into concrete terms the vague discontents I have been discussing in the previous sections. It provides one of the easiest ways of talking about a failed marriage because it presupposes the existence of an other, and it assumes that the blame for the failed marriage can be placed on the party who is attracted to this other. Rather than suggesting that perhaps some painful and awkward questions ought to be asked about marriage—in general and in particular—this plot allows the husband who has been betrayed to point the finger of blame at his wife, rather than consider what portion of blame might be assigned to him.

So many are so quick to believe in the very circumstantial evidence against Annie for another reason, too—a reason related to the convenient nature of the adultery plot. This reason is supplied by Jack Maldon when he speculates about the nature of the Strongs' marriage:

> "I dare say, my cousin Annie could easily arrange it in her own way. I suppose Annie would only have to say to the old Doctor ... that she wanted such and such a thing to be so and so; and it would be so and so, as a matter of course ... because Annie's a charming young girl, and the old Doctor—Doctor Strong, I mean—is not quite a charming young boy," said Jack Maldon, laughing. "No offence to anybody, Mr Wickfield. I only meant that I suppose some compensation is fair and reasonable, in that sort of marriage ... to the lady, sir." (188)

The phrase "that sort of marriage" refers, of course, to the great discrepancy in age between Annie and her husband, for he is old enough to be her father.[15] Marriages of "that sort" are common in Dickens—David's father was 20 years older than his mother—and marriages of "that sort" are also highly suspect. Consider, for example, *The Cricket on the Hearth* (1845) in which John Peerybingle is quite ready to believe his young wife is having an affair precisely because she is his *young* wife. As Alexander Welsh points out, even the wording of the first of Annie's morals points to a nervousness about this discrepancy. In a brilliant deconstruction of the "triply negative formulation" of the moral "There can be no disparity in marriage like unsuitability of mind and purpose," Welsh argues that "'the disparity of marriage' dismissed in the first term of the comparison under the negative universal ... is a much more staring one than the barely hinted differences in temperament between Annie and Jack: it is the obvious disparity in age between Annie and the man she did marry" (*From Copyright to Copperfield* 136). In other words, Annie is defensively stating that while it is true that she is much younger than her husband, it would be worse if they were incompatible in "mind and purpose" rather than in age.

This "valorization of their obvious disparity," to use Welsh's apt phrase, is a protest against the kinds of reasoning employed by Mr Wickfield, David, Uriah, and Jack Maldon in their easy assumption that "some compensation is fair and reasonable, in that sort of marriage." As Tackleton, the suspicious toy-maker in *The Cricket on the Hearth* says to John regarding his young wife, "She honours and obeys, no doubt, you know ... but do you think there's anything more in it?" (221). Or as Mr Wickfield admits, "I thought ... that, in a case where there was so much disparity in point of years ... a lady of such youth, and such attractions, however real her respect for you, might have been influenced in marrying, by worldly considerations only" (503). All these characters seem to believe that there must have been an ulterior motive behind Annie's marriage to Dr Strong since a marriage based on love and sexual attraction seems out of the question. Clearly, these men are not thinking with their heads when they judge Annie Strong, and the fact that marriages of "that sort" are viewed with suspicion in terms of the sexual love which is assumed to be lacking is an indication of the measure by which all marriages are judged in this novel. The marriages Dora, Emma, and Betsey want to leave are all marriages based on sexual attraction. Yet Dickens insists that these are, at least in some sense, good marriages because they are filled with love. The terms of debate become quite confused and confusing at this point, for we see from Miss Betsey's story and from the marriage of Clara and Murdstone that a union based solely on sex is an unfortunate one, yet the belief that there can be no sexual dimension to marriages like the those of the Strongs and the Peerybingles is strongly routed. So what is the lesson? The explicit conclusion to be drawn is found in Annie's morals, but the implicit message is more disturbing.

Annie's morals preach education, discipline, compatibility of values, and a bedrock of love. One must not marry one's first love, and one must seek to tame one's affections. One must seek a mate who shares one's goals and one's habits of mind. Finally, one's love must be the kind that can stand firm. In short, it all comes down to discipline—discipline of heart, of inclination, of temperament, and, most of all, discipline of desire. Remember the discipline of reading over the marriage service and the discipline of the heart Needham cites as the theme of the novel. Those happy, successful marriages—or at least those marriages which Dickens would have us see as such—are ones in which the wife has been disciplined or subdued to her husband's liking. Annie sits for long hours and listens to her husband read from his everlasting Dictionary, while Agnes sits up late into the night with her husband as he writes—"I turn my head, and see [Agnes's face], in its beautiful serenity, beside me. My lamp burns low, and I have written far into the night; but the dear presence without which I were nothing, bears me company" (717). Serene, patient, attending upon their husbands, these are the model wives of *Copperfield*. (Perhaps Dora had the right idea when she asked to hold David's pens.) The real theme of the novel, in fact, comes from the happily married Matthew Bagnet in Dickens's next novel, *Bleak House*, who is always asserting that "discipline must be maintained," who espouses discipline as a sort of cover story for his own happy, yet decidedly matriarchal, marriage.

By thus relying on discipline Dickens tries to shore up the doubts and inconsistencies of his examination of the marriages, both first and second, which he chronicles in *Copperfield*. And it is a theme that finally does not ring true, for its price is too high and its attainment too pat. Dora must die; Annie must be humiliated, doubted and accused by the serpentine Uriah Heep. Discipline is expensive, and even as Dickens valorizes such a mode of behavior, he cannot fully endorse it for it comes only at the expense of Emma and Miss Betsey, and of Dora and Annie.[16]

The Cultural Work of the Novel of Divorce

The hero and narrator of Dickens's novel of divorce is an apprentice at Doctors' Commons, the ecclesiastical court that deals with all legal aspects of marriage, including legal separation. The first mention of divorce in the novel occurs when David is on his way to meet Dora. Women figuratively divorce their husbands, yet they cannot fall out of love with them. As I have argued in the previous chapters, and as I hope the individual sections of this chapter make clear, Dickens is, in ways that are by turns subtle, comic, disguised, and realistic, pointing to the social ill which is the state of marriage in the mid-nineteenth century. In other words, Dickens's novels are engaged in what Jane Tompkins calls "cultural work": "they offer powerful examples of the way a culture thinks about itself, articulating and proposing solutions for the problems that shape a particular historical moment … in order to win the belief and influence the behavior of the widest possible audience" (xi). As Tompkins's emphasis on audience suggests, an important part of this kind of work has to do with the reader: with how she reads and what preconceptions about the genre she brings with her to that reading. If we read in a certain fashion—a fashion which is alert to the silences and the gaps, which looks for those suggestions and bits of nervousness that bespeak a competing vision, that reveal another novel buried beneath the surface of the fiction we are accustomed to reading—then we can see that the work Dickens's novels do is, in fact, feminist in that their effect is to educate readers about the woeful state of the law respecting women and marriage, that Dickens's novels illuminate the vexing nature of nineteenth-century marriage, especially as it concerns wives. In virtually all of Dickens's fiction we are presented with women who are in need of the reform that would come from the Custody of Infants Act and the several Married Women's Property Acts and Matrimonial Causes Acts. The fact that his novels point to the need for such reform should lead us to view them in a different way. Again, Jane Tompkins speaks to this point in a way that is particularly relevant to Dickens's method, especially in *David Copperfield*. Arguing for "the positive value of stereotyped characters and sensational, formulaic plots," she asserts that the strength of such conventions lies in their predictability:

> When literary texts are conceived as agents of cultural formation rather than as objects of interpretation and appraisal, what counts as a "good" character or a logical sequence of events changes accordingly. When one sets aside modernist demands—for psychological complexity, moral ambiguity, epistemological sophistication, stylistic density, formal economy—and attends to the way a text offers a blueprint for survival under a specific set of political, economic, social, or religious conditions, an entirely new story begins to unfold. (xvii–xviii)

The stereotypical, the pat, and the formulaic are agents of social change, the means by which novels perform cultural work. Thus we see that the conservative nature of the story of Agnes Wickfield and the conventional way in which the potentially subversive story of the married Miss Betsey is shut down are the tools of the reform Dickens implicitly champions. The hackneyed characterization of the child-bride Dora, the pathos of the deathbed wherein she leaves her figuratively adulterous spouse to his lover, the machinations of the villainous Uriah Heep—all these elements of the most popular of Dickens's novels lead the reader to draw conclusions which suggest the gap between the apparent conventionality of this novel and the cultural work which is disguised by that conventionality. It is these gaps which provide proof of the extent to which reading *David Copperfield* can be an act of rebellion, perhaps even of reform. For all its allegiance to the courtship plot and the modest heroine and the loyal wife, the novel reveals the need for both legal reform and the kind of paradigm shift that would enable Miss Betsey to take advantage of the protections the law already affords her. This novel both embraces the conventions of the courtship plot and is fascinated by the extralegal solutions wives find to their unhappy marriages. But in order to grasp that duality, we need to estrange *David Copperfield*; we need to open up a reading of what is so very familiar to us and thus make available a very different—and more complete—story.

Notes

1   As David notes in his retrospective narration, that "ingenious little statute" is "repealed now, I believe"; the loophole was closed by the repeal of the nullity clause in 1823 (391).

2   Yeazell reminds us of Foucault's contention in Volume 1 of *The History of Sexuality* that the most convincing proof of an obsession with sex is the avoidance of the topic, that "the intense effort not to talk about sex is really a mode of heightened attention to it, and the very insistence on silence a form of compulsion to transform sex into discourse" (Yeazell 356). That David, among others, is paying attention to these silences is made clear when he conjures up a picture of Maldon in India, "smoking curly golden pipes— a mile long if they could be straightened out" (198).

3   In "Secrets and Narrative Sequence," Kermode talks about those narratives that do not observe the "proprieties" of connection, closure, and character, and which may reveal their "secrets" to a discerning reader. These secrets are aspects of the story which contradict or complicate such things as the connections in story, the attempt at closure, or the description of character, and which "good" readers are trained to ignore, to dismiss, to (as I put it) read over and past (*The Art of Telling* 135).

4   The prostitute who encounters Amy Dorrit begs a kiss from her, but then pushes her away when she realizes that she is a woman, not a child. Amy insists that she is not afraid of her, but the prostitute insists that she "had better be," and begs her to "go home," adding, "I never should have touched you, but I thought you were a child" (218). This scene makes it clear that the prostitute has internalized the assumption that fallen women threaten virginal, marriageable young women.

5   I am referring, of course, to Marcus's *The Other Victorians: A Study of Sexuality and Pornography in Mid-Nineteenth-Century England.*

6   Citing a letter of May 21, 1858 from Forster to Dickens's solicitor, Frederic Ouvry, Michael Slater mentions Dickens's concern about the "New Act" (presumably the Matrimonial Causes Act of 1857, the act that legalized divorce in England), a concern occasioned by rumors that Catherine was being encouraged by her mother and sister to divorce Dickens (147–8).

7   The Biblical injunction against remarriage after divorce is based on the logic that such an action would make the newly-wedded couple adulterers: "If a man divorces his wife for any cause other than unchastity he involves her in adultery; and anyone who marries a divorced woman commits adultery" (Matthew 5: 32).

8   For a suggestive and insightful reading of the relationship between knowledge and childhood in *Maisie*, see "What Fauntleroy Knew" in Beverly Lyon Clark's *Kiddie Lit: The Cultural Construction of Children's Literature in America*, especially pages 38ff.

9   The fact that Dora "clasp[s] Agnes by the hand" during the marriage ceremony (and "still keeps her hand" in the carriage after the wedding) suggests that she has been making room for Agnes in David's life all along (516).

10 It could be argued (only slightly perversely) that Dora has all the necessary grounds for divorce. David's figurative adultery and his cruelty in making her understand that he

wishes they had never married symbolically fulfill the legal requirements for a divorce under the 1857 Act.

11 When we learn that Miss Betsey's husband is suspected of having remarried, it is tempting to assert that he has married Mr Dick's sister, for the ways in which she is mistreated are quite similar to the ways in which Miss Betsey was abused, and there is a strong correspondence between the pain this gives Mr Dick and that which Miss Betsey feels. Further, we might argue that this "relationship" is what brought Mr Dick to Miss Betsey's attention in the first place, for the explanation we are given for her having taken him under her wing—"Mr Dick is a sort of distant connexion of mine—it doesn't matter how; I needn't enter into that"—is vaguely suggestive of a familial relationship and reminds us that Miss Betsey keeps a very closed mouth on a great many subjects (166). We should also remember that, on his way to meet his aunt for the first time, David encounters a tinker who knocks his wife down and bloodies her face. Thus Miss Betsey's story of abuse is prefaced by a similar instance of matrimonial cruelty.

12 For the most compelling study of the convention of the modest heroine, see Ruth Yeazell's *Fictions of Modesty*. Most relevant to my point here is her stunning analysis of Cleland's *Fanny Hill* (1748–49), in which she argues that this work of pornography is in fact the story of a modest heroine who "loves only once: the man whom she eventually marries is the first who takes her virginity and the 'dear possessor' of her 'virgin heart'" (104).

13 As I explain in detail in Chapter 1, before 1857 Miss Betsey could not obtain a divorce unless she went through an expensive three-court process and could prove her husband guilty of aggravated adultery. Miss Betsey would have to wait until 1923 to be able to sue for divorce solely on the grounds of adultery and until 1937 to sue on grounds other than adultery. She would have to wait more than 100 years—until 1950—before affordable divorce became a reality in England.

14 Doctors' Commons was a residential college of doctors of Civil Law who served as judges and advocates in the ecclesiastical courts; it is where David and Mr Spenlow practice law. That Doctors' Commons is held out as a threat indicates that the separation agreement Rawdon offers Becky has not been obtained through an ecclesiastical court and is a private, as opposed to a judicial, separation. Becky and Rawdon are still fully and completely married, then, just as Miss Betsey and her husband are, though both couples are living apart. There is no guarantee of the behavior of either Becky or Miss Betsey's husband since the law has not been invited to intervene in their matrimonial disputes. Rawdon takes the law into his own hands in order to avoid the scandal that suing Becky for a judicial separation would create.

15 According to Alexander Welsh, she is young enough to be Dr Strong's granddaughter, "being only about one third the age of her husband Dr. Strong. She is the contemporary of Agnes Wickfield but married to a man older than Agnes's father" (*From Copyright to Copperfield* 121, 137).

16 Dickens's fondness for these characters is suggested by the fact that he named his third daughter, born in August 1850, Dora Annie.

Chapter 5
Hard Times and the Indictment of Marriage

I want to begin this chapter by establishing a dialectical relationship between *Hard Times* and the novel that immediately precedes it, *Bleak House*. In *Bleak House*, even those marriages that seem "ill-advised" (Vholes's assessment of Richard's and Ada's marriage) or ill-assorted (the discrepancy of age and of class between Sir Leicester and Lady Dedlock) are striking pictures of fidelity (921). Even the comic marriages of the Jellybys, the Pardiggles, and the Snagsbys are, ultimately, demonstrations of the adhesiveness of marriage, an adhesiveness that *Hard Times* seems determined to take apart. In fact, marriages are as remarkably permanent in *Bleak House* as they are temporary and flimsy in *Hard Times*. Because even those stories of apparently failed marriages in *Bleak House* are revealed to be stories of undying love, unshakeable faith, and firm commitment, this novel's matrimonial ethos needs to be read against *Hard Times*' similarly exaggerated ethics of marriage. While I am not arguing that there are no examples of failed marriage in *Bleak House* (for we certainly cannot call the Dedlocks' union a success, nor can we nominate the domineering Mrs Jellyby or the suspicious Mrs Snagsby a model wife), I do want to draw attention to how reluctant *Bleak House* is to entertain that plot: the novel suppresses the story of Lady Dedlock's love for Captain Hawdon and insists that Sir Leicester has no desire—though he certainly has the right—to divorce Lady Dedlock; it keeps the Jellybys together through the vicissitudes of Borrioboola-Gha and the rights of women; and it restores Mrs Snagsby's faith in her husband and leaves her, at novel's end, repentant and obedient. As these examples make clear, suggestions of the failed-marriage plot abound, but they are tamped down, only hinted at in oblique, albeit telling, ways, or resolved in a fashion that rebukes the reader for having even considered the possibility that a marriage could end in anything but the much-mourned death of a spouse. Just as Dickens depicts women who want to leave their husbands, and even women who manage to do so after a fashion, yet does not depict a woman who fails to love the husband she manages to leave in *Copperfield*, in *Bleak House* he seems similarly unable or unwilling to plot the failure of marriage. But the plot Dickens cannot articulate or admit (in)to his avowedly bleak house becomes the one he relies on in *Hard Times*. His dogged insistence on marital love turns into a determined avoidance of, and then an obsession with, matrimonial failure, as the novel that celebrates romantic love becomes the novel of compulsory matrimony and then the explicit novel of divorce.[1]

Bleak House's insistence on plotting marriages for its characters finds it apotheosis in Miss Wisk, the crusader for women's rights we meet at Caddy's wedding. It is Miss Wisk's engagement to Mr Quales (the philanthropist and enthusiastic supporter of Mrs Jellyby's work who originally wanted to marry Caddy) that leads me to call *Bleak House* a novel of compulsory, even compulsive, matrimony. The narrator admits how strange it is to see Miss Wisk at a wedding, for she makes it clear that "such a mean mission as the domestic mission, was the very last thing to be endured," and, at the ceremony itself, she "listened to the proceedings, as part of Woman's wrongs, with a disdainful face" (482, 483). The fact that a woman who believes "that the idea of woman's mission lying chiefly in the narrow sphere of Home was an outrageous slander on the part of her Tyrant, Man" is engaged to be married to one of those tyrants is so absolutely incredible that it suggests that plotting his characters' engagements and weddings is either a tic Dickens is afflicted with in this novel, or something he does almost automatically (482). Tic or habit, this pervasive plot suggests, as Mill does in *The Subjection of Women*, that marriage is the only plot for women, that they have nothing to do but marry, and thus Dickens has no choice but to find them husbands.[2]

Such a reading would begin to make sense of Caddy's marriage, for despite the fact that it is surrounded with foreboding portents and counterplots that suggest it would be much better for her to remain single, she marries her Prince. The chapter in which Caddy gets married begins with Mrs Woodcourt's oblique but detailed enumeration of all the reasons Allan and Esther's marriage is an impossibility, moves to a frenzied scene in which Ada and Esther try to impose some kind of order on the domestic chaos of the Jellybys, and ends with Esther asking Jarndyce two revealing questions: "I hope this marriage is for the best, guardian?" and "Is the wind in the East to-day?" (485). Jarndyce's answer to her first question is straightforward and reflects Esther's concerns ("I hope it is, little woman"), but he ignores the worry her second question implies, "He laughed heartily, and answered 'No.'" (486). This answer does not put to rest Esther's fears about Caddy's marriage, however, for she repeats her question, with more specificity, and without the interrogative: "But it must have been this morning, I think" (486). Jarndyce again says no, and is this time supported in his refusal to admit that the East Wind blew during Caddy's wedding by Ada, who "confidently answered 'No,' too" (486). In this very brief exchange, we see the question of a failed marriage raised, only to be scotched immediately. But Esther is wiser than Jarndyce in this case (and certainly wiser than Ada when it comes to marriage), and her questions remind us that the ceremony itself was attended by those who most emphatically do not subscribe to the importance of the domestic sphere and that the night before her wedding, Caddy had confessed, "I can't help thinking, to-night, Esther, how dearly I hope to be happy with Prince, and how dearly Pa hoped, I dare say, to be happy with Ma. What a disappointed life!" (480). Finally there is the comic but not unimportant fact that Peepy bites Prince on the eve of his wedding. Thus, this chapter is shot through with and bookended by pronouncements against marriage, though these pronouncements are oblique and, ultimately, ignored.

Ada's and Richard's courtship is similarly framed, from Ada's first confession of their love, which she makes to Esther after their evening at the Bayham Badgers (where she learns of Laura Badger's undying love for her first husband, though she is now married to her third), to the fact that we begin to suspect they have married in the same chapter that we learn of the birth of Caddy's "poor little baby," not to mention Vholes's vampire-like presence hovering over them throughout their brief marriage (768). Here again, Esther's first impression of a marriage is the correct one, but it is one that she—and the novel—hastens to correct. When she learns that Ada and Richard are married, all she can think is that she "pitied her so much," a phrase she repeats three times in describing her reaction, and then again when confessing to Jarndyce that "my first impulse had been to pity her" and "so was his" (786, 790). There is also the fact that Ada and Richard marry secretly (clandestinely, we might say) and that Ada continually seeks Esther's and Jarndyce's forgiveness for her marriage.

But to call their marriage a failure is something the novel refuses to do. Rather, we are told that Ada shines in her marriage "like a beautiful star" and that her face is "unshadowed" (921). Vholes is the only one allowed to suggest that their marriage is "ill-advised" (which he does four times in two pages), and when Ada suspects that he has been sharing his opinions with Esther, she makes it clear both why she married Richard, "ill-advised" though the wedding may have been, and why we are to side with her, not Vholes, in honoring her marriage:

> When we were married, I had some little hope that I might be able to convince him of his mistake; that he might come to regard it in a new way as my husband, and not pursue it all the more desperately for my sake—as he does. But if I had not had that hope, I would have married him just the same, Esther. Just the same! … I want him, when he comes home, to find no trouble in my face. I want him, when he looks at me, to see what he loved in me. I married him to do this, and this supports me. (928)

And, of course, it supports Richard, too, and allows him to die cheerfully, with "a smile irradiat[ing] his face" as Ada bends down to kiss him (979).

In much the same fashion, the suggestions throughout the novel that the Snagsbys' marriage is in serious trouble culminate in a scene of discipline that makes the shrewish, suspicious Mrs Snagsby instantly obedient and full of "a good deal of contrition" (911). When we first meet Mrs Snagsby, we are told that she is "jealous and inquisitive; and that Mr Snagsby is sometimes worried out of house and home, and that if he had the spirit of a mouse he wouldn't stand it" (157). Her jealousy escalates to such a degree that she believes Jo, the ragged crossing-sweeper, to be Mr Snagsby's illegitimate son, and she goes to great lengths to bring about "Mr Snagsby's full exposure, and a matrimonial separation" (827). However, her efforts also inadvertently help unravel the mystery of Esther's parentage, and, as Bucket makes clear to her when he delivers the lecture that makes her "falter" and "relent," she is responsible for the fatal delays in the search for Lady Dedlock. "Not to put too fine a point upon it," then, her marital unhappiness is indirectly to blame for the fact that Esther only reaches her mother when she is "cold and dead" (915). The comic plot of the henpecked husband and the shrewish wife culminates in the tragic conclusion of another plot of failed marriage, though neither failed-marriage plot is articulated as such. Bucket's dressing-down is so successful that our last glimpse of Mrs Snagsby is of a woman who has clearly registered the error of her jealous ways; if we had, even for a moment, taken her seriously, if we had attended to that one brief mention of her desire for "a matrimonial separation," we are now left secure in the belief that she, like the plot, has abandoned all desire to leave her husband.

Similarly, while the aristocracy assumes that Sir Leicester will divorce Lady Dedlock once her sinful past has been revealed, the suggestion of divorce is raised only to be rejected. While "one of the peachy-cheeked charmers with the skeleton throats, is already apprised of all the principal circumstances that will come out before the Lords, on Sir Leicester's application for a bill of divorce," this is a rumor that will not, the omniscient narrator makes clear, "go down into Lincolnshire" (886). For Sir Leicester insists on "full forgiveness" and is desperate to find Lady Dedlock, not to divorce her (859). In other words, while all the evidence points to the failure of their marriage, it is anything but a failure in Sir Leicester's mind. Indeed, their marriage is described in the most poignant terms of loyalty and respect even as it moves to what would seem to be its inevitable disintegration. Tulkinghorn, in counseling Lady Dedlock not to flee and thus make her past public, reminds her that Sir Leicester has such trust in her that "with anything short of this case that I have, I would as soon have hoped to root up, by means of my own strength and my own hands, the oldest tree on this estate, as to shake your hold upon Sir Leicester, and Sir Leicester's trust and confidence in you" (657). When she does flee, an event that almost completely incapacitates Sir Leicester, he summons all his strength, and by a superhuman effort manages to articulate—clearly—his faith in and love for her: "I desire to say ... that I am on unaltered terms with Lady Dedlock. That I assert no cause whatever of complaint against her. That I have ever had the strongest affection for her, and that I retain it undiminished" (895). This is his finest hour, and he is, for once, described in terms of manly virility rather than foolish impotence:

> his formal array of words might have at any other time, as it has often had, something ludicrous in it; but at this time it is serious and affecting. His noble earnestness, his fidelity, his gallant shielding of her, his generous conquest of his own wrong and his own pride for her sake, are simply honourable, manly, and true. (895)

Boythorn wonders "whatever can have induced that transcendent woman to marry that effigy and figure-head of a baronet," and Tulkinghorn is quite certain that Sir Leicester should not have married: "most of the people I know would do far better to leave marriage alone. It is at the bottom of three-fourths of their troubles. So I thought when Sir Leicester married, and so I have always thought since" (286, 658). But the narrator emphasizes that Sir Leicester "has loved, admired, honoured" his wife, and that "it is she, who, at the core of all the constrained formalities and conventionalities of his life, has been a stock of living tenderness and love" (838). Despite what Deborah Nord identifies as "the sterility of the Dedlock marriage" and Sir Leicester's "paternal relationship" to his wife, despite even the threatening parallels between Lady Dedlock and the earlier Lady Dedlock, wife of Sir Morbury Dedlock (the figure Hilary Schor identifies as "a specter both dogging and designing her path"), the novel insists on celebrating their marriage with an almost monomaniacal insistence that it is a loving, caring union (Nord 104, n.33, Schor 108). Indeed, while Honoria Dedlock is certainly ironically named, the novel tries to convince us both of her honor (which Schor is right to call "a sham") and of her connection to a more famous Honoria in Victorian literature, Coventry Patmore's angel in the house (Schor 108). While it is true that Lady Dedlock bears no resemblance to "the tranquil Angel in the House, who is seemingly untroubled by sexual desire," when we remember that, as Laurie Langbauer so perceptively notes, "she is introduced gazing longingly at a domestic scene," it becomes clear that her plot, like Patmore's poem, signals both "a renewed appreciation of the domestic" and "a reassertion of its claims" (148, 152).

This is the domestic scene Lady Dedlock is looking at when we first see her: "a keeper's lodge … the light of a fire upon the latticed panes, and smoke rising from the chimney, and a child, chased by a woman, running out into the rain to meet the shining figure of a wrapped-up man coming through the gate" (21). She is looking at what seems to be an idyllically happy family, a mother and child eager to greet the "shining" father coming home to light and warmth and all the comforts of home. Perhaps she is right to stare at it so intently, for it is one of the few scenes of happy domesticity the novel contains. There is, it is true, the muted domestic comfort of Ada's and Richard's apartment and of Caddy's and Prince's home, though both are tainted—by obsession, by impending death, and by disability. There is the happy home we assume awaits Charley when she marries her miller. And there are the Bagnets. Arguably the best picture of marriage in all of Dickens (perhaps in all of Victorian fiction), the Bagnets have it all figured out. They have a happy home, thriving children, and are secure in their working-class comfort. True, they manage to make their marriage work by working creatively within the confines of their patriarchal world, paying lip-service to the doctrine of separate spheres and, as Elizabeth Langland so aptly puts it, "enact[ing] a parodic drama of the cultural myth of dominant husband and submissive wife" (90).

But even their domestic comfort is threatened, and the threat is both imagined, when Mrs Bagnet worries that George Rouncewell's bachelor influence will be a bad influence on her domesticated husband, and real, when George puts the family in financial danger by allowing Mr Bagnet to co-sign a loan from Smallweed. In both cases, Mrs Bagnet exclaims "Oh! Why didn't he marry Joe Pouch's widder in North America? Then he wouldn't have got himself into these troubles" (542). Thus in this register, too, the novel insists that marriage is the answer and that those who refuse the domestic threaten the social order. As Robert Newsom calculates, "the number of celibate people in the novel (those who have been disappointed in love, the bachelors, spinsters, widows, and widowers) is awesome," and he points to both the celibate and the barren (the Dedlocks, the Snagsbys, the Badgers, the Chadbands, and the Buckets) and to the children who are "hardly fortunate in their births" as evidence of "faults of dislocation in love life, home life, and in the relations between parents and children" (*Dickens on the Romantic Side of Familiar Things* 83). The celibate, the barren, and the unfortunate children (the orphans, "the crippled," and "the little monster" children of the Jellybys, Pardiggles, and Skimpoles) are posed in this novel as very real threats to a productive domestic economy, and their scapegoating reveals the novel's investment in healthy, procreative marriage (even Richard and Ada produce a child). The fact that, as Newsom reminds us, "there are only three families of any prominence at all in the novel that are not in some way mutilated or deficient" suggests both how imperiled the domestic is, even as it is everywhere celebrated in this novel (84).

Newsom's examples of healthy marriages are the Bagnets, the Ironmaster's family, and, of course, Allan and Esther, and I want to end my analysis of marriage in *Bleak House* with a consideration of the marriage that marks the end of the novel. While it would be churlish to argue that there is anything failed about the union of Esther and Allan, even parenthetically or elliptically, the fact that their courtship plot ends successfully even as the novel's other plots come to their devastating ends (the deaths of Richard and of Lady Dedlock, Sir Leicester "invalided, bent, and almost blind," Caddy now her family's sole support, with a "deaf and dumb" baby and a lame husband who is "able to do very little") suggests that success comes at great cost (981, 987). As Hilary Schor argues, *Bleak House*

> does not promise healing, or forgiveness, although it does promise its own (dark, warped, bleak, lost) version of love: a love that, if still accomplished (as is Esther's marriage) in the language of debt, exchange, and property, at the least promises that the self can be exchanged for what the self really wants (in Esther's case, Allan) even if that exchange costs the giver (John Jarndyce) a pain the text can hardly fathom. (121)

While Esther gets "what [she] really wants," (and Allan, too, gets his heart's desire), theirs is not a happy ending, but rather a "dark, warped, bleak, lost version of love." Small wonder, then, that the novel does not describe to us their wedding day, for it would be bleak indeed, with the newly-widowed Ada attending as matron of honor and the self-denying Jarndyce acting as "father" of the bride. Garrett Stewart reads this ending in similarly dark terms, and he, like Dickens, stays away from any talk of weddings:

> When the father figure Jarndyce presents Esther to her destined husband, the doctor Woodcourt, and to her new version of Bleak House, this locus of consolation seems rather cryptically dubbed in honor of the unforgotten dead:

"Alan [*sic*] Woodcourt stood beside your father when he lay dead—stood beside your mother. This is Bleak House." (*Death Sentences* 374, n.13)

Bleak indeed: Stewart describes the establishment of a new domestic setting for the novel's heroine and the successful conclusion of her courtship plot not as home and marriage, but rather as a "locus of consolidation," as if the picture were too morbid to describe in connubial terms and was more appropriately expressed in the distancing language of business or geometry.

It is not, then, that *Bleak House* does not recognize the failure of marriage, but rather that it determinedly plots over that failure, moving, for instance, from the bleak scene of Esther's "engagement" to Allan to the resolutely cheerful conclusion, in which Esther confesses to her husband (to whom she has been married for "full seven happy years"), "I thought it was impossible that you *could* have loved me any better, even if I had retained [my old looks]," and he lovingly responds, "And don't you know that you are prettier than you ever were?" (910, 914). In *Hard Times*, however, Dickens just as determinedly lays bare the shortcomings of the institution, taking up those plots he so insistently suppressed in his preceding novel and developing them to their tragic conclusions. It could, in fact, be argued that *Hard Times* does not so much plot the failure of marriage as it takes that failure for granted as the condition that generates the plot. Not only does the novel focus on what Stephen Blackpool calls "th' supposed unpossibility o' ever getting unchained from one another," assuming from the outset that the institution is a crashing failure and taking up immediately the question of how to extricate its characters from the wreckage, but it was also written and published as Parliament was debating the first Divorce and Matrimonial Causes Bill in 1854 (57). Similarly, *Hard Times* is remarkable in that it contains not a single courtship plot, focusing its attention instead on how to effect the end of a legal (and supposedly sacramental) relationship. We meet the Gradgrinds well after their courtship and failed-marriage plots are over, arriving only in time to witness the last bits of life in Mrs Gradgrind and to find scattered evidence of the unhappiness of her marriage. Similarly, we meet Mrs Sparsit long after her husband has left her, and we are introduced to Stephen long after his drunken wife has abandoned him. Finally, while we do witness Bounderby's proposal to Louisa (or, to be precise, we see her father relay that proposal to her), Louisa's and Bounderby's courtship plot is chronicled obliquely (mostly through hints thrown out by her father and brother) and very briefly. By the same token, while Mrs Sparsit imagines she is watching the downfall of Louisa's marriage and the fall of her moral character, that failed-marriage plot is more a creation of Mrs Sparsit's wishful imaginings than it is a chronicling of the discontented union of Louisa and Bounderby.[3]

Those marriages whose failure the novel takes for granted include virtually all of the marriages in the novel. The only ones that seem even remotely happy or healthy are those of the circus families, which we see only in passing, and the suggestion of Sissy's happy marriage we find in the phrase "happy Sissy's happy children" in the novel's penultimate paragraph. But because the aborted divorce plots of Stephen and Louisa seem so central to the novel's overarching design, critics have paid little attention to the other marriages in the novel, nor have they considered the significance of the fact that Stephen's and Louisa's unhappy marriages are framed, as it were, by marriages so failed that the spouses are all but invisible.[4] When we first meet Mrs Gradgrind, we are told that she is "a little, thin, white, pink-eyed bundle of shawls, of surpassing feebleness, mental and bodily; who was always taking physic without any effect, and who, whenever she showed a symptom of coming to life, was invariably stunned by some weighty piece of fact tumbling on her" (12). She is so insignificant—to her husband and to the plot of the novel—that it seems as if the narrator can barely see her, describing her as "an indifferently executed transparency of a small female figure, without enough light behind it" (12). Devoid of light and life, small, feeble, and hard to make out, Mrs Gradgrind is the (dis)embodiment of a wife under the system of coverture. "Nobody minded her," the narrator tells us, and so when she responds to the news of Louisa's engagement to Bounderby by suggesting that she is not to be envied her affianced position, no one even thinks to ask her what she means (14).

"If your head begins to split as soon as you are married, which was the case with mine," Mrs Gradgrind replies, "I cannot consider that you are to be envied, though I have no doubt you think you are, all girls do" (78). This is not only part of the longest speech she makes in the novel, but it also reveals her own marital miseries and her sense that they may be visited upon Louisa, as well. Her reply also suggests that "all girls" naively believe that to be married is to be happy (and "to be envied"), and while Louisa is not one of those naïve girls, she certainly does not realize what she is getting herself into in marrying Bounderby. Indeed, after Louisa leaves Bounderby, she confesses to her father that her marriage was a "wild escape into something visionary" and that she "slowly found out how wild it was" (166). Mrs Gradgrind's indirect warning to Louisa is *Hard Times'* version of Caddy's realization, as she prepares for her own ill-advised wedding, that her parents were once as hopeful as she is now about the promise of matrimonial bliss. In both cases, the betrothed young women have cautionary tales right in front of them, and in both cases their unhappy parents have been so diminished by their years of marriage to overbearing spouses that they have been deprived of basic bodily functions: Mr Jellyby has almost entirely lost the ability to speak, while Mrs Gradgrind rarely leaves her couch.

The other invisible spouse in *Hard Times* is Mrs Sparsit's ex-husband. The narrator calls him "Mr Sparsit, deceased" and "the late Mr Sparsit," but this locution serves to gloss over the fact that, before he died, "he had been separated" from Mrs Sparsit, who was his senior by 15 years (33). Indeed, he leaves her "soon after the honeymoon," a fact that, taken together with the specifics of their marriage ("contrived" by Mrs Sparsit's great aunt, the marriage took place "when Sparsit was just of age" and when he was in considerable debt), suggests it was as failed as it was brief (32). The little we learn about their marriage also suggests that it was a mercenary marriage, that, like Gradgrind, who married his wife because "she was most satisfactory as a question of figures," Mr Sparsit was motivated to marry by his tremendous debt rather than by any emotional attachment he might have had to his bride-to-be (14).

The parallels between Mrs Gradgrind and Mrs Sparsit, whose husbands marry them for their money, between Mrs Gradgrind and Mr Sparsit, who both seem to have disappeared from their marriages almost as soon as they entered them, between Stephen's alcoholic wife and Mrs Sparsit's husband ("the cause [of his decease], brandy"), between Louisa and Mr Sparsit, who enter into marriages arranged by a parental figure, and between Louisa, Mr Sparsit, and Stephen's wife, who all seem to have left their spouses without worrying about the legality of their desertion, are striking, and they suggest a number of strangely parallel plots (33). They also suggest that the novel, in plotting the ways in which characters can get "unchained from one another," takes up some very specific things: the possibility of disappearing from your marriage with impunity, the relationship between marriage, debt, and drinking, mercenary marriages more generally, and the disparity in age between husband and wife (while Mrs Sparsit is 15 years older than her husband, Bounderby is twice that much older than Louisa). Looking at the failed marriages that surround Stephen and Louisa also suggests that while oppressive spouses are just as often husbands (Bounderby and Gradgrind) as they are wives (Mrs Sparsit and Stephen's wife), the only husband to desert his wife (if that is indeed what he did) is Mr Sparsit. To the already long list of wives who leave their husbands in Dickens we can now add Louisa, Mrs Gradgrind, and Stephen's wife.

Hard Times is, in many ways, critical of and antithetical to the novel tradition. It denies readers of the domestic novel so many things that they want: not only a divorce for poor Stephen or a satisfying ending to Louisa's plot, but also even a scene or two of happy home life, or just one courtship plot that ends happily for us to console ourselves with and to distract us from the nuptial nightmares on every other page. *Hard Times* is bleak and unrelenting in its portrait of marriage, and while Leo Bersani is certainly right to identify the structures within which the nineteenth-century novel represses its disorder,[5] Dickens seems to have abandoned those structures entirely in this novel, giving way to the disorder of marital failure. As I suggest above, he plots no courtships, nor does he plot the failure of marriage; he rejects those conventions and plots, choosing instead to concentrate on what is almost always relegated to the scandalous sidelines of a Victorian novel: how to sever the matrimonial tie.

In *Hard Times* there are several ways to extricate yourself from your marriage. You can, like Mr Sparsit, "be separated" and then die before the novel even begins. You can, like Mrs Gradgrind, retire from your marriage and enjoy such a "limited capacity for being in any state" that when you do, in fact, die, it does not seem to make much difference (150). You can leave your husband, as Stephen's wife does (and you can "coom back," too, when you need money, and you can take the money he pays you to "keep awa' fra'" him) (55). Or you can "steal away" from your husband's house and return to your father, as Louisa does (162). In none of these cases will your spouse try to get you back. There is certainly no indication that Mrs Sparsit is even remotely interested in having her husband ("a slender body, weakly supported on two long slim props, and surmounted by no head worth mentioning") return to her. In fact, it is not clear whether he leaves her or she leaves him; the narrator resorts to the passive voice and evasively says that Mr Sparsit "had been separated" from his wife "soon after the honeymoon" (32–3). But, given that he died in Calais, that he spent all his inheritance before he came of age, and then spent it all again "twice over" once he came of age, and that his mother was a Powler ("an ancient stock" much given to "horseflesh, blind-hookey, Hebrew monetary transactions, and the Insolvent Debtors' Court"), it stands to reason that he was more interested in gambling than in patching up his marriage, and that Mrs Sparsit was less than eager to have him back (33, 32).

More pathetic is Mrs Gradgrind; her family seems so willing to let her go that she is reduced to empty, absurd threats, not that she will leave, but that she will repent of her domestic situation. When Mr Gradgrind rebukes her for Tom's and Louisa's interest in the circus, she "whimper[s]" to her children, "you're enough to make one regret ever having had a family at all. I have a great mind to say I wish I hadn't. *Then* what would you have done, I should like to know?" (13). Mr Gradgrind seems to think they would have done (perhaps that they are in fact doing) just fine, for his only response is to "frown impatiently" and resume his conversation with Bounderby. While Mrs Gradgrind only threatens to repent of having had a family on this occasion, she repeats her threat with more conviction when she overhears Louisa "wondering" and worries that Gradgrind will learn that she has been "talking in this absurd way" again. This time she whimpers (the verb is again Dickens's), "I wish … yes, I really *do* wish that I had never had a family, and then you would have known what it was to do without me!" (42). I draw attention to her threats not only because they suggest that she is at least obliquely aware of the fact that they already "do without" her, but also because her threats, like her character in general, are ignored. Her family does not respond to her whimpering any more than they respond to her virtual absence in their lives. They let her imagine what it would be like never to have had a family, they allow her to relinquish the role of wife and mother in everyday practice, and when she dies, the novel barely takes notice. Mrs Gradgrind is such a cipher, in fact, that critics pay her little attention, a dismissive gesture that reveals how unobtrusively this novel about "getting unchained" manages the end of the Gradgrinds' marriage. It is no surprise, then, that when she dies, her children do not mourn her, and her husband does not even seem to notice that she is gone.

Stephen Blackpool does notice when his wife is gone, and it is with such a sense of relief that he pays her to stay away. In fact, his payments suggest a kind of extralegal separation agreement, leading us to wonder, as we do about the Sparsits' marriage, who leaves whom? But the novel is so committed to ending Stephen's marriage (and that of the Gradgrinds and the Sparsits) that it does not seem to matter much who leaves whom. In all three cases, both parties are so eager for their marriages to end that it seems beside the point to remark that these spouses are allowed to leave their marriages with impunity. This is not a novel that concerns itself with trying to rescue a failed marriage or forcing a woman to return to her husband or even suggesting that Stephen's wife has no legal right to abandon him. This is a novel that assumes that marriages are frequently mercenary, that knows all too well how debt compounds, and that understands that an intemperate spouse is such a burden that her disappearance or his death is nothing to complain about. As I suggested at the beginning of this chapter, in its interest in plotting how its characters can break the wedded lock, *Hard Times* skips over courtship and failed marriage, and concentrates on the matter of setting husbands and wives free from the bonds of matrimony.

Similarly, this is novel that takes for granted that a disparity in age signals all sorts of other problems, that is uninterested in exploring what else that disparity might mean or in suggesting that a May–December romance is frequently a fine arrangement. Unlike the advanced age of Dr Strong, in *David Copperfield*, and John Peerybingle, in *The Cricket on the Hearth*, which poses no impediment to Annie's and Dot's deep, abiding love for them, Mrs Sparsit's age is a good deal of the problem, as is Bounderby's. Though it is just one of "those causes of disparity" Louisa cites for her "rebellion against the tie," the fact that Bounderby is 48 while Louisa is only 18 does have something to do with the problems in their marriage, as we see when Stephen comes to ask him for legal advice (166). Mrs Sparsit is aware that her age told against her, too, for when Stephen begins to tell the story of his unhappy marriage, Mrs Sparsit interrupts to ask if his was "an unequal marriage, Sir, in point of years." Learning that it was not (Stephen was 21, his wife almost 20), she explains, "with great placidity," that she "inferred, from its being so miserable a marriage, that it was probably an unequal one in point of years." Mrs Sparsit's inference is, of course, a jab at Bounderby's affections for the young Louisa as much as it is a reflection on her own failed marriage,[6] and he takes it as such, for in response, he "looked very hard at the good lady in a sidelong way that had an odd sheepishness about it" and poured himself another drink (56).

Hard Times is just as uninterested in exploring the fine points of gender as it is unconcerned with the particulars of age. While the law respects the rights of a husband and does not recognize those of a wife, that double standard does not translate into a husband's ability to hold on to his wife in *Hard Times*. This is not to say that the double standard of divorce law, the patriarchal system of coverture, and the confining doctrine of separate spheres do not contribute to a wife's unhappiness, do not put into motion many a failed-marriage plot, do not cry out for reform. And Dickens has done much, in his novels pre- and post-*Hard Times*, to draw attention to the legal plight of the wife. But because the husbands in this novel have very little interest in holding on to their wives, *Hard Times* has little to contribute to the debate over the double standard of divorce law as it relates to gender. It is, of course, intensely interested in that double standard as it relates to class, dedicating much of its energies to insisting that there should be an affordable way for Stephen to divorce his wife and protect his property from her drunken invasions. But it does not make the analogous suggestion that Louisa should be able to divorce Bounderby.[7] Critics try to make the novel interested in exploring the double standard of class and of gender, just as they try to find parallels between the two failed marriages that are central to the plot. But it strikes me that the correspondences between Stephen's and Louisa's plots and the failed marriages of the Sparsits and the Gradgrinds are much more productive and more revealing than the similarities critics try to find between the Stephen and the Louisa plots. Indeed, as John Baird points out, "Bounderby's marriage presents an ironic reversal of Stephen's situation" rather than a parallel to it:

> Stephen and his wife were about the same age; she has betrayed him, and returns to plague him; he is poor, and so cannot divorce her. Bounderby, on the other hand, is thirty years older than his wife; she does not betray him, and refuses to return to him; he has plenty of money, but no adequate grounds, and apparently no desire for a divorce. (410)

One of the things I mean to suggest, then, in drawing attention to the other marriages in *Hard Times*, is that any understanding of this novel's position *vis-à-vis* marriage must not only take into account all its depictions of matrimony, but also discard the false assumption that Louisa's plot is importantly analogous to Stephen's. One of the dangers of drawing that false analogy is that it leads critics to extrapolate from the novel's conclusion a moral about the relationship between marriage and the society it is believed to shore up. But, as I discuss in detail in the epilogue, not only is *Hard Times* a novel with a famously inconclusive conclusion, suggesting the futility of drawing any kind of moral from it, but it is also true, more generally and generically, that any novel that questions the courtship model must also question the belief that marriage works to relieve both individual and societal anxieties. That is, a novel with any kind of failed-marriage plot is always already skeptical of both marriage's ability to shore up society and the threat the rupture of marriage poses to a social structure.

In the remaining pages of this chapter, then, I suggest what I find to be more effective strategies of contextualizing Louisa's and Stephen's plots; rather than read them as analogous to each other, I briefly consider Stephen's plot alongside the parliamentary debates that occurred as the novel appeared in 1854, and I read Louisa's plot in terms of the articles published in the weekly numbers of the novel in *Household Words* and alongside *The Subjection of Women*—alongside, in other words, essays that provide us with a way of understanding her plight as a casualty of the patriarchal institution of marriage. *Hard Times* has, of course, been contextualized in all three ways before, and while I find much to admire in the work that relates the novel to the realms of law, journalism, and political economy, this work still succumbs to the lure of the false analogy in one way or another. The temptation to find parallels between the Stephen plot and the Louisa plot, which we can trace from J.W. Kaye's "The 'Non-Existence' of Women" (1855) to Alexander Welsh's *Dickens Redressed* (2000), has proven to be as irresistible as it is unproductive. Indeed, I think that tendency is in large part responsible for the novel's lackluster reception, for such an approach inevitably reveals that the novel is based on a failed parallel, and it thus often finds the novel itself to be a failure. The only thing failed about *Hard Times*, I would argue, is the marriages of its characters: of Louisa and Bounderby and of Stephen and his unnamed wife, certainly, but also, and importantly, of the Sparsits and the Gradgrinds.

In his 1855 article in *The North British Review*, J.W. Kaye makes this complaint of the novel:

> It seems to have been Mr. Dickens' original design, in this tale, to illustrate the evils of the existing laws of divorce, but the idea, we know not for what reason, was not worked out to its legitimate conclusion. ... There are few, we suspect, of Mr. Dickens' more thoughtful readers, who did not imagine that he was working up towards an illustration of the inequality of the laws of divorce, as they affect rich and poor, by showing how Mr. Bounderby was enabled, by dint of money, to shake off a wife, guilty only of an indiscretion, and too on the evidence of an interested witness, while poor Stephen Blackpool could not rid himself of the degraded being who was the curse of his life, though her offences against him and against God and man were notorious all the country round. (297n)

In the chapter entitled "Louisa Gradgrind's Role," Alexander Welsh argues that Louisa "will implicitly be denied divorce, even as [Stephen] has explicitly been informed that no law can help him" (*Dickens Redressed* 174). While Kaye is careful to stipulate that "it seems" to have been Dickens's original intent to parallel the Stephen and Louisa plots, and while Welsh specifies that Louisa is only "implicitly" refused a divorce, both fill in details in order to find similarities between the two plots. Kaye resorts to what he admits is an act of imagination in comparing Louisa's indiscretion to Stephen's wife's "offences against God and man," while Welsh, in explaining his comparison, emphasizes how very implicitly Louisa is denied a divorce. Referring to the scene when Louisa returns to her father's house and confesses her interest in Harthouse, the utter failure of her marriage, and the uselessness of her father's teaching, and asks him to "save me by some other means," Welsh considers what she might be thinking:

> It is not immediately clear what other means she could have in mind. As for being received at Stone Lodge and thus physically separated from both her husband and her lover—this much she has achieved already. Remotely, "other means" might refer to divorce, like the one Stephen Blackpool asked for: Louisa is now face to face, after all, with her own member of Parliament. But most likely the means is love, a tall order for Gradgrind. (*Dickens Redressed* 179)

Welsh is ultimately too careful a critic to suggest a possibility the novel does not entertain. But in asserting that Louisa is denied a divorce, albeit implicitly, and in suggesting, even "remotely," that Louisa "might" be asking her father to help her divorce her husband, Welsh reveals the typical desire to read Louisa's and Stephen's plots in terms of each other. Even to suggest, however briefly, that Louisa might be thinking of divorcing Bounderby is fanciful in the extreme. Louisa has absolutely no grounds for divorce, nor would she have until 1969, when divorce effected by mutual agreement on the grounds of incompatibility would be made legal in England. If anything, Bounderby could perhaps petition for a divorce, using, as Kaye suggests, that "interested witness" Mrs Sparsit to attest to Louisa's supposed infidelity. But that reading, speculative and outside the text as it is, suggests another reason to resist comparing the Stephen and Louisa plots: to compare them with any accuracy would be to compare the two wronged husbands and thus to suggest a likeness between the bullying Bounderby and the meek and forgiving Stephen. It would also suggest that Louisa could be compared to Stephen's wife as the unfaithful partner.[8]

This comparison is ludicrous, but it is just a more extreme version of what critics do when they compare Louisa, Edith Dombey, and Lady Dedlock as adulteresses who leave their husbands. True, one reason Louisa's plot is so frequently misread as an adultery plot is that she is accorded the punishment typical of adulteresses in the Victorian novel: "herself again a wife—a mother ... Such a thing was never to be" (226). Like Edith Dombey and Lady Dedlock, Louisa is compromised by the suggestion of adultery and by the fact that she marries a man she did not love for reasons her brother calls "mercenary." While she does not marry Bounderby because she wants his money, she does marry him because Tom wants his money; thus her marriage, according to George Bernard Shaw "is none the less an act of prostitution because she does it to obtain advantages for her brother and not for herself" (336–7).[9] Angus Wilson put these three heroines in "the woman who had already sold herself into loveless marriage" category, while Barbara Hardy sees in them "the corruption of love, marriage, and maternity." Françoise Basch goes even further and refers to them, in a chapter entitled "Dickens's Sinners," as "women of industrial society as impure as the Newgate prostitute," a description that is both inaccurate and unfair given that neither Louisa nor Edith is guilty of adultery, while Lady Dedlock's only sin is that of fornication, a sin nonetheless, but certainly not one that warrants comparing her to a "Newgate prostitute" (Wilson 16, Hardy 59, Basch 220).

After Louisa's flight, Gradgrind confesses to Bounderby, "I doubt whether I have understood Louisa" (182). Louisa's important difference from Lady Dedlock and Edith Dombey suggests that critics, too, have not quite "understood Louisa" or her plot. The most significant difference is the simple fact that she does not leave her husband. While Edith leaves Dombey because she can no longer endure the coldness with which he treats her and because of his use of Carker as a go-between, and while Lady Dedlock leaves Sir Leicester in order to spare him the humiliation that the truth of her past will cause, Louisa's flight has nothing to do with her husband. She is not leaving him; she is escaping from Harthouse. She does not go to meet James, as Edith does—although Mrs Sparsit thinks that is her purpose—nor does she flee her would-be seducer in order to save her husband's pride or reputation. She gives no thought to her husband in her flight. And once she reaches her father's house, she does not blame her condition on her marriage or on having been, in some sense, forced to marry, but on her upbringing.

Rather than emphasizing the similarity between Louisa's fate at the end of the novel and that of other characters denied marriage and children because of their sexual sins, I want to suggest that Louisa's *only* punishment is that she is denied marriage and children: she is not transported from England[10] or killed, and she is allowed to play a significant and nurturing role in the domestic sphere. Indeed, reading what "was to be" Louisa's future in terms of punishment deflects our attention from the fact that Louisa is allowed to break the wedded lock, even though her husband is still living and has the legal right to insist that she return to his home (which he does, but only in a half-hearted manner). This fact is important, for it suggests not only that her plot has more in common with Mrs Blackpool's, the Sparsits', and her mother's (in that she is allowed to leave her marriage with impunity) than it does with Stephen's (who dies trying to extricate himself from his wife's sporadic clutches), but also that this novel is more interested in Stephen's plight and in the divorce law's double standard of class than it is in exploring Louisa's right to a divorce.

Louisa neither wants nor needs a divorce; what she wants is to be saved from herself, to be re-educated in the "wisdom of the Heart" and to find her way to "peace, contentment, honour" (170, 172). Bounderby does not want a divorce either, though Mrs Sparsit would like to think that he does. As I suggest above, while he has the right to compel Louisa to return to him, and while he might also, as Kaye imagines, construct a case and divorce her, he seems remarkably willing, eager even, to "resume a bachelor life" (186). Indeed, the only effort he makes to save his marriage is to tell Mr Gradgrind that "if she don't come home to-morrow, by twelve o'clock at noon, I shall understand that she prefers to stay away, and I shall send her wearing apparel and so forth over here, and you'll take charge of her for the future" (186).

In view of the way Dickens plots the end of their marriage, Kaye's objections are especially striking, and they shed important light on the aspects of divorce and failed marriage in which *Hard Times* is most interested. Kaye seems to be disappointed that Dickens did not make the class bias even more clearly a travesty by showing that Bounderby could obtain a divorce on a technicality while Stephen could not "rid himself of ... the curse of his life" (Kaye 297n). Yet most critics agree that Dickens stacks the deck in favor of Stephen's right to divorce his wife, so to complain that the Stephen plot "was not worked out to its legitimate conclusion" seems odd. It is more likely that it is Bounderby's unfair advantage with respect to the law that Kaye finds "not worked out to its legitimate conclusion," but, as Rosemarie Bodenheimer points out, he does "manage to wipe away both his parents and his failed marriage, while Stephen's whole life is confined and distorted by the legal shell of a marriage" (196–7). Again, the double standard of class is quite clear. Why does Kaye want Dickens to make this plot even more pronounced?

I am tempted to argue that Kaye pushes this plot because it is precisely the dimension of divorce reform that the MPs so resolutely ignored in the debates on the Divorce Bill in 1854.[11] And I am quite convinced that Parliament's avoidance of this issue led Dickens to stack the deck in favor of Stephen. The debates of 1854 make it clear that the double standard of class is what needs to be addressed, what is determinedly not being considered, and what—along with the sexual double standard—makes divorce law in the mid-nineteenth century such a legal charade. It is also a dimension of the failed-marriage plot that Dickens had not yet plotted, an important supplement to the picture of the institution he begins to paint in *Pickwick* and will continue to embellish until his death. In addressing Stephen's inability to obtain a divorce, then, Dickens takes up the crucial and all-too-often overlooked matter of class as it relates to both the conventions of the novel and the ideology of Victorian marriage. I thus turn to the debates that occurred as the novel appeared in *Household Words* in order to draw attention to the way in which those debates ignored the matter of class, even as the plot of *Hard Times* calls our attention to it.

In 1850 the Prime Minister, Lord Russell, appointed a Royal Commission to evaluate the state of marriage and divorce law. The ostensible reasons for establishing such a body were procedural in nature; as I describe in Chapter 1, at mid-century there was a great deal of concern about the confusing legal procedures necessary to obtain a divorce.[12] Further, the enormous financial cost, of which Bounderby correctly warns Stephen in the chapter of *Hard Times* aptly entitled "No Way Out," had been the object of some concern, as was the fact that so much of Parliament's time was taken up in hearing private bills. These, then, were the concerns that supposedly gave rise to the Royal Commission, and they are neatly mirrored in the Commission's 1853 report, which, in turn, became the basis of the Divorce Bill of 1854. The Commission's three-volume report recommended no change in the law itself, but rather a reconstruction of the courts so that the action for divorce, formerly taking place in common law courts, ecclesiastical courts, and parliament, could be streamlined.

The Divorce Bill of 1854 was introduced into the House of Lords by Lord Chancellor Cranworth on June 13, three days after the eleventh number (in which Bounderby explains the law of divorce to Stephen) of *Hard Times* appeared in *Household Words*. The bill proposed to remove *divorce a mensa et thoro* from the ecclesiastical courts and *divorce a vinculo matrimonii* from Parliament, turning the former over to Chancery and the latter over to a new divorce court. One of the major effects of this bill would be to require all litigants to come to London for a divorce or separation. The bill would, therefore, actually increase, rather than decrease, the cost of a matrimonial case, but since, as Lord Redesdale reasoned, there had not been "the least expression of a desire for a cheap tribunal for granting divorces … there was no necessity for extending this licence to the poor." The issue of affordability was not debated, and the fact that the bill distinctly did not address the inequity of one law for the rich and one for the poor, which was the case with both the present divorce law and its proposed revision, was not perceived as being at all problematic. In fact, at the end of the day's debate on the bill Cranworth fairly accurately observed that "the only objections which had been made to the Bill in the course of the discussion appeared to him to have reference to the nature of the tribunal to which questions of matrimony and divorce were in future to be referred."[13] Indeed, throughout the debate, MPs opposing the Divorce Bill frequently claimed that the people had no desire for the reforms proposed by the bill, and, specifically, that the poor were not asking for access to any sort of court for divorce or separation. Yet the first time divorce is mentioned in *Hard Times* it is by a poor laborer who is desperate to rid himself of his wife. (As I point out above, the only time divorce comes up in *Hard Times*, it is with respect to Stephen and his plight.) Later in the novel Stephen makes it clear to Bounderby, with Harthouse ("a singular politician") standing close at hand, exactly what the relationship between the government's conception of the poor and the actual state of affairs amounts to: "Look how you considers of us, and writes of us, and talks of us, and goes up wi' yor deputations to Secretaries o' State 'bout us, and how yo are awlus right, and how we are awlus wrong, and never had'n no reason in us sin ever we were born" (99, 114). Here is one of those poor, who supposedly have not asked for reform, making it quite clear what he thinks of the government's methods of determining his wants and needs. Indeed, as Rosemarie Bodenheimer argues, Stephen's "life history contends against ... middle-class ways of thinking about the working class satirized by the narrator. None of the 'tabular statements' proving that workers drink, don't drink, take opium, and frequent 'low haunts' touches Stephen's experience of marriage to a drunkard" (195).

Similarly, Redesdale could only claim there had not been "the least expression of a desire for a cheap tribunal for granting divorces" because, as Lawrence Stone points out, legal relief was far too expensive even to be considered an alternative by the poor: the lower classes

> contrived their own quasi-legal or illegal means of self-divorce—such as desertion, elopement, private separation, or the occasional wife-sale. So long as both parties were satisfied, the illegality of the procedure was irrelevant, and any subsequent act of bigamy carried few serious risks of discovery or of serious punishment if exposed. (21)

Stone's findings reveal the naïve conservatism of Redesdale's subsequent argument that divorce should not, in fact, be made more affordable because such a move "would have a most prejudicial effect on the morals of the country, and upon the domestic happiness of the people" (134:20). Further, when Bounderby reminds Stephen of the "sanctity in this relation of life" which must be maintained, Stephen is quick to correct him: "No, no, dunnot say that, Sir. 'Tan't kep' up that way. Not that way. 'Tis kep' down that way" (57). Aware that the class inequity of divorce law which prevents him from obtaining any sort of relief from his own spouse is more likely to pollute the "sanctity" of marriage than it is to preserve it, Stephen goes not once but twice to Bounderby's to seek information about "the law that helps me" (57). In fact, he is so far from believing that divorce would harm his morals that he actually thinks it would improve his character. Walking home late one rainy night in fear of finding his wife there and musing on how different his life would be if he were divorced from his drunken spouse and married, instead, to Rachael, Stephen "thought of the home he might at that moment have been seeking with pleasure and pride; of the different man he might have been that night; of the lightness then in his now heavy-laden breast; of the then restored honour, self-respect and tranquillity all torn to pieces" (62). He also recognizes that the impossibility of obtaining a divorce "brings blood upon this land, and brings many common married fok to battle, murder, and sudden death" (57). In contrast, Redesdale argues that divorce will not lead to happiness. "If their Lordships were to examine the history of twenty or thirty divorces," he cautions the House two years later, "they would not find more than two or three instances in which anything like happiness had been enjoyed by the parties who had obtained a divorce" (*Hansard* 143: 238). Again, Stephen's situation suggests otherwise: "He thought of the waste of the best part of his life, of the change it made in his character for the worse every day, of the dreadful nature of his existence, bound hand and foot, to a dead woman, and tormented by a demon in her shape" (62). Perhaps he thinks he would be one of the "two or three instances" that Redesdale admits.

But what are Stephen's chances of happiness? Novels that do grant their characters divorces do not suggest they are thus made happy.[14] After *Mansfield Park*'s Maria Bertram Rushworth is divorced by her husband, she is banished from England, rejected by her lover, and consigned to the care of her aunt, Mrs Norris, where "shut up together with little society, on one side no affection, on the other, no judgment, it may be reasonably supposed that their tempers became their mutual punishment" (424). While Clara Pulleyn finally gets to marry the man she loves in *The Newcomes*, the fact that she is a divorcée ruins her happiness:

> the very man who loves her, and gives her asylum, pities and deplore her. She scarce dares to look out of the windows of her new home upon the world, lest it should know and reproach her. All the sisterhood of friendship is cut off from her. If she dares to go abroad she feels the sneer of the world as she goes through it, and knows that malice and scorn whisper behind her. (624)[15]

Lady Vernon, in Charlotte Bury's *The Divorced* (1837), also finds herself an outcast from society, and she must also endure her husband's increasing resentment:

> you must remember that you knew, when you left your first estate, the consequences, the humiliating consequences which, in despite of my tenderest care, must become your portion. Neither have you suffered alone; the man who ties a mill-stone about his neck cannot expect to swim on the surface. (15)

Unlike the adulteresses Maria, Clara, and Lady Vernon, however, Stephen is guiltless, not to mention scrupulously moral. Dickens stresses the purity of his relationship with Rachael; Rachael and Stephen are careful even of how often they walk home together, lest their reputations suffer. In Stephen Blackpool—the poor honest, hardworking, non-union laborer married to an alcoholic, thieving, adulterous, spiteful woman—we find a character who surely ought to be able to enjoy the relief of divorce. In creating Stephen, Dickens presents his readers with such a compelling case against the classist double standard of divorce law that it would seem that even the institution's staunchest opponent could not fail to admit his right to "be ridded o'" his wife.

I suggested in Chapter 4 that divorce is a taboo subject for the Victorian novel, and that when it finds its way into a text, it is—as the examples above bear out—presented as something disgraceful and forbidden, almost always marginalized as a subplot (even as those who obtained divorces were marginalized by Victorian society) and presented in a way that made it clear how damaging it was to one's finances and one's reputation. *Hard Times* breaks those conventional patterns in that it puts divorce at the forefront of its concerns and exposes the social systems that make divorce so shameful, so expensive, and virtually impossible to obtain. While *Hard Times* may seem to subscribe to the conventional pattern in that presents divorce as a solution out of Stephen's reach (and a solution in which Louisa is uninterested), I would argue that those unsatisfying conclusions to Stephen's and Louisa's plots are actually manifestations of the novel's deep commitment to a realistic portrayal of the realities of divorce at mid-century, and that in refusing to effect a legal divorce for any of its characters, it reveals the structural inflexibility of Victorian law and culture.

I have been arguing throughout this chapter that *Hard Times* is interested in exploring Stephen's right to obtain a divorce, but that it is not concerned with what seems to be the parallel case of Louisa's right to divorce Bounderby, that while the novel addresses the double standard of divorce law as it relates to class, it is not interested in the sexual double standard. This is not, however, to say that the novel is uninterested in exploring how a wife might escape her marriage, as I hope my analysis of Mrs Gradgrind's, Mrs Blackpool's, and Louisa's plots have made clear. It is also not to say that Dickens abandoned the plight of the wife after *Copperfield*. The articles that appeared in *Household Words* alongside the weekly numbers of *Hard Times* bear out that continued interest and provide us with a way of contextualizing the marriages of those unhappy women married to Gradgrind and Bounderby. Two articles in particular demand to be read in terms of the wives' plots in *Hard Times*: "The Rights and Wrongs of Women," which appeared alongside the first number of the novel, and "One of Our Legal Fictions," which appeared four weeks later, alongside the fifth number of *Hard Times*, in which Tom urges Louisa to "Look sharp for old Bounderby" (47). Written by Eliza Lynn Linton, a problematic figure in terms of the Woman Question but one who, at least in 1854, espoused views quite similar to those Caroline Norton advocated in her novels and political essays, these articles supplement the plots of failed marriage in *Hard Times* and suggest that while Dickens is concerned with addressing the double standard of class in his novel, he has by no means forgotten the double standard of gender written into the law of coverture.

In "The Rights and Wrongs of Women," Linton argues that many of the rights on which women insist—"teaching, preaching, voting, judging, commanding a man-of-war, and charging at the head of a battalion"—-are inappropriate to their sex and pervert their femininity. Yet she goes on to rail against those "laws which deny the individuality of a wife, under the shallow pretence of a legal lie," and fiercely maintains that a woman ought to be classified as a capable, rational adult, not a child or a criminal or an idiot, not as part of her husband, but as a person in her own right (158, 159). Thus, while she argues vehemently against equal rights for women in terms of work and suffrage (suggesting that giving the vote to women would be as absurd as asking them to command a battleship or lead a battalion), Linton also points to the inequity of coverture and the sexual double standard of the law of divorce. This position, contradictory as it seems by today's feminist standards, was in fact representative of a fairly common position on the issue of women's rights at the mid-century and should remind us of Caroline Norton's paternalistic arguments about the rights of women to be protected by the law. As she argues in *English Laws for Women*, "Is there any reason why (attention being so called to the subject) Women alone, of the more helpless classes,—the classes set apart as not having free control of their own destinies,—should be denied the protection which in other cases supplies and balances such absence of free control?" (14) Linton and Norton both argued that it was women's very inferiority to men, their divinely ordained inadequacy and subservience, that necessitated the reform of laws relating to marriage, divorce, and wives' rights to their property, their earnings, and the custody of their children.

Linton makes a similar argument in "One of Our Legal Fictions," an essay that not only resembles the rhetoric Norton employs in telling her own story and arguing for legal reform, but is in fact another version of Norton's life story:

> The prayers were made, the benediction given, the bells rang out their lusty epithalamium, and by the law of the Church and the law of the land, Charlotte and Robert Desborough were henceforth one—one in interests, one in life. No chill rights or selfish individuality to sow disunion between them: no unnatural laws to weaken her devotion by offering a traitorous asylum against him: but, united by bonds none could break—their two lives welded together, one and indivisible for ever—they set their names to that form of marriage, which so many have signed in hope, to read over for a long lifetime of bitterness and despair. (257)

So begins Linton's (deliberately) thinly disguised account of Caroline Norton's marital misfortunes. As Linton tells it (which is not very different from the way Norton tells it, as I explain in Chapter 3), this is the story of a wife who believed in men's superiority to women, who believed that her husband should be her ruler and should have control over her. This is a story of a woman who "would have looked with horror on any proposition for the revision of the legal poem. Liberty would have been desolation to her, and the protection of the laws she would have repudiated as implying a doubt of her husband's faith" (258). But when he takes advantage of her powerlessness under the law rather than protecting her, as a husband should, it becomes necessary for her to fight for custody of her children, for the right to her own earnings and her own property, and for her reputation, dirtied by "Robert's" attempt to prove her guilty of adultery.

These two essays thus supplement the marriage plots of *Hard Times* in that they draw attention to the law of coverture that sets those plots in motion; reading these essays alongside the wives' plots in *Hard Times* reveals, as Mill argued in *The Subjection*, that it is the inherent injustice of the law that leads, almost inevitably, to marital misery for a wife. But unlike Mill, who is reluctant to take up the question of divorce in his essay on the subjection of wives, Linton weaves it into both of these pieces. Not surprisingly, she argues that Charlotte Desborough should be able to divorce her husband. While Mill defers the question of divorce in the hopes that the reformation of the institution of marriage will do away with any need for divorce, Linton tells the story of a situation that needs to be remedied now, suggesting that wives like Charlotte/Caroline cannot wait for the kind of reform Mill advocates. In chronicling their story, she argues that women deserve custody of their children and the protection of their property and their earnings, and that it is "the entire annihilation of all her rights, individuality, legal existence, and [the husband's] sole recognition by the law" that is the problem (257). It is only after Charlotte has been deprived of her children, her property, and her earnings, dragged through an adultery suit, and assaulted by her husband (Linton refers not only to his "rough deeds" and "personal violences," but also to the fact that "more than once she was in mortal fear, with marks of fingers on her throat, and cuts and bruises on her head") that she seeks a divorce (258). But because she once forgave her husband and returned to his house after leaving him (due to his violent behavior), the law found that she had condoned his behavior and thus could not sue for a divorce.

By telling the story of Charlotte/Caroline, Linton makes a case for divorce designed to sway the strongest opponent, just as Dickens does by stacking the deck in favor of Stephen. At the end of her story of a wife so persecuted through her legal non-existence that she is denied a divorce and access to her children, Linton explains that she merely advocates

> Justice to women. No fanciful rights, no unreal advantages, no preposterous escape from womanly duty, for the restless, loud and vain; no mingling of women with the broils of political life, nor opening to them of careers which nature herself has pronounced them incapable of following; but high-flown assertion of equality in kind; no simple justice. The recognition of their individuality as wives, the recognition of their natural rights as mothers, the permission to them to live by their own honourable industry, untaxed by the legal Right and moral Wrong of any man to claim as his own that for which he has not wrought— reaping where he has not sown, and gathering where he has not strawed. Justice to women. This is what the phrase means; this is where the thing is truly wanted;

here is an example of the great Injustice done to them, and of their maltreatment
under the eyes of a whole nation, by the Law. (260)

Linton's quarrel, like Dickens's in the Stephen plot, is with the state of the law, with
the existence of a system that makes it impossible for the perfectly innocent and
miserably wronged (i.e. Charlotte and Stephen) to find relief from their miserable
marriages. She is not, she insists, arguing for rights for women or careers for
women, but simply for "justice."

Like Dickens's story of Stephen's desire for a divorce, Linton's story of this
lamentable "legal fiction" is a moving one, not a polemic. It is hard to imagine
reading Charlotte's story without agreeing that this, surely, is a clear-cut case,
an exceptional case, a case for which the law must have a remedy. "One of Our
Legal Fictions" does not agitate for radical reform; it presents the sad story of an
unfortunate victim of marriage as it exists under the patriarchal law of coverture.
This is the version of the Louisa plot that reviewers (and readers) seem to want.
It is Stephen's story: a story of wronged innocence that creates sympathy for the
unhappy spouse and thus suggests the need for a more lenient divorce law in an
unthreatening manner. In this regard, it is especially significant that Dickens placed
this essay alongside the fifth number of *Hard Times*, in which Tom urges Louisa to
"Look sharp for old Bounderby" and in which we are also introduced to Stephen
Blackpool and his unhappy marriage (47). This number ends with our first glimpse
of Stephen's wife ("a creature so foul to look at ... but so much fouler than that in
her moral infamy") and thus provides an appropriate introduction to the parallel
story of Charlotte Desborough, who is married to a man similarly foul in his moral
and physical degradation. This story, not Louisa Bounderby's, is the one that rails
against the double standard of gender and thus provides the parallel to Stephen's
plot and its articulation of the double standard of class.

While Linton confines herself to gesturing towards generalities ("rights" and
"careers") in "One of Our Legal Fictions," she is more specific in "The Rights and
Wrongs of Women," where she enumerates some of the careers that those foolish
emancipated women want to be able to pursue. As I suggest above, she chooses
careers that reveal how unreasonable women are in their desires, imagining that
they want to be women warriors and "sea captains" (158). She also mentions
their desire to be "barristers, members of Congress, and judges," and while she
manages to attack both American and British women in that litany, she reserves
special vitriol for the British, and she imagines a very specific kind of barrister
British women want to be (158). In a heavily sarcastic passage she sneers, "they
are to be barristers, too, with real blue bags, pleading for murderers and sifting
the evidence of divorce cases"—an occupation which she, not surprisingly,
warns will damage their morals and their purity (159). Toward the end of her
essay she drops the sarcasm and pleads with women to consider the wisdom and
rightness of occupations such as earning their families' love, marking references
for their husbands, or perhaps even correcting their sermons—tasks which are
"fitter occupation than arguing divorce cases in a wig and blue bag" (160). Even

leaving aside the obvious facts—that barristers do a great deal more than hear divorce cases (especially in 1854) and that a great deal of social reform would have to take place for women to be admitted to the bar—Linton's introduction of a divorce lawyer into her essay seems most curious. Why does Linton choose these particular tasks ("sifting the evidence of" and "arguing divorce cases") and this particular occupation to hold up as the antithesis of true womanhood?

"The Rights and Wrongs of Women" appeared a year after the Royal Commission issued its findings and two months before the Divorce Bill of 1854 was introduced into the House of Lords. Linton's female barrister, complete with wig and blue bag, dirtying her hands and her mind as she "sift[s] the evidence of divorce cases" is a figure that is certainly topical in one sense, though visionary in another. Linton's barrister is a highly resonant and suggestive image, for the idea that women would be allowed to argue divorce cases is both fabulous and an extreme version of what Parliament would eventually make possible in codifying a wife's right to petition for divorce, as it did in passing the Divorce Bill in 1857. That is, Linton's female barrister presents us with an exaggerated example of a woman taking divorce into her own hands. The 1857 Act allowed women to make their case for divorce and to have it articulated in public; similarly, the female barrister articulates another woman's case for divorce in public. Indeed, in inventing this particular occupation for women, Linton presents what is only a more extreme version of her own argument about divorce in "One of Our Legal Fictions." In arguing that Charlotte Desborough should be allowed to sue for divorce, Linton is doing just what a female barrister would do: pursuing a divorce on behalf of another party. Similarly, in asserting that "the laws which class women with infants and idiots ... are the real and substantial Wrongs of Women," she (inadvertently) reveals the need for female "barristers, members of Congress, and judges," not to mention women who have the right to vote. For if women were allowed to "rush to the polling-booth, and mount the hustings" and serve as "judges on the bench," those "Wrongs of Women" would most certainly be addressed (159, 158).

In presenting us, however scathingly, with a woman who has the power to argue divorce cases, Linton imagines a woman who has so overcome the disabilities of her gender that she can articulate her views about marriage and participate in the legal amelioration of the wrongs of wives. Appearing as she does alongside the first number of *Hard Times*, introducing, as it were, the stories of women trying to extricate themselves from their marriages (and succeeding, albeit in extralegal fashion), Linton's divorce lawyer looks forward to a time when women will be able to take the law into their own hands and solve their marital problems legally, rather than relying on paternal protection as Norton, Linton, and Louisa all attempt to do. For we must also admit that in their paternalism Norton and Linton argue for protection more than for emancipation, and protection is what Louisa ultimately wants. As I suggest above, Louisa's plot is not about divorce, it should not be set alongside Stephen's, and it is not one that calls for a legal solution. Indeed, Louisa not only effects her own private solution but she also, in returning to her father's house to find that solution, suggests how we should read her plot and how we should understand its solution.

In returning to her father's house, Louisa is returning to the root of the problem to find its solution. In "curs[ing] the hour in which [she] was born," she draws attention to the fact that she was raised in such a way that made her marriage to Bounderby inevitable (164). "In this condition," she reminds her father, "you proposed my husband to me. I took him" (166). Her "deadened state of mind," the fact that her father "never nurtured" her, that "the garden that should have bloomed" in her heart was never planted, resulted in a "hunger and thirst ... which have never been for a moment appeased" (166, 165, 164, 165). Mixed metaphors aside, Louisa draws attention in this scene to her upbringing and connects its shortcomings to her present predicament. Like Mill, who reminds us that women are "brought up from their very earliest years" in a system that inculcates a belief in their inferiority to men and that offers them no choice but to marry, Louisa suggests that her education has made her incapable of making wise choices with respect to her marriage, her involvement with Harthouse, or her future (*The Subjection of Women* 141). She confesses to her father that she does not know what she feels (and thus does not know what to do), and that it is up to him to guide her:

> If you ask me whether I have loved [Harthouse], or do love him, I tell you plainly, father, that it may be so. I don't know ... I do not know that I am sorry, I do not know that I am ashamed, I do not know that I am degraded in my own esteem. All that I know is, your philosophy and your teaching will not save me. Now, father, you have brought me to this. Save me by some other means! (167)

Like Mill's insistence that "nobody knows [women's capabilities], not even themselves, because most of them have never been called out," Louisa here points to the fact that her father's teaching and philosophy has made it impossible to know herself or to know what to do next (*The Subjection of Women* 151). Similarly, Mill's insistence that men do not know their own wives, even in the best of marriages, for "authority on the one side and subordination on the other prevent perfect confidence. Though nothing may be intentionally withheld, much is not shown" echoes Gradgrind's admission, "I doubt whether I have understood Louisa" (Mill 152, *Hard Times* 182). Gradgrind also realizes that it is the way in which he raised her that is to blame for the failure of her marriage: "I doubt whether I have been quite right in the manner of her education" (183). As Mill would write 15 years later, the reasons for marital unhappiness are systemic; "the abuse of the power cannot be very much checked while the power remains" (216–17).

In much the same fashion, Linton's essays in *Household Words* rail not against Robert Desborough, but against the doctrine of coverture that gives him the power to persecute his wife; they identify the system itself, "the laws which deny the individuality of a wife under the shallow pretence of a legal lie" as "the real and substantial Wrongs of Women" ("The Rights and Wrongs of Women" 159). Linton's diatribes against the doctrine of coverture shed light on the failed-marriage plots of the wives in *Hard Times*, just as Mill's identification of the patriarchal nature of marriage sheds light on Louisa's confession and helps us understand why she returns to her father. The end of her marriage returns her to the system that raised her to enter into that marriage; she thus goes to her father to be re-educated, to compel him to try again "by some other means." In seeking a solution to her plight, then, Louisa is not concerned with how she might put an end to her marriage (which she manages to do quite easily), but about how she might be re-educated, how she can be saved "from the void in which my whole life sinks" (164). The end of Louisa's marriage returns her to Stone Lodge, to the person she believes responsible for her plight, and thus the only person she can think of asking for help, just as it returns us to *The Subjection*, to the text that makes it so clear that the failure of marriage is endemic to the patriarchal structure of society. It has been my argument throughout *Dickens and the Rise of Divorce* that novel theory should take Mill's systemic indictment of marriage into account, that an understanding of the domestic novel is incomplete if it does not consider the important and pervasive role the failed-marriage plot plays in the realistic novels that depict the social structure. It could thus be argued that she and we have come full circle. But it could also be argued that we are back where we belong: staring the failure of marriage full in the face and recognizing its powerful, persistent narrative force.

Notes

1   It is tempting to chart a kind of progression for Dickens's treatment of the failed-marriage plot. That is, in early Dickens, we find the failure of marriage in the margins and hidden in the mazes of his plots, and the monstrous and ill-assorted marriages we find in the shadows and on the periphery are almost always mercenary marriages or marriages of convenience—marriages for money, not for love, and marriages that suggest a kind of belated response to the Marriage Act of 1753 which mandated parental consent, if not control, as the prerequisite for matrimony. Dickens develops his attack on mercenary marriage in *Dombey*, but while the failure of marriage now comes front and center, the melodrama of the Dombeys' marriage suggests the failure of the institution is an isolated and spectacular occurrence (even as the genre in which he casts this plot suggests the paradigmatic nature of the Dombeys' union). In *Copperfield*, Dickens moves beyond a consideration of arranged and mercenary marriages and takes up the affectionate union, revealing that it, too, is flawed in some deep and irremediable ways. *Copperfield*, then, like *The Subjection of Women*, suggests that the problem lies not in opportunistic marriages or in isolated instances of marital breakdown, but rather that the system itself is corrupt and corrupting. Made nervous by this discovery, we might argue, Dickens refuses to consider the failure of marriage in *Bleak House*, tamping down the oblique suggestions of connubial unease that creep into the novel in which he "purposely dwelt upon the romantic side of familiar things" (7). Such a progression positions *Hard Times* as a brave triumph against Podsnap's and Mudie's, for it reveals

Dickens plotting loveless marriages and mercenary marriages again, but this time as the focus of his plot, not as spectacle, but as the characteristic form of the institution. Further, he explicitly takes up the question of divorce as a remedy, developing the implications of the figurative divorces he plotted in *Copperfield* and bringing them to the center of his narrative overtly and straightforwardly.

2   He finds three husbands for Mrs Bayham Badger, and while Laura certainly seems happy with Mr Badger, her third, the fact that she feels compelled to tells Esther and Ada "that she had never madly loved but once; and that the object of that wild affection, never to be recalled in its fresh enthusiasm, was Captain Swosser" makes us wonder just how happy she was in her marriage to her second husband, Professor Dingo, and how contented she really is with her third (208).

3   Hilary Schor calls this a "plot of mistaken adultery," and she argues that "the reader who follows Louisa's plight is drawn on through another fantasy altogether, that crafted by Mrs Sparsit" (72, 73). Similarly, Rosemarie Bodenheimer reminds us that "at the moment when Harthouse expects [Louisa's] suppressed feeling to issue in an adulterous elopement, she returns home to tell her father the sad story of her childhood and marriage" (204). Bodenheimer goes on to argue that the "seduction and fall story" only occurs "in the craven fantasies of Mrs Sparsit," and that it is replaced by "Louisa's 'true' story [which] ends in a literal fall at Gradgrind's feet" (204).

4   Anne Humpherys is one of the very few critics to take up the question of Mrs Sparsit's and Mrs Gradgrind's marriages. She also reminds us that we are treated, if ever so briefly, to a peep at the happy marriage of Sissy's parents. However, like the critics I discuss below, she succumbs to the temptation of comparing Stephen's and Louisa's plots, though she does acknowledge that the "parallelism between Louisa and Stephen is broken at a crucial point" (183).

5   Bersani argues in *A Future for Astyanax* that "realistic fiction serves nineteenth-century society by providing it with strategies for containing (and repressing) its disorder within significantly structured stories about itself" (63). And, as I note in Chapter 4, the marriage plot is typically viewed as one of those stories that provide order.

6   We know, though apparently Bounderby does not, that Mrs Sparsit was also the victim of "so miserable a marriage" and that it was, like the marriage Bounderby contemplates, "an unequal one in point of years." So it stands to reason that Mrs Sparsit's immediate reaction to Stephen's tale of woe would be to assume that it resembled hers in some respect. This assumption is borne out by the fact that Stephen has already confessed that the misery of his marriage is due to his wife's drinking and that she continues to torment him for money. These are, as we know, the basic facts of Mrs Sparsit's marriage, too, so it is hard not to conclude that she is thinking as much about her own failed marriage as she is about Bounderby's desire to marry Louisa when she interrogates Stephen. Indeed, Mrs Sparsit's reaction throughout this scene should be read in light of what we know about her own marital history. When Stephen broaches the subject of divorce, "Mrs Sparsit uttered a gentle ejaculation, as having received a moral shock." Moments later we find her "much dejected by the immorality of the people" while Bounderby pontificates on the "sanctity" of marriage (56–7). While her responses suggest that she is quick to uphold the notion of an individual's duty to society and the threat that

divorce poses to the social fabric, they also reveal that she conveniently ignores the social ramifications of her own separation from Mr Sparsit.

7   I am not arguing that Dickens did not believe women should be able to sue for divorce. I think the plot of *Dombey*, not to mention all the wives who leave their husbands from *Pickwick* onward, suggests that he most certainly did. The articles that he commissioned and/or wrote for *Household Words* during the debates over the Divorce Bill in 1856 and 1857 also suggest that he was very much in favor of redressing the double standard of gender. These articles include Dickens's "The Murdered Person," Linton's "Marriage Gaolers," and Marguerite Powers's poem "A Wife's Pardon."

8   For either Bounderby or Stephen to be able to divorce their wives, they would, of course, have to prove them guilty of adultery. As I have suggested above, following Kaye in his imaginings about the novel Dickens meant to write, Mrs Sparsit would certainly swear to Louisa's adultery with Harthouse, and in "'Divorce and Matrimonial Causes': An Aspect of *Hard Times*," John D. Baird very convincingly argues that Stephen's wife is an adulteress, in the novel Dickens actually wrote.

9   But of course Louisa's marriage is motivated more by her desire for Tom's love than anything else; accordingly, I want to draw attention to the fact that Shaw here follows Tom's lead, for Tom, in calling his sister's marriage "mercenary," implies that Louisa has prostituted herself and leaves out the fact that she is doing so for him.

10 It is Tom, not Louisa, who is exiled from the novel and from England.

11 This claim is not pure speculation. Kaye's criticism of *Hard Times* appears as a footnote to his article on Caroline Norton's *Letter to the Queen on Lord Chancellor Cranworth's Marriage and Divorce Bill*. In this article, he admits the injustice of the law that so mistreats wives, but he takes Norton to task for what he calls " the continual repetition of her grievances" and rebukes her for her "anger and bitterness" and her "indignation and scorn" (301, 302). The footnote about *Hard Times* comes as he invokes Blackpool's phrase ("a muddle") to describe the state of divorce law, and he introduces Blackpool as a way of making the argument that "there are 'hard times,' and hard lines, for man as for woman" and "men have their wrongs as well as women" (297). He is especially incensed by those scenes in which Stephen's wife returns to take more of his property, and he links her to Becky Sharp, who "suffered her husband to go to prison, and mainly too for her extravagance, whilst a bank-note of a large amount lay hoarded up in the recesses of the little lady's writing-desk" (297). Thus in the middle of an argument about the injustice of coverture ("the 'non-existence' of women" to which his title refers), he takes up the case of married women's property from the husband's point of view, and he gestures more generally to the economic double standard of divorce law.

12 For an excellent and concise account of the social and economic factors which worked together to bring divorce to Parliament's attention, see Mary Poovey, "Covered but Not Bound: Caroline Norton and the 1857 Matrimonial Causes Act" in *Uneven Developments*. See also Lawrence Stone, *Road to Divorce*; Lee Holcombe, *Wives and Property*; Mary Lyndon Shanley, *Feminism, Marriage and the Law in Victorian England*; and Dorothy Stetson, *A Woman's Issue: The Politics of Family Law Reform in England*.

13 *Hansard's Parliamentary Debates*, 3rd series, vol. 134; June 13, 1854, 20, 25. All
   further references to the Parliamentary Debates will appear in the notes by volume and
   column number (e.g., *Hansard* 134: 25).

14 But it is crucial to keep in mind the class status of those who divorce (and are divorced);
   the women granted divorces in Austen, Thackeray, and Bury are women of the upper
   class, women whose husbands can afford to divorce them, while Stephen is located
   firmly and inextricably in the ranks of the working poor. So the matter of the questionable
   happiness afforded by divorce must be considered in the context of class privilege, no
   matter how much that privilege is interrogated.

15 Thackeray, not one to stint when it came to exposing the cruelty and hypocrisy of
   society, elaborates on the scorn with which the divorced Clara Belsize is treated:

> People, as criminal, but undiscovered, make room for her, as if her touch were
> pollution. She knows she has darkened the lot and made wretched the home of
> the man whom she loves best; that his friends who see her, treat her with but a
> doubtful respect; and the domestics who attend her, with a suspicious obedience.
> In the country lanes, or the streets of the county town, neighbours look aside
> as the carriage passes in which she sits splendid and lonely. Rough hunting
> companions of her husband's come to her table: he is driven perforce to the
> company of flatterers and men of inferior sort; his equals, at least in his own
> home, will not live with him. She would be kind, perhaps, and charitable to the
> cottagers round about her, but she fears to visit them lest they too should scorn
> her. The clergyman who distributes her charities, blushes and looks awkward
> on passing her in the village, if he should be walking with his wife or one of his
> children. (*The Newcomes* 624)

How to Read the Failed-Marriage Plot: "Leave Sunny Imaginations Hope"?

But, of course, Louisa's plot in *Hard Times* does not end when she returns to her father, anymore than it ends when Bounderby allows her to remain under Gradgrind's paternal protection. Rather, Louisa's future is projected by the narrator in the chapter that is entitled "Final" but in fact is anything but: "Herself again a wife—a mother. ... Did Louisa see this? Such a thing was never to be" (226). In much the same fashion, I want to conclude this book not with a conclusion, but an epilogue. An epilogue, the *American Heritage Dictionary* tells me, is "a short section at the end of a literary or dramatic work, often discussing the future of its characters." Many Victorian novels end with epilogues, whether labeled as such or not, and it is not uncommon for Victorian novels and novel-readers to have a hard time letting go of their characters; readers and writers often seem to want to follow them into the future, to learn what happened next, and even to suggest that while the novel itself is ended, its characters' lives will continue beyond its pages.[1] In *The Sense of an Ending*, Frank Kermode calls this kind of conclusion "completely perfunctory and traditional" (23), and we find it in novels from *Pride and Prejudice* to *Middlemarch*, from *Jane Eyre* to *Dracula* (1897). Indeed, it is such a *topos* in the Victorian novel that even Mary Elizabeth Braddon looks beyond the plot proper of her sensation novels and tells us what happens in the future to the characters in *Lady Audley's Secret* (1862) and *The Doctor's Wife* (1864).

On occasion, however, novelists resist this kind of (dis)closure, choosing instead to insist, in a hyper(un)realistic manner, that they do not know how things turned out for their characters or that it is up to the reader to figure out, sometimes even to determine, how the story ends. Sometimes, as is the case with Thackeray's *The Newcomes* (1853–55) and Charlotte Brontë's *Villette* (1853), the novelist suggests that readers want to believe in a specific ending and grants them their desire, even while signaling that to accept that happy ending is to succumb to wish fulfillment and ignore all that has been portrayed in the pages leading up to the end of the novel. At the end of *The Newcomes*, after keeping hero and heroine apart for over 800 pages, Thackeray tells the reader in a kind of postscript to the novel proper "that in Fable-land somewhere Ethel and Clive are living most comfortably together" (818) while at the end of *Villette*, Lucy makes it clear that M. Paul's ship has been destroyed in a storm but stops short of saying explicitly that he is dead in order to "leave sunny imaginations hope" (596). Like Thackeray, who tells us that we can imagine the ending we want ("But for you, dear friend, it is as you like. You may settle your Fable-land in your own fashion. Anything you like happens in Fable-land"), Lucy decides that there has been "enough said" and bites her tongue so that the sentimental, conventional reader can "picture union and a happy succeeding life" for her with the man she loves.

As these two examples suggest, this kind of evasive ending tends to concern the marriage of hero and heroine, and the fact that Thackeray and Brontë withhold the marriages of Clive and Ethel and of Lucy and M. Paul from their readers in fact, if not in fancy, suggests their skepticism about the possibility of happy endings. As Joseph Allen Boone argues, "Brontë's refusal to reunite Lucy and Paul Emanuel" offers "a blueprint for an ideological decentering of the contradictions embedded in the marriage tradition" (18, 19). In this epilogue, then, I want to consider the generic implications of this kind of equivocating conclusion, for the failed-marriage plot is invested in precisely the kind of questioning suggested by the (in)conclusion that hedges and hesitates and half-heartedly offers a closure it so manifestly does not believe in. Because questioning the courtship model inevitably leads to questioning whether the happy marriage (that does indeed often appear at the end of the third volume) relieves all the anxieties that have received so much expression along the way, it thus stands to reason that a novel that questions the courtship model would finish its work by suggesting a new kind of novelistic ending or by critiquing closure in some fashion. So just as Louisa's plot does not end when she puts an end to her marriage, my project cannot close without a consideration of the relationship between the failed-marriage plot and the failure (or refusal) of the novel to establish closure more generally.

The last paragraph of *Hard Times* is a good place to begin that consideration, for the last words of the novel constitute an ending that is not an ending, an inconclusive conclusion—what Garrett Stewart calls a "purposeful reach[ing] beyond" the "boundaries of sheer story" (223):

> Dear reader! It rests with you and me, whether, in our two fields of action, similar things shall be or not. Let them be! We shall sit with lighter bosoms on the hearth, to see the ashes of our fires turn grey and cold. (227)

This last paragraph is, obviously, an appeal to the reader, and Stewart argues that in addressing and apostrophizing "the participant reader," Dickens "heroizes" what we do as readers of his novel (222). Dickens empowers his readers when he leaves it up to all of us ("it rests with you"—the reader—"and me"—the writer) "whether, in our two fields of action, similar things shall be or not." In inviting us to go with him beyond the boundaries of *Hard Times*, Dickens opens up the possibility of an unscripted ending and admits our power as readers to supply our own list of things that are to be or not, just as the endings of *Villette* and *The Newcomes* invite us to read their endings as we wish.

The last paragraph of *Hard Times* might thus also suggest that it is up to us, as readers, to decide whether the foreclosure of marriage will be a future that we accept for Louisa. Like those readers who choose to dwell in Thackeray's "Fable-land," we can willfully misread "similar things" as the "things" the novel's preceding paragraphs revealed were to be and were not to be in the characters' futures, and insist on our right to determine the kind of future that we think will make Louisa happy.[2] To do so would be to close our eyes to the unmistakeable, albeit moderate, punishment the novel metes out to Louisa for straying from her marriage, but it is, nevertheless, a possibility the novel offers us. Or we can read the ending as it is written, rather than as we are invited to write it, and accept that M. Paul is dead and that Louisa will not remarry. As Brenda Silver formulates our choices,

> to the extent that we can enter into and accept Lucy's cryptic conclusion, we will join "in friendly company" with the "pilgrims and brother mourners" who acknowledge pain. ... Otherwise, we remain among those readers whose sunny imaginations still demand conventional endings. (111)

Silver's assessment of the ending captures the sense that while more than one reader may want to believe in a conventional, happy ending, M. Paul does in fact die, and the reader who can accept this is one realistic enough to "acknowledge pain" and also one "observant" enough to have noticed that "Lucy's life does not end with Paul's." Silver also draws attention to the fact that Lucy tries to prepare the reader for the unconventional ending she can suggest, but not make explicit:

> she appeals ... to the community she herself has created to grant credence to the highly unconventional ending of her tale. She has by this time given us ample warning that "endings" for women are problematic, and traditional plots no help in assessing her own experience. She has explicitly shared with the reader her final words on the lives of the two more familiar fictional women after their marriages: Ginevra fails to ... develop at all; and Polly ... bears a distinct resemblance to a pampered and adoring spaniel. (110)[3]

Silver suggests that Brontë allows the reader to have it both ways: she makes it clear that hero and heroine do not marry, yet she does not spell out that unsatisfying, but highly realistic ending, thus offering what Stewart calls "a white lie as sop to the popular audience at large" (*Dear Reader* 260).

By the same token, while Thackeray suggests in three different ways that Clive and Ethel do marry, these suggestions are presented first as speculation, then as his "belief," and finally as a deduction he makes rather than his certain knowledge, a mode of presentation that leads Stewart to characterize them as "the confession of pure fabulation by the author" (*Death Sentences* 133). Further, he imagines that all these things may be so in "Fable-land," not in the world of the novel, and that the reader finds them not in the novel proper, but rather in a section begins after the white space and the horizontal line that separate the end of the novel from the final section written in Thackeray's voice, rather than in the voice of Pendennis, the novel's "swiftly dismissed" narrator (*Death Sentences* 133).[4] All these particulars suggest why Welsh calls Thackeray "the novelist most wary of the pitfalls of wish fulfillment in novels," and certainly the jaundiced eye he turns on Amelia's love for George, her too-little-too-late affection for Dobbin, and the loveless first (and I would argue, only) marriage he plots for Clive Newcome suggest not only how apt this description is, in that they reveal the kinds of happy endings he refuses these characters, but also how much his mistrust of wish fulfillment in general has to do with his skepticism about the ability of marriage, in particular, to grant the fulfillment of the reader's wishes (*Dickens Redressed* 208).

The careful reader of *The Newcomes*, like the reader of *Villette* that Silver describes, should know how to read the long and pathetically hopeful speculation about Clive and Ethel's eventual marriage that marks the close of Thackeray's novel. Similarly, the alert reader knows that to insist on a happy ending for Louisa (that is, to insist that she remarries) is to misread the end of *Hard Times*. These three endings do suggest that marriage establishes closure, but there are no marriages in these instances, just as there is no closure. In order to achieve this unconventional ending, to refuse marriage to their heroines, the novelists must situate that ending in another realm ("Fable-land" for Thackeray, the future for Dickens), or they must break into the world of the novel and announce the constructedness of that world (in which the reader has presumably been absorbed) by some other means. Thus these three endings also suggest how to read the failed-marriage plot. That is, they suggest how the novel works, not what readers do. In setting their conclusions in "Fable-land" or the future or letting the reader imagine the "happy succeeding life" of Lucy and M. Paul, Thackeray, Dickens, and Brontë jarringly remind us of what we usually prefer to ignore when we are lost in a book: that the world in which we are so absorbed is a provisional construct. Passages that draw attention to the constructed nature of a novel, like Lucy's abdication of narrative authority to her readers ("let it be theirs to conceive ... let them picture") and Dickens's invocation of the reader highlight the fact that we are (their) readers, and that we are reading a novel that depends on our imaginative collaboration as such. It thus draws attention to the conventions of the novel, rather than allowing readers to escape into its created world. Rather than honoring the readers' absorption in that world by keeping its artificiality to itself, these "admissions of fictionality" "break the novelistic contract with the reader, the reader who should be led to believe in the coherence of the world described" (Stewart, *Dear Reader* 419, n.12). This last formulation is Stewart's assessment of Henry James's well-known irritation at Trollope's continual reminders to his readers that he was telling them an invented and constructed tale.[5] James calls these intrusions "slaps at credulity" and insists that the novelist, "as a narrator of fictitious events," "is nowhere; to insert into his attempt a back-bone of logic, he must relate events that are assumed to be real" ("Anthony Trollope" 1343).

James was infuriated by reminders of the text's constructed nature, and he insisted that "when Trollope suddenly winks at us and reminds us that he is telling us an arbitrary thing, we are startled and shocked" ("Anthony Trollope" 1343). While I am not sure we are exactly "shocked" to be reminded that we are reading a fiction, I would argue that the admission of plot as "an arbitrary thing" serves to expose novelistic conventions as such. Specifically, in making explicit the arbitrary nature of their conclusions, Dickens, Brontë, and Thackeray not only suggest the provisional nature of those endings, but also, by extension, allow us to see that many of the marriages that seem to end Victorian novels more straightforwardly and conclusively are just as constructed—that they are, by definition or by convention, often unearned, routinely plotted, or otherwise habitual, as opposed to thoughtful or considered. In suggesting that it rests with the reader to determine how the novel ends, the endings of *The Newcomes*, *Villette*, and *Hard Times* thus reveal a deep skepticism not only about writing novels and the conventions that define novels, like closure, but also about the institution that is assumed to establish closure for the genre. The evasiveness that characterizes the empty promise held out (and held out explicitly as an empty promise) at the end of *The Newcomes* and of *Villette* suggests the novelists' trepidation at breaking with convention, even as it reveals their conviction that the untraditional endings they are trying to convince their readers to accept are more realistic choices.

In "Realism and the Fear of Desire," Leo Bersani argues that the nineteenth-century novel is "a form which provides [its] society with a reassuring myth about itself," that "the realistic novel gives us an image of social fragmentation contained within the order of significant form—and it thereby suggests that the chaotic fragments are somehow socially viable and morally redeemable" (*A Future for Astyanax* 60). But moments like the ones I am exploring here suggest that the novelist is losing faith in that myth, that, try as he might, he cannot mask a growing skepticism about the realist project and the society it seeks to reassure and to represent. Bersani goes on to suggest that "in a sense, then, the realistic novelist desperately tries to hold together what he recognizes quite well is falling apart. The looseness or elasticity of novelistic form is a sign of that recognition" (61), and I would add that the breakdown of that form, as signaled by the inconclusive ending and the rupturing of what we might call the third wall of fiction, is evidence that the novelist has lost control over the pieces he is holding together, over the art of his novel, and cannot supply us with that "definitive ending" we find so reassuring or even keep up the pretense that he is "relat[ing] events that are assumed to be real" (James, "Anthony Trollope" 1343). Instead of presenting us with marriages that "complete the novel's sense," these novelists articulate, in their own voices, that marriage cannot provide that conclusive meaning (Bersani 54).

The fact that the marriage that brings the domestic novel to a close is often unearned or arbitrary or otherwise revealing of the novelist's doubt and uncertainty over the efficacy and ethicality of the courtship plot (and of the realist project more generally) is also made clear by such textual curiosities as the three endings of *Great Expectations* and the failed marriage of his wife that Crimsworth imagines in the last chapter of Charlotte Brontë's *The Professor* (1846). Like the conclusions that Thackeray and Brontë leave to the reader to write, Dickens's vacillation over Pip and Estella and Brontë's inability to leave the happy marriage of the Crimsworths alone suggest an authorial uneasiness with marital closure, and these revisions and insertions also reveal the hand of the author at work in a way that calls attention to the novel as a fictional construct. They reveal these novelists trying to get it right in a sense; the trouble they have in plotting the endings of their novels suggests the ad hoc and artificial nature of endings in general, which bespeaks an uncertainty about the possibility of marriage to serve this function for the realist novel.[6]

In a passage that anticipates Sydney Carton's imaginings about the failed marriage that he assumes would have been his if Lucie had married him, William Crimsworth, the eponymous professor, wonders how his wife, Frances, would have fared "had she married a harsh, envious, careless man: a profligate, a prodigal, a drunkard or a tyrant." Reflecting on their ten years of happy marriage, he concludes that she was "a good and dear wife to me, because I was to her a good, just, and faithful husband," but he wants to know how she would have behaved if she had found herself unhappily married (235). Crimsworth's interrogation of his wife is curiously prolonged and detailed, and the marriage thus described sounds a great deal like the first one that Anne Brontë plots for her heroine in *The Tenant of Wildfell Hall*. Frances says that she "should have tried to endure the evil or cure it for a while; and when I found it intolerable and incurable, I should have left my torturer suddenly and silently." When her husband counters that solution with another question: "if law or might had forced you back again?" she hesitates ("What to a Drunkard—a profligate—a selfish spendthrift—an unjust fool?") and then temporizes, "I would have gone back; again assured myself whether or not his vice and my misery were capable of remedy—and if not, have left him again" (235).

This imaginary failed-marriage plot may seem out of place in what is arguably Charlotte Brontë's most pedestrian novel, but it is of a piece with the other moments of novelistic uncertainty I am concerned with in this epilogue, for, like the multiple endings of *Great Expectations* and the temporized endings of *Villette* and *The Newcomes*, this brief excursion into matrimonial cruelty gives Brontë a chance to lay this (un)scripted version of marriage alongside the putative happy ending she gives the professor and his wife. In other words, this imaginary failed marriage signals Brontë's skepticism about the happy marriage she has scripted for Frances and William, and, by extension, it reveals her skepticism about the happy ending marriage is thought to signal in general. The ending of *Villette* works in much the same fashion, though in her last novel, Charlotte Brontë reverses the presentation of the two options and plots the skeptical ending while she leaves the happy ending to those readers with "sunny imaginations." Even Jane Eyre could be said, in her direct address to the reader, to protest too much and thus to reveal her author's uncertainty about closure. "Reader, I married him," Jane proclaims. But she might as well say, "Reader, if you want to believe that my story ended in marriage; if, despite all the narrative energy it has taken to get me married, you can accept this ending; then, reader, you can accept that I married him." As Rachel Blau DuPlessis points out, "the tension of achieving the resolution is palpable" (8).[7] Like my other examples, Jane Eyre's address to the reader, "the breakthrough into story of novelistic utterance per se," breaches the novelist's contract of fictional integrity and suggests the artificiality of the story Brontë is telling (Stewart, *Dear Reader* 13). This textbook example of the courtship plot thus reveals its awareness of the uncertainties and instability of matrimony even as it announces its heroine's nuptials, for Jane's brazen advertisement of her marriage draws attention to all it leaves out and everything it asks us to overlook.

In *The Sense of an Ending*, Frank Kermode suggests that what he calls "fictions of concord" "meet a need. They seem to do what Bacon said poetry could: 'give some show of satisfaction to the mind, wherein the nature of things doth seem to deny it'" (59, 62–3). But he goes on to caution that "the show of satisfaction will only serve when there seems to be a degree of real compliance with reality as we, from time to time, imagine it" (63). Extrapolating from Kermode, we might say that we need the courtship plot and the "fiction of concord" it depicts, even as the nature of marriage "doth seem to deny" that concord. But, as I hope this project has begun to suggest, "a degree of real compliance with reality," which is a good way of talking about the project of the realist novel, necessitates other plots, as well. The courtship plot alone cannot provide "satisfaction to the mind," and in order to comply with reality, we also need what might be called "fictions of discord"—what I have been calling the failed-marriage plot, and what Dickens, Thackeray, and Charlotte Brontë write throughout their career and draw explicit attention to when they reject closure and advertise their discomfort with a plot that can only exist in the "sunny imaginations" of those who believe in "Fable-land." In *Narrative and Its Discontents*, D.A. Miller proposes that "the problematic of closure" "enjoys unique prominence and pertinence in the novel—particularly, in that epoch of the novel that finds its center of gravity in the nineteenth century" (277). The "prominence and pertinence" of the failed-marriage plot in the Victorian novel is revealed nowhere more clearly than in the "problematic of closure" that typifies the project of Dickens, Thackeray, and Charlotte Brontë at mid-century and leads them to announce to their readers their inability and their unwillingness to plot successful courtships for their heroes and heroines.

Notes

1   In *Narrative and its Discontents*, D.A. Miller finds that "the narratable inherently lacks finality. It may be suspended by a moral or ideological expediency, but it can never be properly brought to term. The tendency of a narrative would therefore be *to keep going*, and a narrative closure would be, in Mallarmé's phrase, a 'faire semblant'" (xi).

2   In *Dickens Redressed*, Alexander Welsh reminds us that, like Thackeray's vacillations at the end of *The Newcomes*, at the end of *Vanity Fair* "he worked out a second marriage for the better of his two heroines but then withdrew belief in it: 'Which of us is happy in this world? Which of us has his desire? or, having it, is satisfied?'" (208).

3   Amanda Anderson points out that "the years without M. Paul were, by [Lucy's] own assertion, the happiest years of her life, and precisely because she worked" and that

the "ending's equivocation can be seen" "as a way to forestall attempts to read her into conventional narratives" (*The Powers of Distance* 61).

4   Similarly, Welsh reminds us that that "in calling upon himself and his reader to determine what things 'shall be or not,' Dickens clearly looks to the future," thus writing an ending that Welsh calls "openended," one that, like the ending of *The Newcomes*, goes beyond the novel itself (*Dickens Redressed* 208).

5   This epilogue is indebted to Garrett Stewart's groundbreaking work on the Victorian reader and specifically to his emphasis on the way in which texts "used instead their readers" (*Dear Reader*, 11). I read interpolation as a sign of narrative dis-ease, whereas Stewart celebrates "the structure of participation" "which floats an entire fictional institution," but my argument about the implications of the inconclusive ending for the failed-marriage plot was quite literally made possible by Stewart's study of the "conscripted audience in nineteenth-century British fiction" (*Dear Reader* 19).

6   In this respect, it is more than a little interesting that Brontë struggled with the ending of *Villette* much like Dickens did with the ending of *Great Expectations*. As Garret Stewart tells us, in the draft version of the penultimate paragraph, after Lucy allows her readers to "picture union and a happy succeeding life," Brontë added "So be it." She deleted this passage in proof, but Stewart points out that the deleted sentence, "like so much in the passage, straddles the options of closure" (*Dear Reader* 261). "Straddles" is a particularly awkward verb, and it thus conjures up nicely the very awkward position that Brontë, Thackeray, and Dickens felt themselves to be in when it came to plotting marriages for their protagonists.

7   Blau DuPlessis goes on to describe the "landmine of cunningly intertextual false marriages" that surround Jane and Rochester's courtship plot:

> There is a hidden wed*lock* with Bertha into which Rochester has been tricked and … that same entrapment he proposes to repeat in a far more subtle form on Jane. Rochester also has a charade "wife," Blanche Ingram, from a masquerade wedding tableau. We are present at a dramatically arrested false marriage ceremony, with Jane as fearful, decorated, enraptured bride. In the array of mid-book "marriages," Brontë has created a critical context in which the normal activities of courtship (and the normal narratives as well) take on a lurid and foreboding quality. (9)

Bibliography

Ackroyd, Peter. *Dickens*. London: Sinclair-Stevenson, 1990.

Adams, James Eli. *Dandies and Desert Saints: Styles of Victorian Manhood*. Ithaca, NY: Cornell University Press, 1995.

Aiken, Susan Hardy. "Scripture and Poetic Discourse in *The Subjection of Women*." *PMLA* 98 (1983): 353–73.

Altick, Richard. *The Shows of London*. Cambridge, MA: Harvard University Press, 1978.

Anderson, Amanda. *The Powers of Distance: Cosmopolitanism and the Cultivation of Detachment*. Princeton, NJ: Princeton University Press, 2001.

———. *Tainted Souls and Painted Faces: The Rhetoric of Fallenness in Victorian Culture*. Ithaca, NY: Cornell University Press, 1993.

Armstrong, Nancy. *Desire and Domestic Fiction: A Political History of the Novel*. New York: Oxford University Press, 1987.

Auerbach, Nina. "Dickens and Dombey: A Daughter After All." *Dickens Studies Annual* 5 (1976): 95–114.

———. *Woman and the Demon: The Life of a Victorian Myth*. Cambridge, MA: Harvard University Press, 1982.

Austen, Jane. *Mansfield Park*. Ed. James Kinsley and John Lucas. Oxford: Oxford University Press, 1980.

———. *Pride and Prejudice*. Ed. James Kinsley and Frank W. Bradbrook. Oxford: Oxford University Press, 1990.

Axton, William. *Circle of Fire: Dickens' Vision and Style and the Popular Victorian Theater*. Lexington: University of Kentucky Press, 1966.

Baird, John D. "'Divorce and Matrimonial Causes': An Aspect of *Hard Times*." *Victorian Studies* 20 (1977): 401–12.

Baldick, Chris. *In Frankenstein's Shadow: Myth, Monstrosity, and Nineteenth-Century Writing*. Oxford: Oxford University Press, 1987.

Basch, Françoise. *Relative Creatures: Victorian Women in Society and the Novel*. Trans. Anthony Rudolf. New York: Schocken, 1974.

Bennett, Rachel. "Punch versus Christian in *The Old Curiosity Shop*." *Review of English Studies* 22 (1971): 423–34.

Bersani, Leo. *A Future for Astyanax: Character and Desire in Literature*. 1976. Reprint. New York: Columbia University Press, 1984.

Blau DuPlessis, Rachel. *Writing beyond the Ending: Narrative Strategies of Twentieth-Century Women Writers*. Bloomington: Indiana University Press, 1985.

Bodenheimer, Rosemarie. *The Politics of Story in Victorian Social Fiction*. Ithaca, NY: Cornell University Press, 1988.

Boone, Joseph Allen. *Tradition Counter Tradition: Love and the Form of Fiction.* Chicago: University of Chicago Press, 1987.

Bowen, John. "Performing Business, Training Ghosts: Transcoding *Nickleby.*" *English Literary History* 63 (1996): 153–75.

Braddon, Mary Elizabeth. *Aurora Floyd.* Ed. P.D. Edwards. New York: Oxford University Press, 1996.

Brannan, Robert Louis, ed. *Under the Management of Charles Dickens: His Production of "The Frozen Deep."* Ithaca, NY: Cornell University Press, 1966.

Brodhead, Richard. *Cultures of Letters: Scenes of Reading and Writing in Nineteenth-Century America.* Chicago: University of Chicago Press, 1993.

Brontë, Anne. *The Tenant of Wildfell Hall.* Ed. Herbert Rosengarten. New York: Oxford University Press, 1992.

Brontë, Charlotte. *Jane Eyre.* Ed. Q.D. Leavis. Harmondsworth: Penguin, 1966.

———. *The Professor.* Ed. Margaret Smith and Herbert Rosengarten. New York: Oxford University Press, 1991.

———. *Shirley.* Ed. Margaret Smith and Herbert Rosengarten. New York: Oxford University Press, 1981.

———. *Villette.* Ed. Mark Lilly. Harmondsworth: Penguin, 1979.

Brooks, Cleanth. *The Well Wrought Urn: Studies in the Structure of Poetry.* San Diego, CA: Harcourt Brace and Company, 1942.

Brooks, Peter. *The Melodramatic Imagination: Balzac, Henry James, Melodrama, and the Mode of Excess.* New Haven, CT: Yale University Press, 1995.

———. *Reading for the Plot: Design and Intention in Narrative.* New York: Knopf, 1984.

Brown, Homer Obed. "*Tom Jones*: The 'Bastard' of History." In *Institutions of the English Novel: From Defoe to Scott.* Philadelphia: University of Pennsylvania Press, 1997. 82–115.

Browning, Robert. "My Last Duchess." In *The Poems, Volume One.* Edited by John Pettigrew. Harmondsworth: Penguin, 1993. 349–50.

Bury, Lady Charlotte. *The Divorced.* London: Henry Colburn, 1837.

Butt, John and Kathleen Tillotson. *Dickens at Work.* London: Methuen, 1957.

Calder, Angus. "Appendix A: The End of the Novel." In Dickens, *Great Expectations.* Edited by Angus Calder. 494–6.

Carey, John. *The Violent Effigy: A Study of Dickens' Imagination.* London: Faber & Faber, 1973.

Carr, Jean Ferguson. "Dickens's Theatre of Self-Knowledge." In *Dramatic Dickens.* Edited by Carol Hanberry MacKay. London: Macmillan, 1989. 27–44.

Chapman, Pauline. *Madame Tussaud in England:* London: Quiller Press, 1992.

Chapman, Pauline and Anita Leslie. *Madame Tussaud: Waxworker Extraordinary.* London: Hutchinson & Co., 1978.

Chase, Karen and Michael Levenson. *The Spectacle of Intimacy: A Public Life for the Victorian Family.* Princeton, NJ: Princeton University Press, 2000.

Chedzoy, Alan. *A Scandalous Woman: The Story of Caroline Norton*. London: Allison & Busby, 1992.

Christ, Carol. *Victorian and Modern Poetics*. Chicago: University of Chicago Press, 1984.

Clark, Beverly Lyon. *Kiddie Lit: The Cultural Construction of Children's Literature in America*. Baltimore, MD: Johns Hopkins University Press, 2003.

Clarke, Micael M. "William Thackeray's Fiction and Caroline Norton's Biography: Narrative Matrix of Feminist Legal Reform." *Dickens Studies Annual* 18 (1989): 337–51.

Collins, Wilkie. *Armadale*. Ed. Catherine Peters. New York: Oxford University Press, 1989.

———. "Introductory Lines." In *The Frozen Deep and Mr Wray's Cash-Box*. Phoenix Mill, UK: Alan Sutton, 1996. 3–5.

———. *The Woman in White*. Ed. Julian Symons. Harmondsworth: Penguin, 1985.

Corbett, Mary Jean. *Family Likeness: Sex, Marriange, and Incest from Jane Austen to Virginia Woolf*. Ithaca, NY: Cornell University Press, 2008.

———. *Representing Femininity: Middle-Class Subjectivity in Victorian and Edwardian Women's Autobiographies*. Oxford: Oxford University Press, 1992.

Costello, Dudley. "History in Wax." *Household Words* 9 (1854): 17–20.

———. "Our Eye-Witness in Great Company." *All the Year Round* 2 n.s. (1860): 249–53.

Dickens, Charles. *Bleak House*. Ed. Norman Page. Harmondsworth: Penguin, 1971.

———. *The Cricket on the Hearth*. In *Christmas Books*. New York: Oxford University Press, n.d. 191–286.

———. *David Copperfield*. Ed. Nina Burgis. Oxford: Oxford University Press, 1983.

———. *Dombey and Son*. Ed. Peter Fairclough. Harmondsworth: Penguin, 1970.

———. *Great Expectations*. Ed. Angus Calder. Harmondsworth: Penguin, 1965.

———. *Hard Times*. Ed. George Ford and Sylvère Monod. New York: W.W. Norton & Company, 1966.

———. *The Letters of Charles Dickens*. The Pilgrim Edition. Volume 5. Edited by Graham Storey and K. J. Fielding. Oxford: Clarendon Press, 1981.

———. *The Letters of Charles Dickens*. The Pilgrim Edition. Volume 8. Edited by Graham Storey and Kathleen Tillotson. Oxford: Clarendon Press, 1995.

———. *Little Dorrit*. Ed John Holloway. Harmondsworth: Penguin, 1967.

———. *Martin Chuzzlewit*. Ed. Patricia Ingham. Harmondsworth: Penguin, 1999.

———. *Miscellaneous Papers*. Volume II. London: Chapman & Hall, 1911.

———. "The Murdered Person." *Household Words* 342 (1856): 289–91.

———. *Nicholas Nickleby*. Ed. Michael Slater. Harmondsworth: Penguin, 1978.

————. *The Old Curiosity Shop*. Ed. Angus Easson and Malcolm Andrews. Harmondsworth: Penguin, 1972.

————. *Oliver Twist*. Ed. Peter Fairclough. Harmondsworth: Penguin, 1966.

————. *The Posthumous Papers of the Pickwick Club*. Ed. Robert Patten. Harmondsworth: Penguin, 1982.

————. *A Tale of Two Cities*. Ed. George Woodcock. Harmondsworth: Penguin, 1986.

Doggett, Maeve. *Wife-Beating and the Law in Victorian England*. Columbia: University of South Carolina Press, 1993.

Dowling, Andrew. "'The Other Side of Silence': Matrimonial Conflict and the Divorce Court in George Eliot's Fiction." *Nineteenth-Century Literature* 50 (1995): 322–36.

duCille, Ann. *The Coupling Convention: Sex, Text, and Tradition in Black Women's Fiction*. New York: Oxford University Press, 1993.

Edwards, P.D. "Introduction." In Braddon, *Aurora Floyd*. Edited by Edwards. vii–xxii.

Eigner, Edwin M. "*David Copperfield* and the Benevolent Spirit." *Dickens Studies Annual* 14 (1985): 1–15.

————. *The Dickens Pantomime*. Berkeley: University of California Press, 1989.

Ellis, Mrs [Sara Stickney]. *The Prose Works of Mrs. Ellis*. Author's Edition. New York: Henry G. Langley, 1844.

Eliot, George. *Middlemarch*. Ed. W.J. Harvey. Harmondsworth: Penguin, 1965.

Ferrier, Susan. *Marriage*. New York: Penguin Books/Virago Press, 1986.

Fielding, Henry. *Joseph Andrews*. Ed. R.F. Brissenden. Harmondsworth: Penguin, 1985.

Forster, John. *The Life of Charles Dickens*. 2 vols. New York: Scribner's, 1900.

Foyster, Elizabeth A. *Marital Violence: An English Family History, 1660–1875*. Cambridge: Cambridge University Press, 2005.

Freedberg, David. *The Power of Images: Studies in the History and Theory of Response*. Chicago: University of Chicago Press, 1989.

Freud, Sigmund. "The 'Uncanny.'" In *The Standard Edition of the Complete Psychological Works of Sigmund Freud*. Volume 17. Trans. James Strachey. London: The Hogarth Press, 1955. 219–52.

Ganz, Melissa J. "'A Strange Opposition': *The Portrait of a Lady* and the Divorce Debates." *The Henry James Review* 27 (2006): 156–74.

Gillis, John. *For Better, For Worse: British Marriages 1600 to the Present*. Oxford: Oxford University Press, 1985.

Green, Katherine Sobba. "The Heroine's Blazon and Hardwicke's Marriage Act: Commodification for a Novel Market." *Tulsa Studies in Women's Literature* 9 (1990): 273–90.

Hadley, Elaine. *Melodramatic Tactics: Theatricalized Dissent in the English Marketplace, 1800–1855*. Stanford, CA: Stanford University Press, 1995.

Hammerton, James. *Cruelty and Companionship: Conflict in Nineteenth-Century Married Life*. London: Routledge, 1992.

————. "Victorian Marriage and the Law of Matrimonial Cruelty." *Victorian Studies* 33 (1990): 269–92.

Hansard's Parliamentary Debates. 3rd series. Volume 134 (1854), Volume 143 (1856).

Hardy, Barbara. *The Moral Art of Dickens*. 1970. Reprint. London: Athlone Press, 1985.

Hardy, Thomas. *The Mayor of Casterbridge*. Ed. Norman Page. Petersborough, Ontario: Broadview, 1997.

Harris, Janice Hubbard. *Edwardian Stories of Divorce*. New Brunswick, NJ: Rutgers University Press, 1996.

Harth, Erica. "The Virtue of Love: Lord Hardwicke's Marriage Act." *Cultural Critique* 23 (1988): 123-54.

Heilbrun, Carolyn. "Marriage Perceived: English Literature 1873–1941." In *What Manner of Woman: Essays on English and American Life and Letters*. Edited by Marlene Springer. New York: New York University Press, 1977. 160–83.

Herbert, Christopher. "*He Knew He Was Right*, Mrs. Lynn Linton, and the Duplicities of Victorian Marriage." *Texas Studies in Literature and Language* 25 (1983): 448–69.

Hibbert, Christopher. *Queen Victoria in Her Letters and Journals*. New York: Viking Penguin, 1985.

Hodgson, E. *The Trial at Large of Rhynwick Williams*. London: R. Butters, 1790.

Holcombe, Lee. *Wives and Property: Reform of the Married Women's Property Law in Nineteenth-Century England*. Toronto: University of Toronto Press, 1983.

Homans, Margaret and Adrienne Munich, eds. *Remaking Queen Victoria*. Cambridge: Cambridge University Press, 1997.

Horstman, Allen. *Victorian Divorce*. London: Croom Helm, 1985.

Houston, Gail Turley. "Reading and Writing Victoria: The Conduct Book and the Legal Constitution of Female Sovereignty." In Homans and Munich, *Remaking Queen Victoria*. 159–81.

Huet, Marie-Hélène. *Monstrous Imagination*. Cambridge, MA: Harvard University Press, 1993.

Hughes, Linda and Michael Lund. *The Victorian Serial*. Charlottesville: University of Virginia Press, 1991.

Humpherys, Anne. "Louisa Gradgrind's Secret: Marriage and Divorce in *Hard Times*." *Dickens Studies Annual* 25 (1996): 177–95.

Hurley, Dan. "Divorce Rate: It's Not as High as You Think." *New York Times*. April 19, 2005: F7.

James, Henry. "Anthony Trollope." In *Henry James: Literary Criticism: American Writers, English Writers*. New York: Library of America, 1984. 1330–54.

————. *The Portrait of a Lady*. Ed. Nicola Bradbury. Oxford: Oxford University Press, 1995.

————. *What Maisie Knew*. Ed. Paul Theroux. Harmondsworth: Penguin, 1985.

Jameson, Fredric. *The Political Unconscious: Narrative as a Socially Symbolic Act*. Ithaca, NY: Cornell University Press, 1981.

Johnson, Claudia. "The Divine Miss Jane." In *Janeites: Austen's Disciples and Devotees*. Edited by Deidre Lynch. Princeton, NJ: Princeton University Press, 2000. 25–44.

Johnson, Edgar. *Charles Dickens: His Tragedy and Triumph*. 2 vols. New York: Simon and Schuster, 1952.

Kaplan, Fred. *Dickens: A Biography*. New York: William Morrow, 1988.

Kaye, J.W. "The 'Non-Existence' of Women." *The North British Review* 46 (1855): 288–302.

Kermode, Frank. *The Art of Telling: Essays on Fiction*. Cambridge, MA: Harvard University Press, 1983.

———. *The Sense of an Ending*. New York: Oxford University Press, 1967.

Kincaid, James. "The Darkness of *David Copperfield*." *Dickens Studies* 1 (1965): 65–75.

King, Amy M. *Bloom: The Botanical Vernacular in the English Novel*. Oxford: Oxford University Press, 2003.

Landes, William-Alan, ed. *Punch and Judy*. Studio City, CA: Players Press, 1995.

Langbauer, Laurie. *Women and Romance: The Consolations of Gender in the English Novel*. Ithaca, NY: Cornell University Press, 1990.

Langland, Elizabeth. *Nobody's Angels: Middle-Class Women and Domestic Ideology in Victorian Culture*. Ithaca, NY: Cornell University Press, 1995.

Lasch, Christopher. "The Suppression of Clandestine Marriage in England: The Marriage Act of 1753." *Salmagundi* 26 (1974): 90–109.

Lawson, Kate and Lynn Shakinovsky. *The Marked Body: Domestic Violence in Mid-Nineteenth-Century Literature*. Albany, NY: State University of New York Press, 2002.

Leach, Robert. *The Punch and Judy Show: History, Tradition and Meaning*. Athens, GA: The University of Georgia Press, 1985.

Leavis, F.R. "The First Major Novel: *Dombey and Son*." In F.R. and Q.D. Leavis, *Dickens the Novelist*. London: Chatto & Windus, 1970. 1–30.

Leavis, Q.D. "Dickens and Tolstoy: The Case for a Serious View of *David Copperfield*." In F.R. and Q.D. Leavis, *Dickens the Novelist*. 34–117.

Leckie, Barbara. *Culture and Adultery: The Novel, the Newspaper, and the Law, 1857–1914*. Philadelphia: University of Pennsylvania Press, 1999.

Lemmings, David. "Marriage and the Law in the Eighteenth Century: Hardwicke's Marriage Act of 1753." *The Historical Journal* 39.2 (1996): 339–60.

Linton, Eliza Lynn. "Marriage Gaolers." *Household Words* 13 (1856): 583–5.

———. "One of Our Legal Fictions." *Household Words* 9 (1854): 257–60.

———. "The Rights and Wrongs of Women." *Household Words* 9 (1854): 158–61.

Litvak, Joseph. *Caught in the Act: Theatricality in the Nineteenth-Century English Novel*. Berkeley: University of California Press, 1992.

Loesberg, Jonathan. "Deconstruction, Historicism, and Overdetermination: Dislocations of the Marriage Plots in *Robert Elsmere* and *Dombey and Son.*" *Victorian Studies* 33 (1990): 441–64.

Lonoff, Sue. "Cultivated Feminism: Mill and *The Subjection of Women.*" *Philological Quarterly* 65 (1986): 79–102.

Luftig, Victor. *Seeing Together: Friendship Between the Sexes in English Writing from Mill to Woolf.* Stanford, CA: Stanford University Press, 1993.

Luhmann, Niklas. *Love as Passion: The Codification of Intimacy.* 1982. Trans. Jeremy Gaines and Doris L. Jones. Stanford, CA: Stanford University Press, 1998.

Lynch, Deidre and William Warner. "The Transport of the Novel." In *Cultural Institutions of the Novel.* Edited by Lynch and Warner. Durham, NC: Duke University Press, 1999. 1–10.

Marcus, Sharon. *Between Women: Friendship, Desire, and Marriage in Victorian England.* Princeton, NJ: Princeton University Press, 2007.

Marcus, Steven. *Dickens from Pickwick to Dombey.* 1965. Reprint. New York: Norton, 1985.

———. *The Other Victorians: A Study of Sexuality and Pornography in Mid-Nineteenth-Century England.* New York: Basic Books, 1964.

Mayhew, Henry. *London Labour and the London Poor.* Volume 3. New York: Dover, 1968.

McGregor, O.R. *Divorce in England: A Centenary Study.* Melbourne: William Heinemann, 1957.

Menefee, Samuel P. *Wives for Sale: An Ethnographic Study of British Popular Divorce.* New York: St Martin's, 1981.

Mill, John Stuart. *The Subjection of Women.* In *Essays on Sex Equality.* Edited by Alice Rossi. 125–242.

Miller, Andrew H. *Novels Behind Glass: Commodity Culture and Victorian Narrative.* Cambridge: Cambridge University Press, 1995.

Miller, D.A. *Narrative and Its Discontents.* Princeton, NJ: Princeton University Press, 1981.

———. *The Novel and the Police.* Berkeley: University of California Press, 1988.

Miller, J. Hillis. *Charles Dickens: The World of His Novels.* 1958. Reprint. Bloomington: Indiana University Press, 1969.

———. *The Form of Victorian Fiction.* Cleveland, OH: Arete Press, 1968.

Moglen, Helene. "Theorizing Fiction/Fictionalizing Theory: The Case of *Dombey and Son.*" *Victorian Studies* (35) 1992: 159–84.

Morse, Deborah Denenholz. "'I Speak of Those I Do Know': Witnessing as Radical Gesture in *The Tenant of Wildfell Hall.*" In *New Approaches to the Literary Art of Anne Brontë.* Edited by Julie Nash and Barbara A. Suess. Aldershot: Ashgate, 2001. 103–26.

Needham, Gwendolyn B. "The Undisciplined Heart of *David Copperfield.*" *Nineteenth-Century Fiction* 9 (1954): 81–107.

Newsom, Robert. *Dickens on the Romantic Side of Familiar Things: Bleak House and the Novel Tradition*. New York: Columbia University Press, 1977.

————. "The Hero's Shame." *Dickens Studies Annual* 11 (1983): 1–24.

Nord, Deborah Epstein. *Walking the Victorian Streets: Women, Representation, and the City*. Ithaca, NY: Cornell University Press, 1995.

Norton, Caroline. *Caroline Norton's Defense*. Edited by Joan Huddleston. Reprint of *English Laws for Women*. Chicago: Academy Chicago, 1982.

————. *A Letter to the Queen on Lord Chancellor Cranworth's Marriage and Divorce Bill*. In *Selected Writings of Caroline Norton*. Edited by James O. Hoge and Jane Marcus. Delmar, NY: Scholars' Facsimiles & Reprints, 1978.

————. *Stuart of Dunleath. A Story of the Present Time*. New York: Harper & Brothers, 1851.

Nunokawa, Jeff. *The Afterlife of Property: Domestic Security and the Victorian Novel*. Princeton, NJ: Princeton University Press, 1994.

Partridge, Eric. *A Dictionary of Slang and Unconventional English*. New York: Macmillan, 1970.

Perkins, Miss Jane Gray. *The Life of Mrs. Norton*. 1909. Reprint. London: John Murray, 1910.

Peterson, Linda. "The Female Bildungsroman: Tradition and Subversion in Oliphant's Fiction." In *Margaret Oliphant: Critical Essays on a Gentle Subversive*. Edited by D.J. Trela. Selinsgrove, PA: Susquehanna University Press, 1985. 66–89.

Phillips, Adam. "On Tickling." In *On Kissing, Tickling, and Being Bored: Psychoanalytic Essays on the Unexamined Life*. Cambridge: Harvard University Press, 1993. 9–11.

Phillips, Roderick. *Putting Asunder: A History of Divorce in Western Society*. New York: Cambridge University Press, 1988.

Poovey, Mary. "Recovering Ellen Pickering." *Yale Journal of Criticism* 13 (2000): 437–52.

————. *Uneven Developments: The Ideological Work of Gender in Mid-Victorian England*. Chicago: University of Chicago Press, 1988.

Powers, Marguerite A. "A Wife's Pardon." *Household Words* 14 (1856): 276.

Psomiades, Kathy Alexis. "*He Knew He Was Right*: The Sensational Tyranny of the Sexual Contract and the Problem of Liberal Progress." In *The Politics of Gender in Anthony Trollope's Novels: New Readings for the Twenty-First Century*. Edited by Margaret Marwick, Deborah Denenholz Morse, and Regenia Gagnier. Aldershot: Ashgate, 2009. 31–44.

Rossi, Alice S., ed. *Essays on Sex Equality*. Chicago: University of Chicago Press, 1970.

————. "Sentiment and Intellect: The Story of John Stuart Mill and Harriet Taylor Mill." In *Essays on Sex Equality*. 1–63.

Sadoff, Dianne. *Monsters of Affection: Dickens, Eliot, and Brontë on Fatherhood*. Baltimore, MD: The Johns Hopkins University Press, 1982.

Schlicke, Paul. *Dickens and Popular Entertainment*. London: Allen & Unwin, 1985.

Schor, Hilary. *Dickens and the Daughter of the House*. Cambridge: Cambridge University Press, 1999.

Schor, Naomi. "Duane Hanson: Truth in Sculpture." In *Reading in Detail: Aesthetics and the Feminine*. New York: Methuen, 1987. 131–40.

Shanley, Mary Lyndon. *Feminism, Marriage, and the Law in Victorian England*. Princeton, NJ: Princeton University Press, 1989.

———. "Marital Slavery and Friendship: John Stuart Mill's *The Subjection of Women*." *Political Theory* 9 (1981): 229–47.

Shaw, George Bernard. Introduction to *Hard Times*. In Dickens, *Hard Times*. Edited by George Ford and Sylvère Monod. 332–9.

Showalter, Elaine. "Family Secrets and Domestic Subversion: Rebellion in the Novels of the Eighteen-Sixties." In *The Victorian Family: Structure and Stresses*. Edited by Anthony Wohl. London: Croom Helm, 1978. 101–16.

———. "Subverting the Feminine Novel: Sensationalism and Feminine Protest." In *A Literature of Their Own: British Women Novelists from Brontë to Lessing*. Princeton, NJ: Princeton University Press, 1977. 153–81.

Silver, Brenda R. "The Reflecting Reader in *Villette*." In *The Voyage In: Fictions of Female Development*. Edited by Elizabeth Abel, Marianne Hirsch, and Elizabeth Langland. Hanover, NH: University Press of New England, 1983. 90–111.

Slater, Michael. *Dickens and Women*. London: J.M. Dent, 1983.

Stetson, Dorothy. *A Woman's Issue: The Politics of Family Law Reform in England*. Westport, CT: Greenwood Press, 1982.

Stewart, Garrett. "'Beckoning Death': *Daniel Deronda* and the Plotting of Reading." In *Sex and Death in Victorian Literature*. Edited by Regina Barreca. Bloomington: Indiana University Press, 1990. 69–106.

———. *Dear Reader: The Conscripted Audience in Nineteenth-Century British Fiction*. Baltimore, MD: The Johns Hopkins University Press, 1996.

———. *Death Sentences: Styles of Dying in British Fiction*. Cambridge, MA: Harvard University Press, 1984.

———. "Narrative Economies in *The Tenant of Wildfell Hall*." In Nash and Suess. *New Approaches to the Literary Art of Anne Brontë*. 75–102.

Stewart, Susan. *On Longing: Narratives of the Miniature, the Gigantic, the Souvenir, the Collection*. Baltimore, MD: The Johns Hopkins University Press, 1984.

Stone, Lawrence. *Road to Divorce: England, 1530–1987*. Oxford: Oxford University Press, 1990.

Surridge, Lisa. *Bleak Houses: Marital Violence in Victorian Fiction*. Athens, OH: Ohio University Press, 2005.

Tanner, Tony. *Adultery in the Novel*. Baltimore: Johns Hopkins University Press, 1979.

Thackeray, William Makepeace. *The Newcomes*. Ed. David Pascoe. Harmondsworth: Penguin, 1996.

———. *Vanity Fair*. Ed. J.I.M. Stewart. Harmondsworth: Penguin, 1968.

Thompson, E.P. "The Sale of Wives." In *Customs in Common*. New York: The New Press, 1991. 404–66.

Tillotson, Kathleen. *Novels of the Eighteen-Forties*. Oxford: Clarendon Press, 1954.

Tompkins, Jane. *Sensational Designs: The Cultural Work of American Fiction*. New York: Oxford University Press, 1986.

Tromp, Marlene. *The Private Rod: Marital Violence, Sensation, and the Law in Victorian Britain*. Charlottesville: University Press of Virginia, 2000.

Van Ghent, Dorothy. *The English Novel: Form and Function*. New York: Harper and Row, 1953.

Vicinus, Martha. "'Helpless and Unfriended': Nineteenth-Century Domestic Melodrama." *New Literary History* 13 (1981): 127–43.

Walkowitz, Judith. "Science and the Séance: Transgressions of Gender and Genre in Late Victorian London." *Representations* 22 (1988): 3–29.

Waters, Catherine. *Dickens and the Politics of the Family*. Cambridge: Cambridge University Press, 1997.

Watt, Ian. *Myths of Modern Individualism: Faust, Don Quixote, Don Juan, and Robinson Crusoe*. Cambridge: Cambridge University Press, 1996.

———. *The Rise of the Novel*. Berkeley: University of California Press, 1957.

Weiner, Martin J. *Men of Blood: Violence, Manliness, and Criminal Justice in Victorian England*. Cambridge: Cambridge University Press, 2004.

Welsh, Alexander. *The City of Dickens*. 1971. Reprint. Cambridge, MA: Harvard University Press, 1986.

———. *Dickens Redressed*. New Haven, CT: Yale University Press, 2000.

———. *From Copyright to Copperfield: The Identity of Dickens*. Cambridge, MA: Harvard University Press, 1987.

Williams, Raymond. *Marxism and Literature*. Oxford: Oxford University Press, 1977.

Wilson, Angus. "The Heroes and Heroines of Dickens." *A Review of English Literature* 2 (1961): 9–18.

Worth, George. *Dickensian Melodrama: A Reading of the Novels*. Lawrence, KS: University of Kansas Press, 1978.

Yeazell, Ruth Bernard. *Fictions of Modesty: Women and Courtship in the English Novel*. Chicago: University of Chicago Press, 1991.

———. "Podsnappery, Sexuality, and the English Novel." *Critical Inquiry* 9 (1982): 339–57.

Zemka, Sue. "From the Punchmen to Pugin's Gothics: The Broad Road to a Sentimental Death in *The Old Curiosity Shop*." *Nineteenth-Century Literature* 48 (1993): 291–309.

Index

Partridge, Eric, 73

Patmore, Coventry, *The Angel in the House*, 4, 6, 18, 46 n.16, 50 n.32, 159

Perkins, Miss Jane Gray, 109–10, 129 n.12

Peterson, Linda, 46 n.17

Phillips, Adam, "On Tickling," 78

Phillips, Roderick, 10 n.3

Podsnappery, 21, 133–5, 179 n.1

Poovey, Mary, 10–17, 21–2, 44 n.4, 53 n.42, 120–5, 130 n.19, 181 n.12

Powers, Marguerite A., "A Wife's Pardon," 181 n.7

Psomiades, Kathy Alexis, 50 n.30

Punch and Judy, 7,68, 74–9, 84, 86 n.9 and n.10

Queen Victoria, 1–6, 26, 29, 31, 46, 99, 130 n.19

Redesdale, Lord, 170–2; *see also Hansard's Parliamentary Debates*

Richardson, Samuel, 12, 16–17, 19, 32, 46 n.16

Rossi, Alice S., 3

Ruskin, John, "Of Queens' Gardens," 4, 6, 18, 30

Sadoff, Dianne, 85 n.3

Schlicke, Paul, 74

Schor, Hilary, 55–6, 86 n.6, 129 n.11, 159–60, 180 n.3

Schor, Naomi, 80–2, 88 n.15, 89 n.19

sensation fiction, 5–6, 10 n.4, 26, 48 n.22, 50 n.32, 96, 183; *see also* adultery plot; bigamy plot

Shakinovsky, Lynn, 10 n.4, 52 n.41; *see also* Lawson, Kate

Shanley, Mary Lyndon, 1, 6, 10 n.3, 99, 128 n.7, 181 n.12

Shaw, George Bernard, 168, 181 n.9

Showalter, Elaine, 10 n.4

Silver, Brenda R., 185–6

Slater, Michael, 114, 137, 153 n.6

Smith, Barbara Leigh, 53

Stoker, Bram, *Dracula*, 183

Stetson, Dorothy, 181 n.12

Stewart, Garrett, 27, 47 n.20, 85 n.3, 160–1, 184–6, 189, 190 n.5 and n.6

Stewart, Martha, 69

Stewart, Susan, 70–1

Stone, Lawrence, 36–7, 52 n.38, 53 n.42, 128 n.7 and n.9, 131, 141, 171, 181 n.12

Storey, Graham, 129 n.14

Surridge, Lisa, 10 n.4, 48 n.24, 50 n.31, 86 n.8, 126 n.1, 130 n.20

Tanner, Tony, 21, 45 n.14

Ternan, Ellen, 93, 114

Thackeray, William Makepeace, 50 n.32, 89 n.17

   The Newcomes, 5, 6, 10 n.6, 45 n.14, 50 n.32, 126 n.2, 172, 182 n.15, 183–9

   Vanity Fair, 25, 45 n.14, 47 n.19, 126 n.2, 145, 189 n.2

Thompson, E.P., 128 n.9

Tillotson, Kathleen, 100, 126 n.3

Tompkins, Jane, 151–2

Trollope, Anthony, 45 n.14, 50 n.32, 186–7

   He Knew He Was Right, 5, 26, 30–1

   Palliser novels, 48 n.21

Tromp, Marlene, 10 n.4, 49 n.28

Tussaud, Madame, 78–83; *see also* waxworks

uncanny (Freud), 80–5

Van Ghent, Dorothy, 12, 19, 45 n.8

Vicinus, Martha, 129 n.15

Walkowitz, Judith, 9

Warner, William, 18; *see also* Lynch, Deidre

Waters, Catherine, 59, 64

Watt, Ian, 4, 7, 11–22, 32–3

waxworks, 65, 68, 78–84; *see also* Tussaud, Madame

Weiner, Martin J., 49 n.25

Welsh, Alexander, 13–15, 33, 85 n.1, 117, 132, 138, 146, 150, 166–7, 186, 189 n.2, 190 n.4

wife-sale, 37, 128 n.9, 171

Williams, Raymond, 8

Williams, Renwick, 87 n.13
Wilson, Angus, 168
Wollstonecraft, Mary, *The Emigrants*, 26,
    46 n.17; *see also* Imlay, Gilbert
Woman Question, 4–5, 7–8, 10 n.3, 109,
    126, 173

Worth, George, 95

Yeazell, Ruth Bernard, 12, 21, 57, 85 n.2,
    133, 153 n.2, 154 n.12

Zemka, Sue, 74